W9-ATL-784

THE AGE OF ARISTOCRACY
1688-1830

A HISTORY OF ENGLAND
GENERAL EDITOR: *Lacey Baldwin Smith*

THE MAKING OF ENGLAND 55 B.C.–1399

C. WARREN HOLLISTER
University of California, Santa Barbara

THIS REALM OF ENGLAND 1399–1688

LACEY BALDWIN SMITH
Northwestern University

THE AGE OF ARISTOCRACY 1688–1830

WILLIAM B. WILLCOX
Yale University

BRITAIN YESTERDAY AND TODAY:
1830 TO THE PRESENT

WALTER L. ARNSTEIN
University of Illinois, Urbana

THE AGE OF ARISTOCRACY 1688-1830

Second Edition

WILLIAM B. WILLCOX

Yale University

D. C. HEATH AND COMPANY
Lexington, Massachusetts

Maps by Norman Clark Adams

Copyright © 1971 by D. C. Heath and Company.
Also copyright © 1966 by D. C. Heath and Company.

All rights reserved. No part of this publication may be reproduced or transmitted in any form or by any means, electronic or mechanical, including photocopy, recording, or any information storage or retrieval system, without permission in writing from the publisher.

Published simultaneously in Canada.

Printed in the United States of America.

Library of Congress Number: 70–145693

FOREWORD

Carl Becker once complained that everybody knows the job of
the historian is "to discover and set forth the 'facts' of history." The facts,
it is often said, speak for themselves. The businessman talks about
hard facts, the statistician refers to cold facts, the lawyer is eloquent about
the facts of the case, and the historian, who deals with the incontrovertible
facts of life and death, is called a very lucky fellow. Those who speak
so confidently about the historian's craft are generally not historians
themselves; they are readers of textbooks which more often than not are mere
recordings of vital information and listings of dull generalizations. It is
not surprising that the historian's reputation has suffered; he has become
a peddler of facts and a chronicler who says "this is what happened."
The shorter the historical survey, the more likely it is for the textbook writer
to assume godlike detachment, spurning the minor tragedies and daily
comedies of men, and immortalizing the rise and fall of civilizations, the
clash of economic and social forces, and the deeds of titans. Nimbly he moves
from the indisputable fact that Henry VIII divorced Catherine of Aragon
and married Anne Boleyn to the confident assertion that this helped to
produce the Reformation in England. The result is sublime but emasculated
history. Men wept when Good Queen Bess died, but historians merely
comment that she had lived her allotted three score years and ten. Anglo-Saxon
warriors were sick with fear when Viking "swift sea-kings" swept down
on England to plunder, rape and kill, but historians dispassionately
note that the Norse invasions were a good thing; they allowed the kingdom
of Wessex to unite and "liberate" the island in the name of Saxon and
Christian defense against heathen marauders. British soldiers rotted by the
thousands in the trenches of the First World War, but the terror and
agony of that holocaust are lost in the dehumanized statistic that 750,000
British troops died in the four years of war.

In a brief history of even one "tight little island," the chronology
of events must of necessity predominate, but if these four volumes are
in any way fresh and new, it is because their authors have tried by artistry
to step beyond the usual confines of a textbook and to conjure up
something of the drama of politics, of the wealth of personalities, and even
of the pettiness, as well as the greatness, of human motivation. The price

paid will be obvious to anyone seeking total coverage. There is little in these pages on literature, the fine arts or philosophy, except as they throw light upon the uniqueness of English history. On the other hand, the complexities, the uncertainties, the endless variations, and above all the accidents that bedevil the design of human events — these are the very stuff of which history is made, and these are the "truths" which this series seeks to elucidate and preserve. Moreover, the flavor of each volume varies according to the tastes of its author. Sometimes the emphasis is political, sometimes economic or social; but always the presentation is impressionistic — shading, underscoring or highlighting to achieve an image which will be more than a bare outline and will recapture something of the smell and temper of the past.

Each book was conceived and executed as an entity capable of standing by itself, but at the same time the four volumes were designed as a unit. They tell the story of how a small and insignificant outpost of the Roman Empire hesitantly and not always very heroically evolved into the nation which has probably produced and disseminated more ideas and institutions, both good and bad, than any state since Athens. The hope is that these volumes will appeal both to those interested in a balanced portrait of the more discernible segments of English history — *The Making of England* (55 B.C.–1399), *This Realm of England* (1399–1688), *The Age of Aristocracy* (1688–1830) and *Britain Yesterday and Today* (1830 to the present) — and to those who seek the majestic sweep of history in the story of a people whose activities have been wonderfully rich, exciting and varied. Erasmus once wrote, "The important thing for you is not how much you know, but the quality of what you know." In this spirit these volumes were originally written and have now been revised, not only to keep pace with new scholarship but equally important to keep them fresh and thought-provoking in a modern world which is becoming both more nostalgic and impatient of the past.

Lacey Baldwin Smith
Northwestern University
1970

CONTENTS

1   The Fruits of Revolution   1

2   The Structure of the Oligarchy   25

3   The Walpole Era   47

4   The Winning of Empire   66

5   The Loss of Empire   87

6   Pause Between Storms   107

7   The Struggle against the French Revolution   133

8   The Napoleonic Wars   158

9   The Twilight of Aristocracy   187

   Bibliography   213

   Index   219

ILLUSTRATIONS

"Canvassing for Votes" by William Hogarth   30
"Polling the Blind and the Halt" by William Hogarth   31
Robert Walpole, 1st Earl of Orford   53
George III   81
Blenheim Palace and Kedleston Hall   109
"Gin Lane" by William Hogarth   112
William Pitt the Younger   123
H.M.S. "Victory"   164
The Duke of Wellington   183

MAPS

The Campaign of 1781   103
The Battle of the Nile   148
Naval Dispositions: March 1805   161
The Waterloo Campaign   181

GENEALOGICAL TABLES

The Succession Problem in 1700   6
The Spanish Succession   17

THE AGE OF ARISTOCRACY
1688-1830

1 The Fruits of Revolution

The Glorious Revolution

England, between November 1688 and March 1689, went through the rare experience of a revolution that was initiated and controlled by conservatives. The only major protagonist in 1688 who was a true revolutionary, in the sense of desiring fundamental change, was the King himself, and the change that James II desired was reactionary. He wanted to reestablish a form of government and a church that the British political world had long since rejected. His dream of making the royal prerogative superior to parliament had died on the scaffold with his father, Charles I; his dream of returning Britain[1] to Roman Catholicism had died with his great-grandmother, Mary Queen of Scots, and its ghost had been laid at the time of the Popish Plot, which at the end of the 1670's had almost upset his brother's throne. James, from the moment of his accession in 1685, worked stalwartly and stupidly to realize his dreams; and by the close of 1688 he was an exile in France. His departure set great changes in motion, but the men who overthrew him were no lovers of change. They acted in order to conserve what they had gained since the restoration of the monarchy in 1660. James threatened their gains and consequently, in their eyes, threatened to subvert the established constitution. To defend it they turned against him, and used revolutionary means to *prevent* revolutionary change.

Their course was dangerous. They were agreed on the fundamentals of what had to be done, but on little else. For a decade they had been divided into two embattled parties, Whigs and Tories; only a great crisis could have brought the two together, and even in the crisis they threatened to turn on each other again. Many issues separated them. The Tories were traditionally the champions of the crown and of the Church of England, the Whigs the champions of parliament and the dissenters, or Protestants outside the established Anglican Church. Although both Tories and Whigs disliked

---

[1] *Britain* at this time had of course no precise political meaning, because until 1707 the island of Great Britain remained divided into two kingdoms with a common sovereign, England (including Wales) and Scotland. But the two were deeply involved with each other, and the inclusive words *Britain* and *British* are a convenience in referring to the island as a whole.

1

Roman Catholics, until the Revolution the Tories, professing blind obedience to the Catholic James, muted their hostility to Rome in order to remain obedient. On foreign policy the two parties were as far apart as on domestic. The Whigs, partly because of their ties with the mercantile interests and partly because of their stalwart Protestantism, were belligerent toward France, which was becoming Britain's chief commercial rival and was the major Catholic power of the Continent; the Tories, who drew strong support from the rural gentry, had no desire to be drawn into a French war, from which the merchants would profit and for which the gentry would be taxed. These were major issues, and so divisive that nothing short of a political miracle could have induced the two parties to collaborate.

James worked the miracle. When he tried to use his prerogative not only to establish despotism but to return the church to Rome, he forced the Tories to choose between the two basic articles of their creed, loyalty to the crown and to Anglicanism, for the two were now in conflict. Most Tories responded, however reluctantly, by discarding their theory that the king could do no wrong and by allying with the Whigs to safeguard the familiar institutions of the country. The alliance was precarious, for all the old stresses were still at work within it; but the cost of letting them come to the surface was clear — to put the nation, in all likelihood, on the road it had followed in 1642, through civil war to the destruction of the whole known order. The men of 1688, with the lesson of the Cavaliers and Roundheads fresh in memory, were so determined to keep their own revolution from getting out of hand that they were willing to forget past quarrels and temporarily compromise their differences.

They had their awkward moments. In the autumn of 1688 they faced a real threat of civil war, but James saved them by fleeing the kingdom. Then came the problem of who should succeed him. The Convention Parliament, summoned to determine the question, argued long and bitterly before it agreed to settle the crown on James's elder daughter, Mary, and her husband and first cousin, William, Stadtholder of the Netherlands and grandson, through his mother, of Charles I. Once William III and Mary II were proclaimed as joint sovereigns, the revolution in England was virtually complete. It still had a stormy course to run in Scotland and an even stormier one in Ireland, as will soon be seen; but by the spring of 1689 the danger was over that the attack on James would, like the attack on his father, Charles I, unloose the flood of radicalism.

The Revolution was adroitly managed, but this was not the principal reason why it was orderly. It also commanded a large degree of consensus among the oligarchs, the small group of Whigs and Tories who were the political world of the day. Violently as these men disagreed on specific issues, they agreed on the fundamental point that their own position must be secured against royal encroachment. A few Tories, for whom their old principles were more important than their position as oligarchs, remained loyal to their exiled King; for them, as for Shakespeare,

The breath of worldly men cannot depose
The deputy elected by the Lord.

These nostalgic royalists were known as Jacobites, from the Latin form of
James, and they and their descendants continued to make intermittent trouble
for more than half a century. But they found little support among their fellow
oligarchs, who were satisfied with the Revolution because it confirmed their
power.

The Revolutionary Settlement in England

The men who engineered the accession of William and Mary were
not abstract political theorists, but workaday politicians. Although they agreed
on branding as unconstitutional certain past actions of King James, they
could never hav_ agreed on a definition of how the government should operate
in future; the mere attempt to define would have set them at each other's
throats. Instead they concentrated on the needs of the moment: they asserted
the rights and privileges of the House of Commons; they settled the crown
on William and Mary and then, in default of children, on Mary's younger
sister, Anne; they dealt with the status of Protestant dissenters in England,
and of the church and parliament in Scotland. These were substantial
achievements, but they were also incomplete. The position of the House of
Commons was only one part of a larger question, the relationship between
Westminster and Whitehall or, in other words, between parliament and the
executive; and this relationship remained amorphous for generations to come.
The future of the crown was uncertain, statutes to the contrary notwithstanding, until the accession of the House of Hanover in 1714; and so also
was the position of English dissenters. Anglo-Scottish relations were in flux
until the Act of Union of 1707. All that the Revolution settled, in short, could
have been unsettled during the years that followed.
    Those years were filled with problems. The brief alliance of Whigs
and Tories was dissolved by success, and the old factionalism revived. The
fiscal system of Charles II and James II proved hopelessly inadequate, and
new ways of financing the state had to be found. Behind all the developments
of the period, furthermore, molding them in greater or lesser degree and
rendering their outcome unpredictable, was a great foreign war that lasted,
with one brief intermission, from 1689 to 1713. In the heat generated by
armies fighting abroad and parties fighting at home, the revolutionary
settlement remained fluid; and it did not cohere into a stable system of
government until the war ended and the Stuarts gave place to the Hanoverians.
By then the original architects of the Revolution would not have recognized
their creation.
    Those architects were all agreed upon one cardinal point, that power
should rest with men of property like themselves. They were no more

democrats than Charles I had been; they would have shared his view that the common people have no claim to a part in government, but only the right to have a government that safeguards their lives and goods. The oligarchs were ready enough to speak in the name of the people, and did so in the Bill of Rights of 1689, which holds that all freeborn Englishmen have "their undoubted rights and liberties" and proceeds to list some of them. But participating in government was not a right; it was the privilege of property-owners. If the state itself existed for the preservation of property, as John Locke argued, the conclusion was obvious that only men of substance should have a voice in determining, primarily through the legislature, the actions of the state.

But the constitutional role of the legislature was still undefined. The Revolution established the principle of parliamentary sovereignty: in a basic disagreement between the monarch and the two houses, the monarch must either yield or lose the throne. The means of implementing the principle, however, had not yet been found; the modern concept of responsible government, in which the executive branch is responsible to parliament for the day-to-day workings of administration, was still far in the future. Since the accession of James I in 1603 parliament had learned how to hamstring royal policy by refusing supplies, by impeaching ministers, by scrutinizing accounts, and if nothing else would serve by inaugurating revolution. But this did not mean that parliament *governed,* because it had no way of doing so.

The revolutionary settlement, for all its safeguards against misuse of the king's executive authority, created no mechanism by which that authority could be effectively subordinated to the authority of parliament. The ministers of the crown, although they normally sat in the House of Lords or the House of Commons, were not servants of parliament but of the king. A major part of their service to him, it is true, consisted in marshaling enough votes in the two houses to ensure passage of legislation that was acceptable to him; their position therefore depended in great measure upon their parliamentary influence, and when they lost influence they usually lost office. But the king alone determined their tenure. He could, if he chose, keep for a time the most unpopular ministers to carry out the most unpopular policy; parliament could eventually force him to change his ways, but had no means of securing from him the men and measures of its choice. It might bankrupt a government by withholding funds, overturn a minister by the cumbersome process of impeachment, and in a great crisis even destroy a king. What it could *not* do was control the executive sufficiently to dictate a continuing line of policy. The two houses were able, given time, to eliminate obstacles to their will; they were unable to implement their will through the day-to-day operation of the ministry. Although by now their power was enormous, it was still, as it had been throughout the century, in essence negative.

The final sanction behind that power was revolution, a sanction upon which no constitutional government can rest. The right of revolution is the right to violate constitutional procedure, and substitute force for law. The conservative revolutionaries of 1689 had the conservative's dislike of force, but no substitute for it as their final argument. They were in much the same dilemma that had confronted their remote forebears in 1215: the barons who had extracted Magna Carta from King John had feared, with good reason, that he would break the promises contained in it, and had tried to meet the difficulty by inserting a clause to legalize rebellion against him if he did so; but their attempt to enforce the law by lawlessness had come to nothing. The makers of the Glorious Revolution, moved by the same fear, inserted a similar provision in the Bill of Rights: the oath of allegiance no longer precluded resistance to the crown, and all Protestant subjects were permitted to bear arms. The implication was clear, that sovereigns who owed their throne to one revolution might lose it by another. This was perhaps a salutary warning, but until the right to revolution was forgotten — as it was not for years to come — government could not find its constitutional feet.

The Tories had foreseen the instability that would come from altering the succession. Their insistence on the strict law of heredity had made them, at the time of the Popish Plot, vehement opponents of the Whig plan to exclude James from inheriting the throne; and their position had been rooted in more than traditionalism. To change the descent of the crown was almost as dangerous in the seventeenth century as it had been in the fifteenth, when the deposition of the Plantagenets in the person of Richard II had led to almost a hundred years of instability. The sovereign was still in fact the chief executive, and an executive without a clear title invited conspiracies in the name of a pretender. The Tories had not used this prosaic argument before James's accession, but had talked of divine right and the sin of resisting God's anointed. When the new King's conduct had forced them to realize that such talk was nonsense, and they had joined in ousting him, they had done so with great hesitation; and they now made heroic efforts to invest William and Mary with some shreds of James's legitimate sovereignty. The Tory logic was ridiculous or pathetic, depending on the point of view; but the purpose behind it was practical, to stabilize the settlement by crowning it with a legally valid crown.

The Whigs cared little about such legalism. After 1689 the labels of Whig and Tory, in the words of a modern historian, "distinguished those who welcomed the Revolution as a notable constitutional advance from those who grudgingly accepted it as a sinful and infinitely regrettable necessity." [2] The advance that the Whigs welcomed was primarily in ways of controlling the sovereign, and to gain control they were more than willing to sacrifice the law of heredity. Although they had to admit that the royal prerogative was necessary, they intended to keep it subordinate to the will of the oligarchy as expressed through parliament, that citadel of oligarchic power. Precious little divinity, in consequence, hedged their king.

[2] J. P. Kenyon, *The Stuarts: a Study in English Kingship* (1959), p. 189; this short, well-written, and vivid account is focused, as the title indicates, on the personalities of the sovereigns.

The Whig position was writ large in the statutes of William's reign. The Bill of Rights guaranteed the House of Commons control of its own procedure, and ended the royal claim to suspend or dispense at will with acts of parliament. Judges gained at long last security of tenure, subject only to removal by parliament, and so acquired that independence of the crown for which they had been struggling since the days of James I. The first in a series of Mutiny Acts, in 1689, established parliamentary control over the army by legalizing martial law — the basis of all military discipline — for only a stipulated period; the acts have been renewed continuously from that day to this, usually for a year at a time, and have achieved two purposes at once — to subject the army to periodic parliamentary examination and to ensure that parliament was in session at least once a year. Last but far from least, the course that the Revolution took underlined the Whig principle, largely derived from Locke, that the state rests upon a contract between government and governed. In the Bill of Rights the people of England, represented by the Lords and Commons in parliament, "claim, demand, and insist upon" specific liberties, and *then* declare that William and Mary are joint sovereigns. The point is unmistakable: sovereignty is not an indefeasible right but the result of a bargain, in which the subjects offer their allegiance on condition that the crown maintain their liberties. If the condition is violated, the contract is void.

The enthronement of William and Mary was the beginning, not the end, of the problem of the succession. Mary died without children in 1694; William remained king for his lifetime. At his death, according to the Bill of Rights, the throne would pass to his sister-in-law, James's younger daughter Anne, and then to her offspring by her husband, a dull Danish prince. Anne had thirteen pregnancies in thirteen years, but no child lived to grow up. The last died in 1700, and with him died the hope of carrying on even the semilegitimate line of James's children by his first wife. That line would end at Anne's death, and the question of who would succeed her had to be settled all over again.

There were two possibilities. One was to bring back James or his son by his second marriage, both of whom were Roman Catholics. The other was to turn to the nearest Protestant branch of the Stuarts, which was a remote one; it was represented by James I's granddaughter Sophia, the widowed Electress of Hanover, and her son the Elector George.[3] Bringing

---

[3] The following family tree shows how the problem arose. Sovereigns are in Roman capitals, and the claimants after 1700 in italics.

in the Hanoverians, petty German princes with their wholly German outlook, would not only extinguish the glamor of royalty but embroil Great Britain in the politics of central Europe. Restoring the Catholic Stuarts would be even worse: their faith and their heritage almost committed them to undoing the Revolution. Even the Tories could not stomach that prospect. In 1701, the year after the death of Anne's last child and the year before King William died, a parliament dominated by Tories passed the Act of Settlement, which stipulated that after Anne's tenure of the throne it should pass to the Hanoverian line. Thus the Tories, for the moment, confessed that their doctrine of legitimacy was untenable; for they passed into law their opponents' doctrine that the crown was at the disposition of parliament. But only for the moment. The Tories' creed of legitimacy died hard, and within a decade some of them were intriguing to bring the son of James II back to his father's throne.

If Whigs and Tories could in a crisis be brought together by their hatred of Roman Catholicism, they were poles apart in their attitude toward the Protestant dissenters. The Tories, traditional champions of the Anglican church, were enemies of dissent and wished to maintain the restrictive policy that the Clarendon Code had imposed a generation earlier. The Whigs had long ago realized that the Code had failed in its purpose of making life so unpleasant for its victims that they would return to the fold of the established church. Instead, legal harassment had merely kept the Presbyterians, Congregationalists, Baptists, and other sects a discontented minority. But that minority had proved so loyal to the parliamentary cause, despite all the blandishments of Charles II and James II, that the Whigs considered dissenters to be humble champions of Whiggism who deserved their reward; and by 1689 even the Tories were ready to make some grudging concessions to them. The question was how far to go, and here the two parties were at loggerheads.

The result was a compromise that satisfied no one. The Toleration Act of 1689 was as important for what it did not do as for what it did. It did not cover Jews, Roman Catholics, or a small body of Protestants who denied the doctrine of the Trinity (the later Unitarians); it did not apply to Ireland; it did not give English dissenters political rights, for they remained excluded from local and national government. It did relieve all English Protestants, including Quakers, from the restraints upon their civil liberty and freedom of worship that the Clarendon Code had imposed, and made them for the first time full-scale participants in all aspects of the national life except those that the oligarchs reserved for themselves, politics and officeholding. There the entrée was still the fantastic one set up in the Test Act of 1673 — taking communion in the established Church of England. A particular form of the eucharist remained the hallmark of the ruling class.

The Toleration Act, like so many compromises, failed to settle the problems that it tackled. It did not go far enough for the dissenters or for many of their Whig champions. (The latter, it must be remembered, were at least nominal Anglicans; otherwise they could not have been in politics.) It went too far for the Tories, particularly when some dissenters began to worm their way into office by the practice known as occasional conformity, or taking the Anglican communion once a year to satisfy the letter of the law. On the issue of dissent, more than on most others, the Tories after 1689 were reactionary, trying to undo the measure of toleration that had been granted, while the Whigs tried to maintain and even extend it. This struggle, like the uncertainty over the succession, helped to keep the whole settlement in suspense until the day of Queen Anne's death.

The Revolution in Foreign Policy

Behind these domestic conflicts, and often overshadowing them, was another and far greater conflict. The upheaval that ousted King James was a revolution not only in internal affairs but in foreign policy, for it launched Britain into European involvements she had never known before. Since the 1660s, when Louis XIV had begun to reach for the hegemony of western Europe, the British government had done nothing to stop him. Twice it had helped him by fighting the Netherlands, the power that barred his way to the lower Rhine; the rest of the time Whitehall had preserved a largely benevolent neutrality. As long as Britain's chief executive was Charles II or James II, both of them Louis's first cousins, thoroughgoing war against France was out of the question. Neutrality ended, however, when William became king.

By the 1680s the Netherlands were squarely in the path of French aggression; and their first citizen, the Stadtholder William of Orange, was forging a European coalition against Louis. William was a mediocre soldier but a skilled diplomat, and largely in the cause of his diplomacy he made his bid for the British throne. When he succeeded, he brought his new subjects into the Grand Alliance of 1689 — Sweden, Spain, Savoy, the Holy Roman Empire, Bavaria, Saxony, the Palatinate, the Netherlands, and Great Britain. Europe was in arms. For the first time Britain was an integral part of a vast continental coalition; she was also beginning, unknown to herself, that series of struggles against France that is often called the second Hundred Years War. It was a duel of giants, which occupied almost half of the next hundred and twenty-five years and profoundly affected the history of the world.

The British oligarchs did not go to war merely because they took William for king; they had reasons of their own. Merchants had long been alarmed by the rise of French commerce and naval power; diplomats had realized that Louis, if he secured for France the "natural" frontiers of the Pyrenees, Alps, and Rhine, would upset the balance of power in Europe; politicians had feared his intrigues in Whitehall and parliament; Protestants had come to see in him a new Philip of Spain, scheming to bring the British

Isles back into the arms of Rome. The causes of war antedated the Revolution, and the coming of William made war inevitable.

Tories and Whigs were agreed on opening the struggle, but not on how far to carry it. France was too strong to be brought quickly to her knees, and the Tories had no taste for long years of fighting. Their party did not have its center of gravity in the mercantile interests, which were largely Whig, but in the landed gentry; and the gentry neither knew nor cared much about distant dangers in Europe. Their background and tradition made them isolationists and, even when they themselves were sitting on the benches of parliament and confronting the affairs of the great world, tended to restrict their vision to the rural limits of squire and vicar and justice of the peace. They disliked the French more as foreigners than as a threat to the balance of power; they detested papists, but did not see in Louis the malevolent champion of Rome. In consequence, willing as they were to embark on war, they had no compelling incentive to wage it through thick and thin.

They had one compelling reason not to, which was the taxes that a long war entailed. The system of taxation rested, as it had for centuries, predominantly upon land, the easiest form of property to discover and assess; and by 1689 the land tax stood at twenty percent of assessed value. The landowners who were the backbone of the Tory party paid what many of them considered, with some reason, a disproportionate share of the nation's bills. As the campaigns in Europe dragged on from year to year, and the cost mounted, so did the discontent in Tory circles. Long before the first phase of the conflict ended in 1713, the Tories had become the party of peace.

Yet the struggle, much as the Tories grumbled, brought to them and the rest of the oligarchy enormous benefits. The Revolution was secured at home, primarily by the defeat of James II's attempt to regain his throne from Ireland. Scotland and England, not daring to fly at each other's throats in wartime, came together instead as a single state. The strain that military operations put upon the treasury produced a new financial structure. Britain learned to employ her naval strength, and dazzled Europe with her victories on land. War is always to some degree revolutionary, because it accelerates the rate of change; and these wars were no exception. The kingdoms of England and Scotland entered them in 1689 as two parochial states that had been concerned for centuries with their own affairs. The kingdom of Great Britain emerged in 1713 with new interests in North and South America and in the Mediterranean, with a new status as one of the great powers of Europe, and with the revolutionary settlement deeply rooted at last against the wind of reaction.

The first phase of the conflict, from 1689 to 1697, was known as King William's War; and its chief strategic importance for Britain was naval. The nature of the Grand Alliance created a novel problem, but one that was to recur over and over again in the future — how to hold the alliance together. The states that composed it, because they surrounded France on all sides, were exposed to attack and destruction piecemeal; the French were at the center of a circle, and could strike at the circumference wherever they pleased. The allied war effort depended on effective communications between Spain, northern Italy, central Europe, the Netherlands, Scandinavia, and the British Isles. The distances involved were enormous; but the British had an advantage, if they could develop it, to compensate for the French advantage of position. Moving supplies and armies was slower and more cumbersome by land than by sea, and naval control of the waters around Europe would give the allies the upper hand. A successful war of coalition, in short, depended on the successful exertion of sea power.

As an instrument of sea power the Royal Navy of 1689 seemed to be a weak reed. It had not seen action since the third Dutch War, fifteen years before, and its performance then had been lamentable. Now it was outnumbered by the French and had no apparent advantages; tactics were crude, gunnery inaccurate, and strategic ideas embryonic. But in some ways the navy was more effective than in the days of its past glory under Elizabeth and the Roundheads. The warship had become differentiated from the commercial carrier; no longer could merchant ships be pressed into service in the line of battle, as they had been against the Armada. A naval career had become differentiated from a military; gone were the amphibious heroes of Cromwell's time, like Blake and Monck and Rupert, who had transformed themselves from generals into admirals. The "senior service" was emerging as a specialized profession: a start had been made on a marine corps, on training youngsters systematically for a career at sea, and on maintaining reserve officers in peacetime. What remained to do was build and man more ships and learn how to use them.

King William's War opened with a crisis in which sea power was of paramount importance. In March 1689 King James landed in Ireland, which he intended to use as a base for reconquering the British throne. He was welcomed everywhere except in Ulster, the Protestant north, where a few towns managed by desperate exertions to hold out against him. But the French were superior at sea and landed arms, money, and officers in such force that the reduction of the whole island seemed only a matter of time. William could not come to the rescue unless the navy could clear a way for him, and this the navy had no idea how to do. Fortunately for him, however, the French admirals were as inept as their British counterparts.

The result was what looks by hindsight like a comedy of errors, but was in fact more a comedy of ignorance. In the summer of 1690 the French concentrated against the Anglo-Dutch fleet in the English Channel, defeated it, and then, instead of gathering the fruits of victory by blockading Ireland, did nothing at all. Meanwhile King William had sailed (with a convoy of only six warships) and had landed in Ireland and marched on Dublin, where his father-in-law had set up his capital. James met him in battle on the River Boyne, was defeated, and promptly fled once more to France. The remnants of his army held out until October 1691, still with little support from the sea, and then in the Treaty of Limerick surrendered on reasonable terms. The French had lost the best chance in their history of turning Ireland into a satellite. When they tried again a century later, the British had learned how to handle a navy.

The Revolutionary Settlement in Ireland and Scotland

The effect of James's failure was to save the Revolution at the cost of the Irish. If he had been victorious, or even maintained his hold on part of the island, he might have regained his hold on part of England; for the Dutchman and his wife were newly on their thrones, and many men would have been glad to see them toppled off again. But such thoughts were suppressed as soon as James scuttled back under Louis's wing and became the pensioner of France. The exiled King never again landed in the British Isles, and the Jacobites who waited for him there grew more and more discouraged. They had to nourish their faith on a secret ritual; when one of them toasted "the King," for example, with his wineglass held over a goblet of water, he meant that he was toasting the King-over-the-water. Such antics revealed a loyalty that was overlaid, as well it might be, with circumspection. From the Battle of the Boyne to the end of the wars the Jacobite cause, whether in Ireland or Scotland or England, was the cause of France as well as of James, and therefore tinged with treason.

Scottish and English Jacobites paid chiefly in heartache for their failure, but Ireland paid a heavier price. Three times in a century the Irish had turned on their masters and had always met defeat. They had rebelled against Elizabeth, and been chastised by her and James I; they had rebelled against the Long Parliament, and been chastised by Cromwell; now they had rebelled against King William, and the vengeance exacted was more civilized but more effective than that of the Puritans. The Treaty of Limerick was repudiated, the penal laws against Roman Catholics were strengthened, the Catholic landholding class was slowly strangled by legal restrictions on their property, Catholics were barred from trade and the professions and from the Irish parliament. Even the Protestants of Ulster, who had held a beachhead for William until he could come to the rescue, were swallowed in the general ruin. They were largely Presbyterians, and the benefits of the Toleration Act were not extended to them. They were barred, like the Catholics, from the Dublin parliament, which was limited thenceforth to the tiny minority who belonged to the Church of England.

This Anglican clique, determined to keep its monopoly of power, was responsible for some of the most savage legislation of the period. The Westminster parliament also contributed its share, particularly in economic restrictions; it ruined the Irish woolen industry by high tariffs and virtually stopped Irish trade with the colonies. The island began to sink fast into poverty and despair. The few who could escape did so, in the first of those waves of emigration that went on for the next two centuries and disseminated far and wide the Irishman's hate for Britain.

The Glorious Revolution and the wars that followed it, like the era of revolution and wars between 1640 and 1660, had dramatically different effects in Ireland and Scotland. To Ireland both upheavals brought unmitigated disaster; to Scotland they were, in the long run, a blessing. The reason is largely that the Scots, in dealing with the English, had three great advantages over the Irish: a political system that gave them considerable autonomy, a church that was dourly Protestant, and a fighting force that commanded respect. Seventeenth-century Scotland was not strong enough to avoid defeat and partial domination by England, but was too strong to be exploited like Ireland.

The Restoration in 1660 had been little more popular with the Scots than the "sword government" of Cromwell's Ironsides. Presbyterians had been furious to see the Church of England reestablished, and merchants to see their trade with England and her colonies curtailed. The first of these grievances the Scots took care of in 1689, when they offered the throne to William and Mary on condition that the Presbyterian kirk be recognized as the national church of Scotland. The condition was promptly met, and the northern kingdom finally shook off the rule of the hated Anglican bishops, against which it had been struggling for a hundred years.

The Highlanders remained a problem. In the wild hills and glens of the north, a region without roads or commerce or kirk, the king's writ scarcely ran; there the clans, who cared almost as little for the government in Edinburgh as for that in London, were a tumultuous law unto themselves, swayed by loyalties that had little to do with the religion or politics of the lowlands. Jacobitism was strong among the Highlanders. King James was nominal head of Clan Stuart, and the clansmen were romantics at heart. In 1689 some of them rose and were suppressed by force, the first bloodshed in the hopeless saga of the north that went on for the next half-century. In 1692 the Macdonalds of Glencoe, who had been slow to make their peace with King William, were butchered by soldiers drawn from a rival clan. This massacre, for which William had not been directly responsible but which he condoned, increased his unpopularity in the north. Every Scot who resented the heavy hand of Whitehall was a potential Jacobite.

These troubles coincided with a weakening of the King's political control over Scotland. Before the Revolution the Scottish parliament had been largely under the thumb of the executive; privy councillors responsible to the sovereign had picked a committee of members of parliament that arranged most of its business. After the Revolution this committee disappeared, and parliament changed its character: it was no longer a tool of royal authority, but began to speak for the nation to a distant sovereign. That sovereign now had to work with two legislatures, English and Scottish, each jealous of its own prerogatives; and if friction arose between them the crown would be in an impossible position.

Friction did arise, largely from economic causes. The Scots were turning to trade and commercial ventures overseas with the avidity that they had once shown for the theological niceties of John Calvin. English financial and mercantile interests, entrenched in the Westminster parliament and determined to keep the resources of the empire for themselves, feared Scottish competition even more than Irish. In the 1690s a Scottish company was founded to promote trade with the Isthmus of Panama. The London financial community discouraged English investment in the company, which the Scots then took over as a national enterprise, undeterred by King William's failure to support them. The company collapsed, primarily because there was no trade to be had in Panama. But the Scots, who blamed the debacle on England, were "like raging madmen."

The story had its denouement after Anne ascended the throne in 1702, but can best be completed here at the cost of strict chronology. The new reign coincided with Britain's entry into a new and larger war against France, and the Scottish parliament took the opportunity to assert national autonomy in stronger and stronger terms. The climax came in the Scottish Act of Security of 1704, which provided that the dynastic union of the two countries, unless it were amended in a way to satisfy the Scots, should end at Anne's death; the Scottish crown would then go to a Protestant Stuart, but not necessarily to the same one who wore the crown of England. The Queen refused to sign the act, whereupon the Edinburgh parliament, for the first time in its history, put pressure on her by refusing supplies. She signed, the act became law, and the crisis was at a boil. The English government did not dare coerce the Scots in the middle of a great war for fear of driving them into the enemy's hands. Waiting for time to heal the quarrel was even more dangerous, however, for at any moment Anne's death might open the northern kingdom to the French.

Breaking the ties between the two countries was unthinkable, and their existing constitutional relationship was unworkable. The only other possibility was a closer union. Negotiations began, progressed with great speed, and bore fruit in the Act of Union of 1707. The two nations were amalgamated in the Kingdom of Great Britain, with the Union Jack for its flag. Scotland retained its own courts and legal system, and of course its own church. It received forty-five seats in the House of Commons of the new combined parliament, and sixteen seats in the House of Lords for representatives elected by the Scottish peers. It also received the large economic concession of free trade with England and within the empire; the island of Great Britain thereby became the largest free-trade area in Europe. The union was an act of necessity on both sides, not of choice, and it remained extremely unpopular for years to come. But it was the response to centripetal forces that had been at work for two centuries.

When Henry VII's daughter Margaret Tudor had gone as a bride to Edinburgh, her father had said that in this marriage alliance between the two kingdoms the greater would draw the less. Time proved him right. The first pull came at the beginning of Elizabeth's reign, when the Scots threw off Catholicism, broke away from France, and called on England for aid; the next came when the House of Stuart moved its capital from Edinburgh to London; the third came during the Puritan Revolution, which brought the two countries into more intimate contact than ever before — sometimes in collaboration, sometimes in war — and culminated in a brief political union that was forced on the Scots by the Cromwellian Protectorate. The Glorious Revolution was achieved by both nations together, and after it the idea of a voluntary and lasting union was periodically broached. But what brought the idea to fruition was the outburst of economic and military activity that swept the whole island at the turn of the century. England and Scotland had parallel aims, in war and trade as much as in their search for dynastic security, and their need of each other undercut their jealousies. They could no longer afford individual governments, little as they cared to admit it, and by fusing their sovereignties they gained strength for the future.

Financial Innovations

The activity in war and trade that brought England and Scotland first into collision, then into union, was closely connected with another part of the revolutionary settlement: the reordering of public finance. By 1689 the archaic fiscal system that the Stuarts had inherited from the Tudors, although improved at the Restoration, was still a long way from the system of a modern state. Money was in ample supply, but much of it lay idle; until it could be readily channeled into investment, whether in private enterprise or government securities, commercial growth was restricted and the waging of a prolonged war was impossible. What were needed were mechanisms for tapping the nation's wealth, and these were found. Although complex and undramatic, they were as much responsible as the navy or the Act of Union for Britain's emergence as a great power.

One mechanism was the public debt. By the early 1690s the government, it was clear, could not continue to finance the war by increasing taxation or by short-term loans. The solution that was found was to create a system of permanent borrowing — to issue annuities, not repayable but bearing interest for specified terms of years; investors could thus buy from the state a guaranteed income. By 1696 the system was fully developed, and what had once been a short-term loan to the government had become a government security. So began the national debt. It did not solve at one stroke the financial problems of the state; a debt rarely does. But it did permit the government to utilize private capital more freely than before, and in this case to turn it into war-making.

The evolution of the public debt was intimately associated, almost from the start, with the rise of the Bank of England. Here many factors were at work, of which two were especially significant. One was the government's need for an agency to administer the complicated machinery of the debt; the other was the rising demand for a reliable form of paper currency. Private banking, largely in the hands of London goldsmiths, had grown by leaps and bounds since the Restoration, and had already developed the two techniques that chiefly concern the average citizen of today, the personal check and the bank note (or, in American, the bill) that constitutes paper currency. The check is in essence an order to the banker to pay from money deposited, the note a promise by him to pay from his own resources. By the 1690s bank notes were becoming a kind of informal currency; but their value depended on the financial reputation of the particular bank that issued them and might vary enormously from firm to firm and year to year. What was needed was a bank of issue that was as far above suspicion as Caesar's wife.

In 1694 a group of Whig financiers made a bargain with the government. They lent it £1,200,000 at a lower interest rate than that on the debt, and in return were chartered as a bank with certain unique privileges, which grew as the years passed. Soon the new corporation, the Bank of England, had the entire management of the debt and a monopoly of joint-stock banking, and was the only institution of any size permitted to issue bank notes. Its volume of business was so large, and its connection with the government so close, that it commanded the confidence of the business community; before long its notes became what they have remained to this day, the paper currency of Great Britain. From the beginning the Bank has thus held a unique position, in that it is both a private corporation and an arm of the state.

Many Tories fought the Bank tooth and nail, on the ground that it was a Whig device for tying the financial world to the leading strings of the Whig party. If that party was synonymous with the cause of the Revolution, the point was well taken. Political changes tend to be lasting when men invest money in them; Henry VIII, for example, perpetuated the breach with Rome by transferring the monastic lands to new owners, who thereafter saw in Rome a threat to their pocketbooks as well as their souls. An analogous process was going on in the 1690s: the Revolution was becoming a gigantic vested interest; the more money was poured into government securities and the more powerful the Bank of England grew, the more the new financial structure of the nation was fused with its political structure. The threat of a Jacobite restoration carried with it an implicit threat not only to those who governed under William and later under Anne but to those who invested in government, and security-holders were far more numerous and more formidable than officeholders.

The Bank also strengthened the sinews of sea power, by which the Revolution was secured. The climax of the naval war came in 1692, when Louis attempted an invasion only to have his fleet destroyed under the eyes of his army. Thereafter his resources were more and more drained away from the navy by the needs of the land war, while the British pushed a shipbuilding program that soon gave them predominance at sea. But ships were so expensive that only the creation of the Bank permitted the Royal Navy to function. Half of the initial loan of 1694, with which the Whig bankers bought their charter, went at once to the treasurer of the navy; and throughout the war, and the one that followed it, squadrons plowed through distant seas because suitable arrangements had been made in the London money market.

The thirteen years of William's reign were thus a period of far-reaching change. The constitution was altered, dissent was recognized, Ireland was pacified effectively if brutally, Scotland started on the autonomous road that led to union five years after William died, and the two kingdoms fought their first great European war and achieved the financial wherewithal for waging it. When peace returned to Europe in 1697, the tide of Louis's aggression had been halted; for the first time in his military adventures he gained nothing of significance, and in the peace treaty he recognized William as king and Anne as William's successor.

For these solid achievements the Dutch King might have expected some thanks from his subjects, but he got none. Even the Whigs had never been enthusiastic about him, and he lacked both the virtues and vices by which his uncle, Charles II, had endeared himself to much of the public. William was a cold, withdrawn man, and such heart as he had remained in the Netherlands. He had Charles's political acumen without his laziness, and a deeper insight into European diplomacy than any sovereign since Elizabeth; but these qualities did not appeal to the oligarchs, who were far more interested in managing their king than in learning from him. While the war lasted they were forced to cooperate with him after a fashion, but the moment peace was signed they made his life miserable. Parliament took the bit in its teeth, forced the sale of Irish lands that the King had given his favorites, cut his standing army drastically, and packed home his beloved Dutch guards. After a decade on the throne he was on such bad terms with the men who had called him to it that he talked of quitting the country.

But he could not do so, for the same reason that he had been unable to resist the call in 1688. The storm clouds of a new and greater crisis were boiling up over Europe, and he dared not lose such control as he had over British policy. In the four years of peace after 1697 his gift for diplomacy was stretched to the limit, first in his efforts to ward off the coming storm and then in preparations for it. Parliament was asleep, and he could only hope that it would wake in time to meet the danger.

The War of the Spanish Succession

The question that confronted Europe at the opening of the eighteenth century was what to do with a state that was too weak to determine its own future. The state, or rather collection of states, was the empire of the Spanish Habsburgs. It had Spain for its focus, and included the Spanish Netherlands, possessions in Italy, and most of Central and South America. The crown of these vast dominions was on the head of a weak and sickly king, Charles II, who had no direct heirs. What would happen when he died?

The answer would affect the whole power structure of the continent. By 1700 there were two principal contenders for the inheritance, both claiming it by right of descent: Archduke Charles of Habsburg, a younger son of the Austrian branch of the family headed by the Holy Roman Emperor; and Philip of Bourbon, the grandson of Louis XIV.[4] Neither could succeed to the entire Spanish empire without threatening the balance of power, in one case by reestablishing the old Habsburg predominance of the early sixteenth century, in the other by creating an even more menacing Bourbon predominance. The only way to maintain the balance was to split the prize and give part to each claimant. Even Louis XIV was attracted by this idea as the alternative to a European war, and he and King William agreed to a partition treaty. But the Austrian Habsburgs refused to agree, and the King of Spain was not so weak or so lacking in Spanish patriotism that he was willing to see the empire partitioned. He willed it in its entirety to Philip with the priviso that, if the Bourbon refused, all the empire should go to Archduke Charles. Then, in 1700, the King died.

Louis was faced with a difficult choice. He might respect the partition treaty, which could well mean fighting Austria for his grandson's share, or accept for him the entire empire and fight all who objected. He chose the second alternative and thereby ensured a war against Austria. Britain was far from ready to fight, but during 1701 Louis acted as if he were trying to force her hand: he moved his troops into the Spanish Netherlands, announced that France would henceforth have special trading privileges with Spanish America, and in September, when James II died, formally recognized his cousin's son as James III, King of England, Scotland, and Ireland. Almost simultaneously Louis banned British imports into France and urged his grandson, Philip, to do the same in Spain. These actions gave Britain major war aims — to preserve the Netherlands from French dominance, to redress the balance of power, to safeguard the Hanoverian succession against a Stuart

[4] The following family tree shows how the claims arose. Claimants after 1700 are in italics.

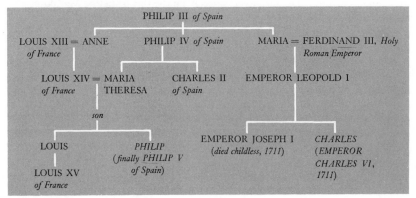

pretender who was the protég' of France, to protect British trade in Europe
and overseas. When King William returned from the continent after
organizing another coalition, he found that parliament at last was solidly
behind him. The War of the Spanish Succession had begun.

William did not live to manage it. He had never been robust, and this
latest crisis drained his stamina. In February 1702, he fell from his horse and
broke his collarbone; a fortnight later he was dead. But, fortunately for both
his countries, he left behind a war leader more talented than he was — John
Churchill, then Earl and soon Duke of Marlborough, the most brilliant
soldier-diplomat of modern British history.

Marlborough, like William, had a cool intelligence and almost infinite
patience; he also, unlike William, was endowed with tact, good looks, and the
charm to melt a basilisk. Under this winning surface he was greedy and
unscrupulous, like most of the men about him. In a peaceful era he might have
left no more of a mark than they did; but in wartime his genius, aided by the
luck that brought him to power, carried his name across Europe. He had
begun as a trusted servant of James II (who had taken his sister for mistress),
had deserted him at the critical moment of the Revolution and been rewarded
with an earldom by the new sovereigns, and had then begun to intrigue with
James again. William never liked or, for good reason, trusted the Earl, but
was compelled as time passed to bring him into prominence. Although the
King did not know what talent lay hidden in his slippery servant, he did
know that Marlborough's wife Sarah was the bosom friend and confidante of
the Princess Anne, and that the Earl and Countess would play crucial parts in
the new reign.

So they did. Anne was born to be dominated by someone, and Sarah
was born to dominate. The Queen was an unattractive person, corpulent, dull-
witted, narrowly pious, and suspicious of all except her few friends. But
friends she had to have, and those she trusted she trusted completely — for the
time being. She decided the many issues that came to her less on their merits,
insofar as she could grasp them, than on the personalities of their advocates.
Her whole-souled admiration for Sarah, spiced with a touch of fear, extended
to Sarah's husband. The Queen was scarcely on the throne before Marlborough
became the power behind it; he was made commander in chief, a duke, and a
Knight of the Garter. His duchess bullied Anne in his interest, and provided
the strange liaison that tied the direction of the war to the source of executive
power in St. James's Palace.

For a liaison with parliament Marlborough trusted primarily to the
manipulations of a moderate Tory, Lord Godolphin, whose chief responsibility
was to hold together a working majority that would support the war. Success
in this task depended in great measure on military success, which depended in
turn in how well the allies could coordinate their efforts. They were again
scattered across the map of Europe: Britain, the Netherlands, Austria, some of
the German states, and before long Savoy and Portugal. The second coalition

had the same weakness that King William's had had, dispersion, while France
had new advantages. Her armies already occupied Spain and the Spanish
Netherlands and commanded the lower Rhine, and she had the alliance of
Bavaria in southern Germany, a wedge thrust between Anglo-Dutch and
Austrian power. She consequently began the war in a vastly stronger position
than in 1689.

Politics and geography created three main theaters of operations, to
which a fourth was soon added. The three were the Low Countries, the Danube
valley, and northern Italy; the fourth was Spain. Each of the continental
allies had its own particular interests. The Austrians were intent on defending
themselves on the Danube while they acquired the Spanish possessions in
Italy, and they wanted to see Archduke Charles made king of Spain only if
they did not have to do the fighting there. Neither the British nor the Dutch,
at the start, dreamed of doing it for them. The Dutch were focused on the
Low Countries and, like the French in the First World War, opposed any
distant operations that weakened the defense of their own soil. Only the
British, secured at home by sea power, were in a position to see the struggle
as a whole and the need to coordinate its many parts. But they were not
inclined to do so, and Marlborough's chief task was to imbue them with
his own broad vision.

Many of them were impervious to his vision, but no one was
impervious to his charm. Lord Chesterfield, who knew him well, has left
a sketch of him that deserves quoting. "He was eminently illiterate, wrote
bad English and spelled it worse. . . . His figure was beautiful, but his manner
was irresistible by either man or woman. It was by this engaging, graceful
manner that he was enabled, during all his war, to connect the various and
jarring powers of the grand alliance and to carry them on to the main object
of the war, notwithstanding their private and separate views, jealousies, and
wrong-headednesses. Whatever court he went to (and he was often obliged
to go himself to some testy and refractory ones), he was constantly prevailed
and brought them into his measures."

During the first two years of the struggle the Duke did not notably
prevail with either parliament or Britain's allies. Although he showed his skill
by parrying the French threat to the Netherlands, the threat to Austria steadily
increased; by the spring of 1704 the French and Bavarians were poised for a
blow at Vienna that might well knock the Habsburgs out of the war. Neither
the Tories nor the Dutch could see the danger. Marlborough did, and he rose
to it. In the deepest secrecy, taking only the Queen and Godolphin into his
confidence, he kidnaped the British, Dutch, and German army in the
Netherlands, for a lightning march to the Danube. There at Blenheim, in
August, he won the first great victory that had come to a British general in
Europe since the Middle Ages. King Louis's army was shattered, his marshal
a captive in Marlborough's coach; and Versailles had its first word of the
disaster in letters from prisoners of war. France was still far from defeated,

but after Blenheim she was forced progressively onto the defensive. The gilded panoply of her regime, which had fascinated and terrified Europe for half a century, was shown at last to be vulnerable.

Meanwhile the workings of British sea power had begun to be felt in the Mediterranean. In the autumn of 1703 the Royal Navy helped to induce the Duke of Savoy, Louis's ally in northwestern Italy, to change sides and bring into the coalition an army of 16,000 men. Almost simultaneously Portugal likewise deserted France for Britain, and thereby changed the whole face of the war. The allies now had a base for the conquest of Spain, and began to take seriously the idea of installing the archduke in Madrid. Here was a war aim to arouse the enthusiasm of the powerful merchants, Dutch and British, who were eager to enlarge their trade; Spain and her overseas empire under Habsburg rule would be their happy hunting ground.

But Philip V, backed by French land power, was reigning in Madrid. To oust him would require attack from the sea and therefore command of the sea. For that purpose the Portuguese harbor of Lisbon was inadequate, because a fleet based there could not control the Mediterranean coast of Spain, or contain the French fleet based at Toulon. What was needed was a base inside the straits, a good harbor immune to land attack and therefore on an island. The obvious place was Port Mahon on Minorca, in the Balearic Islands. Here the British established themselves in 1708 and remained for seventy-five years.

Meanwhile they had picked up another prize. In 1704 a British admiral, frustrated by a cruise in which he had accomplished nothing, had attacked and captured the Rock of Gibraltar. It was not a base like Port Mahon because its harbor was too small, but it was invaluable as an observation point for shadowing any hostile fleet that entered or left the Mediterranean. Gibraltar and Minorca together proved in the long run to be the keys to naval operations off southern Europe: large ships based on Port Mahon could blockade enemy squadrons in the harbors of the mainland; if a squadron ran the blockade and made for the open Atlantic, frigates based on Gibraltar could follow it and call up a battle fleet from Minorca or Britain. This was the strategy of the future, but it took many years to develop. Britain, when she retained her two conquests at the end of the war, had no inkling that they would eventually be worth far more to her than all Marlborough's victories.

Those victories continued after Blenheim, for the Duke never lost a major battle. But those he won were never conclusive, and their principal effect was to breed violent controversy at home about the conduct of the war. As one campaign dragged on to the next, the Tories became more and more restive, the Whigs more and more ambitious. Marlborough's strategy now had for its political aim driving King Philip from Spain, and for its military aim invading France by way of the Spanish Netherlands and Flanders. The Tories believed (and they proved to be right) that these aims were unattainable, and urged instead what they called a "blue-water" policy, concentrating on the war at sea while supporting Britain's continental allies by subsidies, which were less expensive than the interminable land war. The eyes of the Whigs were fixed on the Spanish prize, and Marlborough's victories made them over-confident. They dreamed of France conquered by invasion from the Low Countries, of Louis brought to his knees and his grandson exiled from Madrid, of Spain and Spanish America opened to British trade. Year after year, how-ever, Louis refused to kneel, and the Spaniards held to their Bourbon king. "The Whig formula of 'no peace without Spain' would mean 'no peace till Doomsday'." [5]

During those years Marlborough and Godolphin, in order to carry on the war, had to turn more and more from the Tories to the Whigs, who by 1710 monopolized the queen's ministry. Then came the explosion. Anne had never been a wholehearted believer in the Revolution that had ousted her father (and eventually given her the throne), and distrusted its Whig partisans; her high-church Anglican views, furthermore, inclined her by nature to the Tories. The Duchess of Marlborough had argued her into discarding Tory for Whig ministers, but in the process had overreached herself; Anne was tired of being bullied. And the majority of her subjects were tired of the war. In 1710, when the implacable Whigs had rejected a peace overture and were clearly bent on conquering the unconquerable, discontent came to a head; the queen seized the opportunity to change her ministers again. The Tories swept into power, and at the end of 1711 even Marlborough was brusquely stripped of his command.

The End of the Stuart Era (1711–1714)

The Tories were committed to making peace, and for domestic reasons they had to make it fast. At the Queen's death, which might come at any moment, they dreamed of a Stuart restoration. They had never liked the prospect of a Hanoverian king, even though they themselves had passed the Act of Settlement; and in the years since 1701 their imagination had been increasingly intrigued by the Stuart youngster, growing up in France, whom

[5] George M. Trevelyan, *England under the Stuarts* (1949), p. 413. Although this book, first published in 1904, is now out of date, its insight and vividness still make it a classic example of history-writing as a fine art. The other important general history of the period is G. N. Clark, *The Later Stuarts, 1660–1714* (1934). For more specialized studies see F. C. Turner, *James II* (1949); David Ogg, *England in the Reigns of James II and William III* (1955); G. M. Trevelyan, *The English Revolution, 1688–89* (2nd ed., 1946); and the antiquated, biased, but still magnificent work of Thomas B. Macaulay, edited by Sir Charles Firth, *A History of England from the Accession of James II* (6 vols., 1913–15). The major contributions to the history of Queen Anne's reign are C. T. Atkinson, *Marlborough and the Rise of the British Army* (1921); G. M. Trevelyan, *England under Queen Anne* (3 vols., 1930–34); and Sir Winston S. Churchill's biography of his ancestor, *Marlborough, His Life and Times* (6 vols., 1933–39).

the Jacobites called James III and others called the Pretender. If he could be persuaded to change his religion he might make a Tory king — *provided* that the war was over by the time the question arose. Even the most fevered Tory fancy could not picture the British public's accepting in wartime a king who was a pensioner of France.

Two factors helped the government in its hurried efforts to make peace and force the treaty through parliament. One was that Archduke Charles succeeded to the Habsburg dominions in 1711 as the Emperor Charles VI; his accession vitiated the Whig argument for conquering Spain, because success there would unite the Austrian and Spanish empires under a single crown and thereby upset the balance of power. The other factor was that the queen gave her ministers the support they needed to force the treaty through the House of Lords. The upper house, unlike the lower, was still dominated by Whigs because it was immune to the electorate, and without royal intervention the Lords could not be coerced. But Anne could pack the house, and did so at the end of 1711 by creating twelve new Tory peers. Her action was more momentous than she or her ministers realized. Two other and greater crises of the future, in 1832 and 1911, were resolved by the government's threatening to take the same course, and the fact that Anne had taken it sufficed to bring the Lords to heel.

The final Anglo-French peace was signed at Utrecht in 1713, after Britain had shocked her allies by deserting them in the field; other treaties were concluded in the following year. The whole complex, which goes by the name of the Utrecht settlement, was a landmark in European history; and an examination of its terms will show why it was also a landmark in British history. France accepted the Hanoverian succession and banished the Pretender; in return the allies recognized Philip V as king of Spain and of the Spanish overseas empire on condition that he should never inherit the the French crown. The Habsburgs received the former Spanish possessions in Italy and the Spanish Netherlands, which until the 1790s remained Austrian; and the border between them and France was garrisoned by Dutch troops to protect the road to Amsterdam. Spain ceded to Britain Gibraltar and Minorca, and by an agreement known as the asiento accorded to British merchants a monopoly of importing slaves into Spanish America and limited trading rights there.[6] In North America France ceded to Britain Hudson's Bay, Nova Scotia, and Newfoundland. These were the dry details.

The settlement respected the principle of the balance of power by giving something to every strong belligerent. The Dutch gained security for their frontiers. The Austrian Habsburgs gained the whole of the European Spanish empire, except Spain itself, and so increased their weight in the scales of power to balance the Bourbon accretion. France gained a dynastic, and therefore a political and economic, link with Spain and South America, but lost part of the inheritance for which Louis had originally gone to war. Only

[6] See below, p. 48.

Britain, among the major contestants, seemed to make minor gains: a rock by the Straits of Gibraltar, a Mediterranean island, and some North American wilderness. But appearances were deceptive.

The settlement furthered the long-standing British interest in keeping a strong power out of the Low Countries, for the Austrian Netherlands were henceforth protected by the Dutch and governed by the distant Habsburgs. British merchants gained concessions that started them on their century-long struggle for the trade of Latin America. The Royal Navy, faced with the possibility that the Franco-Spanish fleets might unite against it in overwhelming strength, received in Gibraltar and Minorca the bases it needed for keeping Bourbon forces in the Atlantic separated from those in the Mediterranean. Britain came out of the struggle, in short, with little to show on the surface for eleven years of fighting, but with solid foundations for her power.

The end of the war was the beginning of a final, bitter domestic crisis. Its crux was the succession, but the old quarrel over religious dissent helped to heat the atmosphere. Here the Tories were as intolerant as ever. In 1711 they banned the practice of occasional conformity to evade the Test Act, and three years later gave the Church of England a monopoly of secondary education; dissenters now could neither hold office nor keep their children from Anglican indoctrination. Even their precarious position of 1689 was being undermined, and they looked for deliverance to the Whigs and Hanover. The Tories, in turn, could rely on a large segment of the country squires and the Anglican clergy, whose attitude toward dissent would have won the approval of Archbishop Laud.

Persecuting a minority might win votes for the Tories, but did not touch their basic dilemma over the crown. Time was running out; Anne clearly could not live for many more months, and some preparation had to be made at once for the succession. But for whose? If Hanover was unpopular with the Tory government, the converse was equally true and more important. The Elector George became sole heir to the throne when his mother Sophia died early in 1714, and George believed that the great Tory achievement, the Treaty of Utrecht, had flagrantly betrayed the interests of the German states in general and Hanover in particular. Unless the angry Elector could be shorn of power before he set foot in England, the Tory ministers would be finished, politically if not physically. Yet their only alternative to the Hanoverian was the Pretender, who far from giving them help dashed their hopes, in the spring of 1714, by announcing that he would not abandon his Catholic faith for the sake of a throne.

As spring wore on toward summer, the unity of the Tory ministry began to disintegrate in a quarrel between its two leading members. Robert Harley, Earl of Oxford, was an enigmatic and skillful politician, who wanted to wait on events in the hope of profiting from whatever came. Henry St. John, Viscount Bolingbroke, wanted to gather into his hands the full power of the state, by putting his agents into every position of influence; how he intended to use the power is not clear to this day, because he did not quite have the chance to demonstrate. Lord Oxford stood in his way. The two men, who by now detested each other on a number of grounds, fought for the upper hand. On July 27 Bolingbroke won: Oxford was dismissed. But the victor had only three days in which to try to exploit his victory. By the 30th, when the queen was obviously dying, few men were willing to risk their necks for whatever Bolingbroke's schemes might be. The moderates gained control, and a stream of orders went out to prepare the way for the coming of the Hanoverian. On the morning of August 1 the last of the Stuarts died. Edema and a bad heart, in a woman prematurely old, ended Bolingbroke's career and destroyed his party, and he of all men had reason to remember his *Macbeth:*

> She should have died hereafter;
> There would have been a time for such a word.

The years 1713–14 were a watershed in British history. They marked the end of a quarter-century of wars, from which Britain emerged as the first sea power of Europe and during which the changes set in motion in 1688 were completed and secured. If defeat of the Royal Navy had ever opened the way to invasion and a Stuart restoration, if Scotland had broken the dynastic union and resumed her independence, if the Bank of England had failed, if the Pretender had turned Protestant and Anne had lived a few months longer — these are the *if's* of history, which produce no answer. All that can be said is that the revolutionary settlement was never really safe until King George was proclaimed, and never in serious jeopardy thereafter. The settlement, like the men who made it, was a combination of political wisdom and expediency, principles and grasping self-interest, and was built in the dust of battling parties in Westminster and battling armies in Europe. It was revealed, when the dust finally cleared, as the structure of Britain's Augustan Age.

2 The Structure of the Oligarchy

A society, past or present, can only be described in generalizations, which by their nature are unsatisfactory. The observer of a society today can at least live in it, but the historian cannot; he has to view it through the eyes of men and women long dead, who saw only what they were able to see from their particular positions and with their particular preconceptions. The "facts" that they provide, and on which any general description of a period must in great part depend, are consequently unreliable.

This is no modern discovery. It was clear to a sophisticated observer in the reign of George II, and underlay his skeptical view of the data that make history. "Do we ever hear the most recent fact related exactly in the same way," the Earl of Chesterfield asked, "by the several people who were at the same time eyewitnesses of it? No. One mistakes, another misrepresents, and others warp it a little to their own turn of mind or private views. A man who has been concerned in a transaction will not write it fairly; and a man who has not, cannot."

In this passage, nevertheless, the Earl was urging upon his son the value of studying history. That study was becoming, as never before, the recognized prerequisite for understanding the present, which is why the eighteenth century saw the beginning of history-writing in the modern sense. Chesterfield was in accord with this trend of the times, but he also had a healthy strain of what he called "historical incredulity." He urged his son not to accept at face value historians' generalizations about causes and motives, but to try to pry into them for himself and to remember the complexities and inconsistencies of human nature with which history deals — the fluctuations of passion and will, the accidents of bodily health, the admixture of petty and evil in the best of men, of greatness in the worst. "As for the reflections of historians, with which they think it necessary to interlard their histories or at least to conclude their chapters, . . . do not adopt them implicitly upon the credit of the author, but analyze them yourself and judge whether they are true or not."

His words are a sound caution in approaching his world. We know a great deal about the oligarchs among whom he moved, from their politics and architecture to their farming and views of life; but no one knows enough to generalize confidently about them. This chapter will begin with

their political structure, will touch upon their architecture, their problems
in providing for their families, their ways of using the land, their taste
in literature, and will return at the end to Chesterfield as the exemplar of a
social code by which many of them lived. Generalizations will appear in
abundance, but they will be no more than tentative conclusions. "Analyze
them yourself and judge whether they are true or not."

The Death of Toryism

The political structure of the oligarchy changed after 1714, for the
Hanoverian accession marked the end of parties in the old sense. They had
never been parties in the modern sense, because they had had little national
organization, cohesion, or discipline; they had rather been expressions
of contrasting points of view. Out of the great cleavage that had produced
the civil war of 1642 had come the Whigs and Tories of the Restoration,
one the intellectual heirs of the Roundheads, the other of the Cavaliers; and
from the 1670s until the death of Anne the party struggles had had in them
an undercurrent of violence. Great issues had been at stake in domestic
and foreign policy, and they had all been tied to the disposition of the crown.
Now that the issues were settled, the venom went out of the political world.

So did the old Tory party. The Glorious Revolution had shaken its
twin pillars of principle, the Anglican Church as the sole church of the
nation and the royal prerogative as divinely ordained. Toleration of Protestants
outside the church had been legalized, and God's law of hereditary monarchy
had been subordinated to man's law made in parliament. The Tories had
continued till 1714 to fight bitterly *against* these changes, without knowing
what they were fighting *for*. The idea of a narrow church that persecuted
Catholic and Protestant outsiders with equal fervor had become as unrealistic
as the idea of restoring divine-right monarchy in the person of a Roman
Catholic Stuart. In the frenzied pursuit of these will-o'-the-wisps the Tories
had gone to their destruction.

After 1714 their twin principles and their party were dead and
buried. The Whigs extended the practice of toleration in a typically pragmatic fashion: parliament repealed the legislation of Anne's reign against
dissenters, and annually indemnified those of them who took local office
illegally; but the Test Act and the Clarendon Code, as modified in 1689,
remained on the statute book. Politically ambitious dissenters moved into
the Anglican fold. The rest were still underpriveleged; they had no voice in
national politics, or even in local except in communities where they were
numerous. But they were no longer a minority persecuted to the point where
they excited controversy. Their acute grievances were over and their religious
zeal was flagging. They gradually settled down, alongside the Anglicans, to
what Edward Gibbon in later years called "the fat slumbers of the church."

If dissent was not a major political issue after 1714, neither was monarchy. The person of George I was enough to dissipate the last wisps of Tory romanticism, and his court was as dull as he was. In his early years he had divorced and imprisoned his charming young wife for a love affair, and had probably had her lover murdered; but by the time he came to England, in his mid-fifties, he had lost even the glamor of scandal without acquiring that of royalty. He had nothing regal about him. He never learned English, shunned the pomp that his office demanded, and was gross even in his pleasures. "No women came amiss to him," Lord Chesterfield reported, "if they were very willing and very fat. . . . The standards of his Majesty's taste made all those ladies who aspired to his favor, and who were near the suitable size, strain and swell themselves like the frogs in the fable to rival the bulk and dignity of the ox. Some succeeded, and others burst."

The Tories could not worship a crown that rested on such a head, and George would not have welcomed them if they had. He recognized that he owed his throne to the Whigs, and accordingly gave them the plums of office; to be Tory was to be in permanent and hopeless opposition. A few of the erstwhile Tories turned Jacobite, scheming for the day that never arrived when a Stuart would again be king. Many more came to terms with the new regime, called themselves Whigs, and joined the scramble for office. The rest became disgruntled onlookers, longing for they knew not what.

The extinction of Toryism meant that Britain, for a century after 1714, did not have two parties in any meaningful sense.[1] Everyone who aspired to office was by definition Whig, and the political conflicts of the period were among cliques within this universal party. As the balance of power shifted between the cliques, ministries came and went. There was always an opposition, and its leaders thundered against corruption in government; but they were usually trying to increase their nuisance value in order to force their way into office, and were quick to change their tune when they got there. Although politics remained tumultuous, it was a different kind of tumult from that under the later Stuarts, a struggle for place rather than for principle. Only the Jacobites, with their antiquated principle, could on occasion revive the old threat of civil war. The rest of the time the politics of Whiggism produced only factional skirmishing.

The Cabinet and Parliament

Great causes and principles are not prerequisite for great developments, which often come in undramatic periods. So it was with the first half-century of the Hanoverians, when the very dullness of the new monarchy contributed to the rise of cabinet government. George I and his son, who

[1] The title of one of the major works on the politics of the period seems to belie my generalization, but the author in fact supports it: Keith G. Feiling, *The Second Tory Party, 1714–1832* (1938).

succeeded him in 1727 as George II, had some prestige because they were kings, and more because advancement depended on their favor; but they had neither the brains nor the will for leadership. Consequently a subtle shift of executive power set in, from the sovereign to his ministers. They became less agents of his policy and more makers of policy themselves; under the king's surveillance, sometimes sharp and sometimes perfunctory, they steered through parliament measures that were essentially their own. The eighteenth century was evolving the mechanism, which the seventeenth had lacked, for amalgamating executive and legislative authority through the king's cabinet.

The beginnings of this process went back to the Restoration and can best be sketched here. The cabinet originated as an inner, secret committee of the privy council. Secrecy was vital, because parliament could not call cabinet members to account unless it knew what they had done. As long as they were protected from prying eyes at Westminster, and as long as the king was able to direct them, they were servants of his will. Charles II, when told that

> He never said a foolish thing
> And never did a wise one,

answered that "my words are my own, my acts are my ministers'." But the reply was deftly misleading. He acted for himself, and so did his immediate successors. Just as he forced the Earl of Danby to be his reluctant tool in negotiating with Louis XIV, so William III forced his cabinet to authorize unnamed persons to treat with Louis for unnamed ends. Ministers of the Stuarts had no doubt about who determined policy.

William began his reign by drawing cabinet members from both parties, but in his last years he preferred to draw them from whichever party had a parliamentary majority. The reason was merely that government could function more effectively, and with less legislative interference, if it had a solid base of support than if it depended on segments of both parties. At the end of the reign, however, when parliament was at its most obstreperous, it interfered with a vengeance: it attacked the whole cabinet system as a device for vitiating parliamentary supremacy. The Act of Settlement of 1701 barred the cabinet from offering secret advice to the sovereign, and provided that after Anne's death cabinet members should also be barred from the House of Commons. These two provisions would have made the new experiment unworkable. Prohibiting ministers from advising the crown privately would have ended their usefulness to it. Excluding them from the Commons would have destroyed the essential characteristic of the cabinet, that it is an executive selected from and based in parliament. Both provisions, by good luck, were soon repealed, and the cabinet continued its unplanned growth.

The Hanoverian accession began a new phase of growth. The principle that cabinet members should be drawn from the majority party lost its meaning as soon as everyone became a Whig, and the rise of factions within the all-encompassing party left the king leeway in choosing his ministers. He had to be sure that they commanded the support of a sufficient number of factions in the Commons to carry on his government, but this proved to be a problem that he could leave largely to the men of his choice. The conduct of administration came to be a matter of manipulation, bargaining, and influence, which the Whig politicians soon developed into a fine art. Understanding how they did so, in other words how the Hanoverian political system worked, demands some understanding of the structure of the House of Commons.

The knights of the shire, the two members representing each county, were elected at large by those who held freehold property worth forty shillings a year. Powerful local families, as time went on, learned to control most of the elections by adjusting their differences and balancing their interests so as to present only two candidates, whom the voters were expected to return and usually did. These county members had to hold land worth £600 a year, and therefore belonged to the well-to-do gentry; but they composed only a small fraction of the house. The great majority was the burgesses, or representatives of the boroughs.

A parliamentary borough was any town to which the sovereign had accorded one or more representatives. But "town" was often a euphemism, for boroughs ranged from great cities to decaying hamlets. The way in which they had been apportioned at the beginning of parliament in the Middle Ages had reflected, in a rough and ready fashion, the distribution of urban wealth and population at that time; but the vast changes since had brought no commensurate change in apportionment. An eighteenth-century borough might be a heap of stones in a pasture or engulfed by the sea; it continued to send its member or members to Westminster, whereas many new and bustling towns sent none. The system was logically absurd, and politically indispensable.

Although the qualification for voting in the boroughs varied as widely as their size, in almost all of them the electorate was small. Only three had more than 4,000 voters, most had less than 500, and several had thirteen or fourteen. The possibilities of influencing an election in such tiny constituencies were increased by the fact that a candidate did not need to be a resident. If he had landed property worth £300 a year he might stand for any borough, and he did not have to look far to find one where the voters would return whoever offered them the most. Offers varied from bribes and favors to individuals, through paying for public improvements in the town, to supporting its interests in Whitehall and Westminster.

If the candidate himself did not have the wealth or influence to meet the terms demanded of him, he needed only to discover a patron who had, or better yet a patron who controlled a "pocket" borough. In these the voters were so well in hand that they returned whoever was offered them; at each election the patron reached into his pocket, in effect, and pulled out

Canvassing for Votes. Painting by William Hogarth.

(Sir John Sloane Museum)

Polling the Blind and the Halt.   Engraving by William Hogarth.

(*New York Public Library*)

the member or members for that borough. In such cases no candidate needed
to lift a finger. "Your seat in the new parliament is at last absolutely
secured," Lord Chesterfield wrote his son in 1754, "and that without opposition or the least necessity of your personal trouble or appearance." A patron
had been found, and "he brings you in with himself at his surest borough."
The wheedling and bargaining that preceded such an agreement were often
difficult, but the election itself was a mere formality.

As the century wore on, patronage became a highly developed
system. A Whig aristocrat, himself usually a peer and sitting in the House of
Lords, would work through his agents and friends to gain and keep control
of a group of boroughs. Some needed constant attention and constant guarding against predatory rivals; but with enough persistence and money every
large landholder could build up what the period called his "interest," a
group of members of the lower house who owed him their places and voted
substantially as he told them to. The larger his "interest" the greater his
political weight, and out of the great "interests" ministries were built.[2]
Four or five territorial magnates, pooling their resources in the cabinet, could
command a substantial bloc of votes in the Commons, and many of the
remaining votes they needed would come to them because they were in
office. The king, one of the greatest landholders in the country, had a borough
"interest" of his own to put at his ministers' disposal; as his agents they
also had a variety of other ways in which to influence votes in the Commons.

The key to this influence was the Septennial Act of 1716, which
extended the life of any parliament to a maximum of seven years. Not until
after the American Revolution was a parliament dissolved before the end
of its legal term, and the reason is not far to seek. From the viewpoint of
members of the Commons and their patrons, elections were expensive and
time-consuming, and so to be avoided. From the viewpoint of the cabinet, a
long parliamentary session provided the opportunity to explore the weaknesses and needs of members, to determine those who could be counted on
and those who could be bought with promises and favors, and so to
create a phalanx of government supporters.

Some votes went almost automatically to any administration in
power. Many army and navy officers sat in the House of Commons, and
so did placemen, who would now be called civil servants; these groups were
rarely in opposition — officers because they had their eye on promotion,
placemen because they were themselves a part of government. Other members
responded to more indirect influence: one might have a clerical brother who
hungered for a bishopric, another a father anxious to be raised from the
Irish to the British peerage; a third might want a local henchman made
postmaster or customs collector, and a fourth might have such heavy debts
that only a colonial governorship could keep him out of jail. The king was

---

[2] *Interest* is of course an ambiguous word. When using it in this special sense,
therefore, I enclose it in quotation marks.

still the source of promotion, honors, offices, and cash; his ministers could barter his favors for political support.

But their "interests" combined with his influence could never secure a working majority. For that the government always had to have substantial assistance from the independent members, those men who were beholden to no one in office and voted as they pleased. They are sometimes called the Country Party, as distinct from the ministerial or Court Party; but the phrase is misleading, because they were even less a party in any meaningful sense than the pre-Hanoverian Whigs and Tories had been. The independents, although they included the troublemakers who hoped to harass the ministry into silencing them with an office, were for the most part men who were uninterested in office, who in earlier days might have been Tory, and who were concerned primarily with the needs of their own localities and secondarily with such national questions as they could grasp. They were the solid substratum of the House of Commons, merchants and financiers with a sharp eye on the government's commercial policy, country gentlemen intent on keeping down the land tax and keeping up the prosperity of agriculture. They were largely immune to political manipulation but alert to their own special interests, which no cabinet could neglect for long and stay in office.[3]

Thus a ministerial majority, like an electoral majority in a borough, was the result of careful bargaining and arrangement. To call this way of doing things corrupt is to impose today's moral judgment on the past. Politicians of that day, even when out of office and inveighing against ministerial corruption (by which they usually meant that others were getting the plums they wanted for themselves), would never have called the system itself corrupt. They knew no other. They and their ancestors in the feudal hierarchy had always scrambled for favors from the king, and only their scramble had made government possible; they had given services in return for rewards. This two-way process still operated, with the difference that a small group of the oligarchs, ministers of an acquiescent king, now dispensed the rewards. At a time when parties were in abeyance and the cabinet was delicately balanced between crown and parliament, rewards were the means of securing votes, and votes were the means of getting the king's business done. What the ministers called influence, not corruption, was only a part of the governmental process, but in the circumstances it was an essential part.

The formal, organized opposition that the modern British political system requires was unthinkable under the Hanoverians. In a world where all the ambitious were Whigs, and the symbol of Whiggism triumphant was the new dynasty, loyalty to it — if not enthusiasm — was incumbent on all.

[3] For a fuller analysis of the composition of parliament see Dorothy Marshall, *Eighteenth Century England* (1962), pp. 51–63. This volume in a ten-volume history of England, under the general editorship of W. N. Medlicott, is exhaustive on the political side of the period and sketchy on all the other sides.

Ministers were still the servants whom the king chose to carry out his policy, and opposing them would have smacked of disloyalty to the crown. They were fair game in debate, but only on their specific measures; to attack them on principle, because they were ministers, would have been tantamount to attacking the throne. Although when they fell from power they might criticize the succeeding administration, they rarely if ever attempted to undermine it. What is formally known today as "her Majesty's loyal opposition" can be both loyal and in opposition because majesty no longer plays a personal role in government. The Hanoverians did play such a role, and hence could not have such an opposition.

Once every generation, however, opposition was able to assume a kind of dynastic loyalty. The reason was an odd family characteristic of the Hanoverians: each sovereign in turn became, sooner or later, bitterly estranged from his heir, the Prince of Wales. George I and his son George were at loggerheads as long as the father lived; George II and his wife quarreled furiously with their firstborn, Prince Frederick, whom the Queen once described as "the greatest ass and the greatest liar and the greatest *canaille* and the greatest beast in the whole world." George II outlived his son (a great good fortune for the kingdom) only to find himself at odds with his grandson, the future George III; and a generation later George III in turn was made miserable by his eldest, the prince who eventually became George IV. This repetitive antagonism of father and son had a political significance. Malcontents could rally around the heir to the throne, as long as he opposed his father, and attack the royal ministry in the name of royalty-soon-to-be. The king was the setting sun; those who championed the prince were likely, when the sun set, to be the ministers of the new reign. Meanwhile they could be both loyal and in opposition.

Another trait of the first two Georges had major political repercussions. Both men were more devoted to the Electorate of Hanover than to the Kingdom of Great Britain. George I accepted the throne from a sense of duty to his house, not from love of the island. "His views and affections were singly confined to the narrow compass of his Electorate," said Lord Chesterfield. "England was too big for him." George II spoke English, unlike his father, but with a marked German accent; in his heart he was equally German and longed to escape the cares of British kingship. "I am sick to death of all this foolish stuff," he once burst out, "and wish with all my heart that the devil may take all your bishops, and the devil take your ministers, and the devil take the parliament, and the devil take the whole island — provided I can get out of it and go to Hanover."

Both kings spent part of each year in their electorate, were intent on safeguarding its interests, and expected their British ministers to provide the wherewithal for doing so. This expectation posed a new kind of problem. For the first time since the Middle Ages, except for the brief Dutch connection brought by William III, Britain had a territorial stake in Europe; and the location of Hanover made it far more vulnerable and difficult to defend

than the Netherlands. It lay across the lower Elbe and Weser, the two great
waterways from Central Europe to the North Sea; on the east was the rising
power of Prussia, on the west the Dutch and Austrian Netherlands and
France. Hanover was directly or indirectly involved in every struggle for
power in that part of the continent. Whenever a crisis arose, the great
question was how far Britain would be involved in consequence.

That question, recurring over and over again, emphasized the
equivocal position of the king's ministers. They were responsible to him and
also to parliament, and were therefore in a dilemma whenever Hanoverian
and British interests conflicted. Sacrificing the first to the second would never
be forgiven at court; sacrificing the second to the first would never be forgiven
at Westminster, where the independent country gentry cared little or
nothing about the Electorate and were quickly aroused by the argument that
the Hanoverian tail was wagging the British dog. For half a century the
problem of how to coordinate tail and dog plagued successive administrations.
It was never settled because it was the expression of a more fundamental
problem — how ministers could both serve a king who was pulling in one
direction and keep control of a legislature that was pulling in the other.
That problem was insoluble until the king ceased to pull and became a constitutional figurehead.

So much for the political structure of the regime. It was a confused
and rambling structure, which would have been the despair of a modern
political scientist; and by his standards the government that operated within
it was unbelieveably inefficient. But modern standards of efficiency, like modern
views of corruption, are irrelevant in understanding the past, which has to be
taken on its own terms. Men of the time might realize dimly that there
were constitutional problems and even absurdities in their political system;
yet for half a century they accepted that system because by their standards
it provided effective government.

The Ruling Class

Britain was ruled by amateurs. A professional politician or administrator, in the sense of a specialist who devotes his whole life to that career,
would have struck an eighteenth-century Whig as an aberration of the
human species. Gentlemen had careers and might even spend a great deal
of time at them, but they were not prepared for them by formal education.
If they went into either of the armed services, they did not attend college —
let alone a military or naval academy — but were trained in the regiment or
at sea; one admiral remarked that for forty years his ship "has been the
only university he has been permitted to study at." If they elected a political
career, they were likely to start with an education of sorts at Oxford or
Cambridge, and perhaps an exposure to the law at one of the Inns of Court;
but then, when they secured local office or a seat in parliament or member-

ship in the cabinet, they learned their job as they went along, trusting to their wits and, with luck, an experienced secretary.

This is not to say that gentlemen were uneducated. Almost all of them were versed in the classics and had some command of French; many were well grounded in history and informed by foreign travel and wide reading. What they lacked was a training in principles, in the theory of what they were doing; they were improvisers rather than specialists and would have scorned to be anything else. Their self-assurance, even when they were ignorant, was that of men who know that they are to the manor born; their amateur status was synonymous with their being gentlemen.

Their rule was as expensive as it was successful. They were profligate in wasting time and money; they often made decisions on inadequate information and unexamined premises; they ignored much that cried out to be done. Yet they also achieved surprising results in the hundred-odd years that their regime lasted. They conquered an empire overseas, fought France to a standstill and eventually to defeat in Europe, presided at home over an economic revolution in agriculture and industry, and brought the art of living among the favored few to a high peak. They had faults aplenty, but they also had an energy that made even their system work.

Early Georgian society, for all its self-assurance, was less sophisticated than it become later in the century. The court did much to set its tone, and the sovereign to set the tone of the court. Anne had been no patron of the arts, and by comparison with her the first two Hanoverians were boors — as witness the bluff comment of George II, in his Germanic English, "Damn the Bainters, and Boets Too!" The great magnates were not so philistine as this, for they encouraged painters and poets, musicians and architects. But their taste was far from impeccable, and they often mistook ostentation for elegance.

An example in point is Blenheim Palace, completed at the beginning of the period. Parliament had voted the Duke of Marlborough a great country house; and a fashionable architect, Sir John Vanbrugh, had been commissioned to design it. The Duke himself had much to do with the plans, and after his death his termagant duchess brought the work to completion. It bears the impress of Marlborough's personality. "As the Pharaohs built their Pyramids, so he sought a physical monument which would certainly stand, if only as a ruin, for thousands of years. About his achievements he preserved a complete silence, offering neither explanations nor excuses for any of his deeds. His answer was to be this great house." [4]

Although the "house" — three acres of it — answers no questions explicitly, it does tell something about what the Duke and his age considered to be monumental. The palace is not only huge but as ponderous as the Great Pyramid, and its heaviness is accentuated by the fact that it broods over

---

[4] Churchill, *Marlborough and His Times*, VI, 319. For an illustration of Blenheim and a fuller discussion of its architecture see below, pp. 107–109.

one of the most serene and spacious parks in England. The mass of the
building is enough in itself to explain the epitaph on Vanbrugh, its architect: "lie heavy on him, Earth, for he laid many a heavy load on thee." But
massiveness is not the only characteristic; another is multiplicity. Despite the
symmetrical plan, the sense of unity is lost in a maze of pavilions, wings,
colonnades, and indentations; the eye is kept busy in racing from window to
cornice to statuary to pilaster without ever coming to rest. The interior is of
a piece with the facade: monumental staircases, vast rooms hung with tapestry
or gleaming with marble (some of it real, some painted on the walls), and
never a quiet moment. This is the architecture of show. It is a collection of
impressive parts jostling each other for preeminence, like politicians jostling
for office; and the restless energy within the structure itself results in an
imposing chaos.

   The same restlessness ran through much of society, although it did not
always appear on the surface. The land of England, for example, seemed
to be immune to change; but even there a new energy was stirring, and
before long the effects were felt throughout an oligarchy that had its foundation, social as well as political, in the land. The territorial aristocrats and
their neighbors, the gentry or squires, were the predominant element in the
ruling class, and were essentially rural. Great folk usually had town houses
in London, and many squires came there often on business or pleasure.
But both had their roots in the country, and change in anything that had to
do with land meant change in their lives.

   The eighteenth century was their heyday. They had freed themselves
from the attempts of the Stuart monarchy to control local as well as national
government, and had taken both into their own hands. They ruled the roost
in the countryside, as sheriffs, high constables, justices of the peace; and parliament, controlled by their friends and relatives, left them largely to their
own devices. They might have been expected to settle into placid enjoyment
of their power. But political power was a function of their status as gentry, and
status depended on money; rulers who went bankrupt would cease to rule.
They had to maintain their incomes, and this need kept their world in flux.

   They themselves were not farmers, or they would never have had the
leisure to govern. Their estates were tilled either by hired hands, whom a
steward normally supervised, or by tenants — farmers in the English sense.
The nobleman or squire lived on the labor of others, which enabled him to be
a local official or member of parliament and still have time left over for
the vigorous life of a country gentleman. But the economic foundation of
that life could not be taken for granted. If his estate was entailed, he had only
a life interest in it and had to keep it intact, to go at his death to his eldest
son; if it was not entailed, dividing it between several sons would fatally
lower their positions in the world. How then, could he keep it together and
also provide for his children? Not by sitting still, but only by exploring
every possible way to increase the family fortunes.

   One way was matrimonial. If a father could find rich wives for his

boys and rich husbands for his girls, his troubles would be over. Even if he
could do nothing more than find an heiress for his eldest son, the estate might
then be stretched to take care of the other children. The conscientious father
would rarely try to make a marriage alliance with a monster or a moron,
no matter how well-endowed with earthly goods.[5] But neither could he
be too much swayed by the feelings of the child concerned. His goal was
financial stability, and love was largely irrelevant. Achieving his goal required
luck in finding wealth, diplomatic and business acumen in bargaining with
the other parent, and shrewd lawyers in drawing up the contract. Such contracts, though they could not ensure happy marriages, often ensured the
survival of families.

  The largest market for rich husbands and wives was among those
who had more money than lineage. The *nouveaux riches* of the day, who
had made their fortunes in banking or commerce or the wool trade, or
abroad in the service of the East India Company or one of its lesser competitors, were eager to rise above their origins into the ruling class. The way to
do so was first to settle on the land, then to contract judicious marriages.
No one could begin the climb toward gentility until he severed all active
connection with trade and bought a country estate; then he could inaugurate
the long series of moves by which his son might gain admission to county
society. The boy would go to an acceptable school such as Eton, then to
Oxford or Cambridge, then perhaps to Europe for a year or two of polishing
on what was called the Grand Tour. On his return he would be eligible, if
his father had enough wealth, to marry even the daughter of an impecunious
earl; and such a marriage would in all likelihood make him socially acceptable
by right of his wife. Their son, two generations removed from money-
grubbing, would in any case be a gentleman above reproach.

  In this and similar ways the oligarchy was constantly getting new
blood. "Trade in England," said Daniel Defoe, ". . . has peopled this
nation with gentlemen. . . . The tradesmen's children, or at least their
grandchildren, come to be as good gentlemen, statesmen, parliament-men,
privy councilors, judges, bishops, and noblemen as those of the highest birth
and the most ancient families." One of these newly arrived noblemen,
catapulted into the peerage by his father's wealth, summed up the process
more succinctly: "I am William Lord Craven. My father was Lord Mayor of
London, and my grandfather was Lord knows who."

  If what is now termed upward mobility characterized the ruling class,
so did downward mobility. Not all the younger sons of squires or even
peers could find heiresses to ease their way; families were large and opportuni-

---

[5] Here he was probably an improvement on his Elizabethan ancestors. In *The
Merry Wives of Windsor* Anne Page comments on her imbecilic suitor,

> He is my father's choice.
> O, what a world of vile ill-favored faults
> Looks handsome in three hundred pounds a year!

ties limited. The careful father would use all his connections, relatives and influential friends, to find openings for his boys in the world in which they were reared; but he could not always do it. Take the case of an imaginary country squire, Sir Roger Broadacres, Bart.,[6] who is the father of six sons. The estate is entailed on young Roger, the eldest, who will inherit it along with the baronetcy. No problem there. Secundus, his younger brother, is marked out for the army; and Lady Broadacres's cousin at the War Office will watch out for his advancement. Tertius, a studious boy, will obviously go into the church, for his uncle is a bishop. Quartus is attracted by the sea and has for godfather a captain in the Royal Navy. But connections cannot be overused, and the prospects for Quintus and Sextus are slim. So Sir Roger puts one to work with the family solicitor, to be trained for the law, and the other with the wool merchants who have long marketed the produce of the family's sheep. Two out of the six brothers, in other words, leave the world of the gentry.

Agricultural Change

A man in Sir Roger's position had to do more than provide for his children by arranging marriages and pulling strings; he also had to look sharply to his income. The status, perhaps the survival, of his family depended on how well he used his land, and in the first half of the century both the rewards and the techniques for using it well were on the increase. The population was rising, particularly in the towns; between 1700 and 1760 it is estimated to have grown by just under ten percent, to a total for England and Wales of over six million. Because townsmen clamored for food, farm prices also rose, and under this stimulus new techniques were being found to swell the production of foodstuffs. Those techniques were beginning, slowly but surely, to alter the whole agrarian structure and to bring new wealth to the landed interest.

The revolutionary discovery in agriculture was that land need not lie fallow in order to regain its fertility. This simple fact undermined the system of cultivation that had prevailed from time immemorial, by which the arable land of a manor was divided into two or three great fields, each subdivided into the lord's and tenants' strips; in the two-field system one of the two fields lay fallow each year, in the three-field system one of the three. In any given year, therefore, at least a third of the fertile land of the country was bearing nothing but weeds. There was consequently not enough fodder grown to keep all the cattle through the winter, and many had to be slaughtered every fall. These limitations on the supply of grain and

---

[6] Baronet, a form of knighthood created by James I to make money. It is hereditary, unlike other knighthoods, but is below the peerage. A baronet's wife is known as Lady So-and-So, like the wife of any knight, and is therefore impossible to distinguish at first glance from the wife of a peer.

meat seemed to be imposed by the nature of the soil; century after century no one thought to question whether they might be imposed by human ignorance.

The increase in scientific activity that began with the Restoration was essentially a process of questioning, and one of the earliest inquiries of the Royal Society was into methods of farming. At the same time pioneers were bringing in the idea, long a commonplace in Flanders, that judicious rotation of crops would keep a field producing every year. Wheat one summer, turnips the next, then oats or barley, then clover, then wheat again — this was the cycle that slowly revolutionized British agriculture. The primary reason was that the new crops, turnips or clover, did two things at once: they replenished the soil with nitrogen and provided winter fodder for cattle. Bigger and better-fed herds gave the farmer more meat to sell and more manure for fertilizing, which made for more and better crops and hence still larger herds. Simultaneously came the first experiments with scientific breeding of sheep and cattle for meat. Progress was extremely slow, but by 1750 modern farming was coming to birth.

The rotation of crops and the new emphasis on stock-breeding forced a change in the face of the countryside. Now that the old system, two or three open fields divided into strips, was no longer necessary, landholders gradually came to realize how wasteful it was. The only way to rotate crops efficiently was to consolidate a man's scattered strips into a single holding; the only way to improve farm stock was to prevent the animals' wandering together over the fallow ground as they had always done, a practice that ensured "the haphazard union of nobody's son with everybody's daughter," and to segregate them for breeding purposes. Improving crops and meat, in other words, required enclosed land. The requirement was met by the enclosure movement, which was essentially the conversion of strips and pasture rights in the open field, under communal supervision, into individual fields and pastures, walled or fenced, in which each owner or tenant could do as he pleased. The great age of eighteenth-century enclosures was still ahead. But beginnings were already visible, as the Middle Ages loosened at long last their grip on agriculture.

In a society so deeply rooted in the land these changes were momentous. The predominance of the landed interest, unchallenged until after the Napoleonic Wars, did not rest solely on turnips and clover, mutton and beef; for wealth was accruing from many other sources. But the wealth that was most accessible to the landowner was that which lay in his fields. The more profit his farmers made, the fatter his rent rolls grew. As harvests and herds improved from year to year, so did the income of the progressive squire with his few acres and the great magnate with estates all over England.

Such men were the leaders in agricultural improvement and the chief beneficiaries of it. They of course had an economic incentive, but it was not their only one. Like Antaeus, they drew their strength from the earth, and familiarity with it was in their blood. The discovery that it had greater potential than they had dreamed of was a challenge to their adventurousness, and they responded by innovating with the same energy that they brought to politics and empire-building.

Augustan Calm

Innovation, however, is only part of the picture. The leaders of early Georgian society, energetic as they were, did not make a virtue of energy. They were much more concerned with other values, perhaps chief among them the inner tranquillity that expresses itself in good manners and good form. To be civilized meant to be free of the passions, religious as much as political, that had convulsed the past; and good form was the mark of freedom. The God that had been an overriding reality to both Puritans and Cavaliers was fading into the abstraction of deism, and becoming a life force behind the universe; any individual experience of Him — or It — was branded as "enthusiasm" and bad form. A gentleman's goal, it seemed, was no longer to be saved but to keep calm.

> Void of strong desire and fear,
>   Life's wide ocean trust no more;
> Strive thy little bark to steer
>   With the tide, but near the shore.
>
> Thus prepared, thy shorten'd sail
>   Shall, whene'er the winds increase,
> Seizing each propitious gale,
>   Waft thee to the port of Peace.

This almost complacent serenity appears over and over again in the literature of the period. The savage satire and political pamphleteering of Queen Anne's reign gave way to a quieter mood, in which even satire lost its barb. It is true that the embittered Irishman, Jonathan Swift, published *Gulliver's Travels* in 1726; but this attack on the human race was as exceptional as it was masterly. A much more typical satire, mixed with light nonsense, was *The Beggars' Opera* by John Gay, which appeared in the following year and took the country by storm. This featherweight comedy (for it is not an opera) is peopled with highwaymen, jailers, pickpockets, and their womenfolk, all talking and behaving like — and busily poking fun at — the gentry. A father, for instance, asks his newlywed daughter,

> "Had not you the common views of a gentlewoman in your marriage, Polly?"
> "I don't know what you mean, sir."
> "Of a jointure,[7] and of being a widow."

---

[7] A settlement that the wife received on marriage and retained in her widowhood.

"But I love him, sir: how then could I have thoughts of parting with him?"

"Parting with him? why that is the whole scheme and intention of all marriage articles. The comfortable state of widowhood is the only hope that keeps up a wife's spirits."

This is not great comedy; John Gay's fondest admirers would scarcely rank him with the Elizabethans. But in one respect he has an advantage over them for readers of today: he is completely intelligible. Little more than a century had passed since Shakespeare's death, and in that time the English language had changed its nature. It had lost its wealth of metaphor and simile, its elaborate sentence structure, and at that price had gained in lucidity.[8] Georgian England conversed and wrote in a prose that had already taken on its modern form.

The age was essentially prosaic. Although it had its famous poets, notably Alexander Pope (1688–1744), even he substitutes flawless technique, wit, and occasionally wisdom, all smoothly packed into heroic couplets, for the soaring music of such earlier lyrics as

> Beauty is but a flower
> Which wrinkles will devour;
> Brightness falls from the air;
> Queens have died young and fair;
> Dust hath dimmed Helen's eye;
> I am sick, I must die —
> *Lord, have mercy on us!* [9]

Much of what the Georgians called poetry was in fact pretentious prose, dressed up in rhyme and regular metre and adorned with archaisms and the flowery clichés of which Pope complained:

> And ten low words oft creep in one dull line,
> While they ring round the same unvaried chimes
> With sure returns of still-expected rhymes.

[8] For comparison with the prose of *The Beggars' Opera* take this passage from *Much Ado about Nothing* at the close of the sixteenth century:
"I can tell you strange news that you yet dreamt not of."
"Are they good?"
"As the event stamps them: but they have a good cover; they show well outward. The prince and Count Claudio, walking in a thick-pleached alley in my orchard, were thus much overheard by a man of mine: the prince discovered to Claudio that he loved my niece your daughter, and meant to acknowledge it this night in a dance; and, if he found her accordant, he meant to take the present time by the top and instantly break with you of it."

[9] Thomas Nashe, 1593. To call the age of Pope prosaic would shock his admirers, who argue that he stands comparison with any of the great poets in the language. The issue boils down to the question of what is poetry, and each reader must perhaps answer this for himself.

> Where'er you find 'the cooling western breeze,'
> In the next line it 'whispers through the trees';
> If crystal streams 'with pleasing murmurs creep,'
> The reader's threatened (not in vain) with 'sleep.'

Georgian prose was also marred by clichés, particularly classical tags and allusions. All gentlemen shared a knowledge of the Roman classics (not many were so fluent in Greek), and often poured out their knowledge in a flood of Latinity that drowned the meaning of the English. They give the impression that they were dressing up their prose with Latin just as poets dressed up their verse with flowers of speech. Lord Chesterfield, who was as fond as the next man of invoking the Romans, recognized at least that they did not belong in business correspondence. "Carefully avoid all Greek or Latin quotations," he cautioned his son, "and bring no precedents from 'the virtuous Spartans,' 'the polite Athenians,' and 'the brave Romans.' Leave all that to futile pedants. . . . There is an elegant simplicity and dignity of style absolutely necessary for good letters of business; attend to that carefully."

Chesterfield, like many of his contemporaries, was obsessed with style. He insisted on it in writing, and he insisted on it in living. His *Letters to His Son* are a rambling, discursive exposition of what he conceived to be a gentleman's style of life.[10] In them he revealed a great deal about the values and concerns of his world, and a survey of that world may well end with a glance at what he had to say. The letters preach an egoism as cold as Machiavelli's; they are repetitive and often trivial, and they never probe the depths of experience. For Chesterfield has a narrow vision: he sees only the surface, the outward form, the style. But he sees with the eyes of a hawk, and he is completely honest.

The World of Lord Chesterfield

Philip Stanhope, fourth Earl of Chesterfield (1694–1773), belonged to one of the political dynasties of the period. He was a diplomat, a cabinet member, a friend and patron of French and British writers, and a voluminous author himself; his life bore out his conviction that "any man of common

---

[10] They are published in condensation in the Everyman series, and Oliver H. G. Leigh edited them in full and sumptuous form for the Navarre Society (2 vols., 1926). The period was one of assiduous letter-writing, much of it designed for publication. The most prolific and famous of all correspondents was Horace Walpole (1717–1797), for whose epistolary output see Mrs. Paget Toynbee, ed., *The Letters of Horace Walpole, Fourth Earl of Orford,* (16 vols., 1903–05). I discuss Chesterfield instead, partly because I find him more congenial than Walpole (which is not to say that I find the Earl congenial) and primarily because he knew at first hand, as the dilettante Walpole did not, the politics and diplomacy of his age.

understanding may, by proper culture, care, attention, and labor, make himself whatever he pleases, except a good poet." His primary concern, however, was not with politics or diplomacy or literature, but with being a gentleman. Here by his own rigorous standards he succeeded. But his success did not extend to his illegitimate son Philip, to whom his letters were written; the boy had in him a touch of boorishness, which his father tried for more than a decade to eliminate by sage admonitions. What mattered to Chesterfield was that he failed; what mattered to posterity was that he expressed, in the process of failing, his concept of what a gentleman should be.

The essence of the concept was to be pleasing. "You had better talk trifles elegantly to the most trifling woman than coarse, inelegant sense to the most solid man; you had better return a dropped fan genteelly than give a thousand pounds awkwardly; and you had better refuse a favor gracefully than to grant it clumsily. Manner is all, in everything; it is by manner only that you can please, and consequently rise." The central rule of life, therefore, was never to impose yourself on those around you, or try to make them admire you, but always to cater to their tastes and interests in order to buttress their self-esteem. "Those whom you can make like themselves better will, I promise you, like you very well."

This creed is obviously based on pure if sophisticated egoism. The *Letters,* said Samuel Johnson, "teach the morals of a whore, and the manners of a dancing master." But there is something else as well, a love of form for its own sake. Chesterfield had an almost physical aversion to those who lacked the graces of good breeding, and admitted frankly that he cared more for the clothing of ideas than for their intrinsic worth. Awkwardness was for him the sign of worthlessness. He was honest enough to suspect that he might be wrong, but he resented the suspicion and did all he could to keep from putting it to the test. "If a speaker should ungracefully mutter or stammer out to me the sense of an angel, deformed by barbarisms and solecisms or larded with vulgarisms, he should never speak to me a second time if I could help it." [11]

This worship of form was amoral, because it permitted any kind of dissimulation that was gracefully garbed. Religious belief, for example, was important for the simple reason that society did not trust freethinkers; therefore a wise atheist would pretend to a belief that he did not hold. Women were a much more important case in point, for they also required a gentleman to pretend. Although they were only grownup children, they played a crucial part in the school of good manners; "the concurrence of the two

---

[11] Such fastidiousness was far from universal; otherwise Samuel Johnson, whose manners were notorious, would never have exercised the dominion that he did over the literary world. A tribute to Johnson by a friend provides the common-sense rebuttal of Chesterfield's position: "To reject wisdom because the person of him who communicates it is uncouth and his manners are inelegant—what is it but to throw away a pineapple, and assign for a reason the roughness of its coat?"

sexes is as necessary to the perfection of our being as to the formation of it."
A man must flatter and humor women and, because they always suspect
that they are being dallied with and crave to be taken seriously, must give
them the impression that he is opening his inmost secrets to them. "Weak
men really do, but wise ones only seem to do it."

Females were only a little more gullible than males. Chesterfield, although he lived in an age of rationalism, had no illusions about the role
that reason plays in governing human conduct. "Those who suppose that men
in general act rationally, because they are called rational creatures, know
very little of the world, and if they act themselves upon that supposition will
nine times in ten find themselves grossly mistaken." Everyone is a blend
of reason and passion and appetite; no two blends are identical, and each
contains weaknesses that are waiting to be manipulated. All that is required
of the manipulator is to address himself to the whole man, heart as well as
head, and he will find the weak spots soon enough.

This was Chesterfield's recipe for success in the drawing room and
also in the House of Commons. He had been a member of the lower house
before inheriting his earldom and had soon lost his awe of its members. "I
discovered that, of the five hundred and sixty, not above thirty could understand reason; . . . that those thirty only required plain common sense dressed
up in good language; and that all the others only required flowing and
harmonious periods, whether they conveyed any meaning or not, having
ears to hear but not sense enough to judge." This discovery he carried with
him to the House of Lords, and he believed that it accounted for his high
reputation as a parliamentary orator.

His gloomy view of human intelligence did not, of course, extend to
himself or those he loved. He was an educated man, grounded in the classics,
fluent in modern languages, and with a wide knowledge of history and
what would be called today political science. He sent his son to the continent for a Grand Tour that lasted for a number of years, to acquire not
only polish but information. Over and over again he enjoined Philip to keep
up his French, improve his German, learn Italian and someday Spanish,
and study the ways and institutions of the countries through which he
traveled. A favorite injunction was *approfondissez,* get to the bottom of
things: "learn if you can the *why* and the *wherefore*." This insistence on
learning, like the insistence on good manners, had a practical purpose, for
Philip was being trained for the diplomatic corps. But the rigor of the training shows that his father, the apostle of the graces, set equal store by a well-
stocked and disciplined mind.

Because most men did not have such minds, in Chesterfield's opinion,
they were wrong a great deal of the time. But he was strongly averse to
telling them so, and viewed their mistakes with an almost supercilious pity.
Although — or perhaps because — he was quick to recognize and profit from
their sloppy thinking, he was tolerant of it and held that persecuting or even
mocking it was an egregious breach of taste. No one could help ideas that

came from honest muddleheadedness. "The blindness of the understanding is as much to be pitied as the blindness of the eye; and there is neither jest nor guilt in a man's losing his way in either case. . . . I may as well expect that every man should be of my size and complexion as that he should reason just as I do. Every man seeks for truth, but God only knows who has found it."

Chesterfield obviously believed that he had found as much of it as he needed for using men to his advantage. He would have said that he had taken thoroughly to heart Pope's famous couplet:

> Know then thyself, presume not God to scan;
> The proper study of mankind is man.

The Earl's study was a cool, detached scrutiny that included, as Pope had advised, his own nature, about which he thought that he was as clear-sighted as about the rest of mankind. "I know myself (no common piece of knowledge, let me tell you); I know what I can, what I cannot, and consequently what I ought to do. . . . My only remaining ambition," he confided to Philip, "is to be the counsellor and minister of your rising ambition. Let me see my own youth revived in you; let me be your mentor, and with your parts and knowledge, I promise you, you shall go far."

But what counsel did he actually have to give? Learn the facts; *approfondissez*. Learn to think. Above all learn to charm men and women in order to manipulate them, for without well-mannered manipulation learning and thinking are profitless. This was no creed to fire the mind, let alone the heart. It was focused entirely on superficialities, as Chesterfield would have been the first to admit, and for that very reason he considered it the only realistic guide to life. "The world is taken by the outside of things, and we must take the world as it is; you nor I cannot set it right."

This world was of course much wider in its tastes, and more forceful in its ways, than the Chesterfieldian view of it. The men who listened to the music of Handel or bought the engravings and paintings in which Hogarth commented on the passing scene could scarcely be said to have been "taken by the outside of things." The men who were beginning to transform the English countryside, to create through the cabinet a new form of executive, to build an empire overseas, knew their own minds too well to be swayed by anyone's grace of manner. But this is only to say that the oligarchy was too complex to be seen by a single observer, no matter how shrewd. What Chesterfield saw was there, the love of form and style and the surface of life. Much more was there as well, a self-confidence and energy that were carrying the country ahead to new heights of power. These qualities appear, not in an old man's letters to his son, but in the subject matter of the following chapters, the record of what the oligarchs achieved.

3 The Walpole Era

The Years of Instability (1714–1722)

For the first year of his reign George I sat uneasily on his throne. More than his corpulence made it shake; no one really wanted him for king. The rejoicings that greeted his arrival came from relief and hope, not enthusiasm — relief that the danger of civil war had been averted, hope that the new dynasty might prove to have something attractive about it. As the relief evaporated and the hope proved vain, many men began to wonder whether they had been right to saddle themselves with "King Log." The coronation was scarcely over before Jacobite sentiment was kindling again. The victorious Whigs helped to fan it by their vindictiveness: when George's first parliament met, in the spring of 1715, they opened an attack on Lord Bolingbroke and his colleagues, purged Tory henchmen from office throughout the country, and so convinced many Tories that rebellion was the only alternative to political extinction. By summer unrest was widespread. Jacobite mobs rioted in the west country, the midlands, the north; and Scotland was seething. Local magistrates did nothing to stop the disorders or to enforce the measures taken by the government. Central authority seemed to be breaking down. Eight months of Hanoverian rule, wrote the Prussian minister to London, had done more for the cause of James Stuart, the Pretender, than four years of the Tories under Queen Anne.

But James, like his father, was badly served. He himself had been exiled from France to Lorraine after the Treaty of Utrecht, and at that distance he was powerless; his cause depended entirely on daring leadership in Britain, and this he did not have. Bolingbroke, who had the best chance of rallying the Tories to action, was no more capable of seizing the moment than he had been the year before. At the height of the crisis he bolted across the Channel and took service with the Pretender, and no one of stature replaced him. Risings in the west country melted away; royal troops seized Oxford. Only in the north of England, where great landlords could still rouse their tenantry in a lost cause as they had in the days of Elizabeth, did a sizable number of "Jacks" turn out to fight for King James.

Their chance of success depended on Scotland, which was the focus of rebellion. There the unpopularity of the union, combined with the magic of

the Stuart name, might have touched off a national rising if James himself
had been on hand; and even without him some ten thousand men took up
arms against a force of only thirty-three hundred royal troops. But the
Jacobites again had no competent leader. They failed to join hands with their
friends across the border and marched aimlessly to and fro until the Pretender
finally arrived, just after Christmas. By then his cause was dying, and he was
not the man to revive it. "Throughout his life he was, like his grandfather
Charles I, a great gentleman, but the virtues of a great gentleman are not by
themselves sufficient to regain a lost throne." [1] After six weeks of wandering
in the Highlands, more and more the fugitive and less and less the king,
James VIII of Scotland and III of England, as he called himself, vanished
into the exile's limbo from which he never returned.

    The failure of the rising, known to history as the Fifteen (although it
actually did not end until 1716), secured the Hanoverian succession at a small
price in lives. A few victims, ranging from aristocrats to humble sergeants,
were executed for form's sake. Most of the leaders either were pardoned or
fled before they could be tried; a few were tried and condemned, and then
vanished mysteriously just before their executions, to reappear in France. The
rank and file of the Scottish rebels melted away into the obscurity from which
they had come, and kept the cause alive in the Highlands until the final
Jacobite effort thirty years later. In England, where the movement was not fed
by nationalism and clan loyalties, it rapidly withered away. The country
became used to the Hanoverians, and was willing to give them its loyalty as
long as they looked to its prosperity.

    In the years after the Fifteen, prosperity ran wild, until it produced in
1720 a financial crisis that endangered the new regime. This was the lurid
episode known as the South Sea Bubble. On the surface it was nothing more
than an orgy of speculation and bribery, ending in the worst stock-market
crash in British history; under the surface it was a political threat of the first
order, which bade fair to bring down the government if not the throne itself.
The outcome was quite different: Robert Walpole came to power. During the
next twenty years, under his guidance, the dynasty became so firmly established
and the political world so well systematized that the tumults of the midcentury
— foreign war and Jacobite invasion — could not shake the house of
Whiggism.

    But in 1720 that house was still under construction, and the bursting
of the Bubble shook it badly. The origins of the crisis went back to 1711. In
that year the Tory government, which considered the Bank of England to be
an organ of the Whig party, chartered the South Sea Company as a rival to the
Bank. One of the initial purposes of the Company was to trade with the South

---

[1] Sir Charles A. Petrie, *The Jacobite Movement: the First Phrase, 1688–1716*
(1948), p. 195. This and its companion volume, subtitled *The Last Phase,
1761–1807* (1950), are a convenient history of Jacobitism. The facts are reliable,
but the conclusions are often eccentric; Sir Charles is unduly addicted to the
Stuarts.

Seas — the southern Pacific, or in other words Spanish America. The prospect of making money there grew fabulous when Spain, as part of the Utrecht settlement, granted the Company a major concession, the asiento, to run for the next thirty years. The asiento permitted members of the Company to import up to 4,800 slaves a year into the Spanish colonies, and to sell there duty free such merchandise as could be carried on a single 500-ton ship that was to accompany the annual Spanish treasure fleet from Europe. This trade was confined to the Caribbean (thereby falsifying the name of the South Sea Company), but its merchants had at least an entering wedge with which to break into the Spanish colonial market. They paid little attention to the limits set in the asiento and soon developed a thriving trade in smuggled goods as well as slaves.

The directors of the Company were less interested in trade, legal or illegal, than in what they could make out of high finance. As their corporate position improved, they engaged in large-scale operations connected with the public debt. The climax of these operations, and the beginning of the Bubble, was a coup in February 1720, when parliament empowered the directors to take over the entire national debt. The Company agreed to charge the government a lower rate of interest than the treasury was paying on its annuities, of which the debt largely consisted, and to sweeten the bargain by a cash settlement of more than £7 million.

As this gigantic payment suggests, the directors looked forward to even more gigantic profits. The operation that they had in mind was complex in detail but essentially simple: to convert the national debt into Company stock. The holders of government annuities were to be persuaded to exchange them for stock, abandoning an assured income from their old annuities for capital gains from the expected rise in market value of their new South Sea shares. Everything depended on this rise. The Company was authorized to issue more and more stock as it took over more and more of the debt, and the greater the worth of its shares the more annuities they would buy. The scheme looked foolproof, granted the one basic assumption that the Company could market its stock at a price that would rise and never stop rising. Of this financial miracle the directors were serenely confident. The Company was as closely tied to the state as the Bank of England was, and not only monopolized the South American trade but possessed the largest working capital — some £40 million — ever amassed in England. How could investors resist this opportunity?

For the first few months they could not. Their scramble for shares drove up the price to almost ten times what it had been in February, and the whole market followed the lead of the South Sea stock in a dizzy upward spiral of inflation. New companies burgeoned overnight, and no one cared much whether their aims were real or fanciful; the public was buying shares in anything, for everything was going up. By June a few wise men began to sell, and by midsummer the market was leveling off. The South Sea directors were trying to force it higher by every possible means, honest and dishonest,

including loans to permit stockholders to buy more shares on credit. But by
then the most frantic pump-priming would no longer serve.

The crash came in September. The South Sea Company's bankers
failed, its stock fell even faster than it had risen, paper fortunes vanished, and
those who had bought on credit were faced with ruin. Worse still, the ministry
and the court were involved to the hilt; the directors had been lavish in their
bribes to the influential, and had not neglected even the King's mistresses.
The public, disillusioned with its dream of riches, cried for retribution; but
almost no one in the government had clean hands. Parliament reassembled in
an ugly mood.

This was the opportunity for Robert Walpole. He was a seasoned
politician, who had been in and out of office for years, but at the moment he
held a relatively minor post. He had not foreseen the crash and, like almost
everyone else, had lost a lot of money in it. But it did not smirch his reputation
because he was free from his colleagues' shady dealings with the Company. He
also had the wherewithal for establishing his ascendancy — a clear idea of
what had to be done and the adroitness to get it done. The emergency gave
him, for the first time in his career, full scope for his talents.

He had two objectives. One was to avert panic until investors regained
their confidence in what was still an essentially sound financial system; the
other was to prevent public anger, focused in the House of Commons, from
destroying the government and perhaps the dynasty. In both aims he
succeeded. He proposed a scheme for salvaging what was left of the South
Sea Company by help of the two remaining giants of finance, the Bank of
England and the East India Company; although the plan was never
implemented, it gave time for the market to recover, for men to realize that
they could still make money in sane ways. He did not prevent a parliamentary
inquiry, but he did manage to keep it within discreet bounds. While the
directors' estates were being confiscated and a few ministerial victims thrown
to the wolves, the key figures in the government and court were saved from
awkward questions. These were negative accomplishments, but important ones.

Luck then took a hand in Walpole's rise. He detested his principal
colleague, the rancorous Lord Sunderland, but had defended him for reasons
of expediency; Sunderland now repaid the kindness by suddenly dying. The
next day, April 20, 1722, Walpole became the King's first minister, and Britain
entered a new era. Politics, which for so many generations had been a rough-
and-tumble business that no man or group of men could long dominate,
gradually acquired order and form, and "the country enjoyed a stability of
government such as it had not known for a hundred years." [2]

[2] John H. Plumb, *Sir Robert Walpole: the Making of a Statesman* (1956), p. 379.
This volume and its companion, subtitled *The King's Minister* (1960), are
not only a biography but a study of the period in depth. The second volume ends
in 1734, and a third will presumably complete the story. For other accounts
of the Walpole era see Dorothy Marshall, *Eighteenth Century England* (1962);
Basil Williams, *The Whig Supremacy, 1714–1760* (1939); and C. Grant
Robertson, *England under the Hanoverians* (10th ed., 1930).

The Walpole Machine

Governmental stability derived from a fusion of the two cardinal elements required for administration, support from the king and control of the House of Commons. Walpole had a genius for handling his sovereign, but it was a delicate, time-consuming occupation that required a blend of courage and tact. George was as suspicious as he was stupid. He often had ideas that his first minister would not or could not implement, and rival politicians often insinuated that they, given power, would do exactly as their royal master wished. Walople had to counter these insinuations, retain the King's confidence, and if need be thwart his wishes. And that was not all. If he hoped for a long tenure of power, he had to serve George I without alienating the Prince of Wales. This assignment was difficult enough to tax even his gifts, but he managed to perform it.

He showed himself equally adept at handling the House of Commons, which he understood as well as any politician of the century. Although he could never afford to neglect the House of Lords, he recognized that the Commons had now become the locus of power; for that reason he refused a peerage, and in 1726 became instead a Knight of the Garter. No commoner had received that honor in generations, but neither had a first minister elected to stay a commoner. Sir Robert knew what he was about. He had a hard enough task to control the lower house as a member of it, and would have had an infinitely harder one to control it from the House of Lords.

The methods of control that he developed and systematized remained in force for the rest of the century. The office of prime minister did not yet exist in name; the critical position was that of the first lord of the treasury, who controlled vast patronage through the appointment of customs and excise officers. From the treasury Walpole operated his machine. He organized a phalanx of placemen in the House of Commons, who voted as he told them. He distributed favors and honors and preferment in order to maintain and strengthen his political control. He became the key figure, even under the jealous eye of George I, in determining promotion in the army. He exercised a tighter reign over patronage in the church than any minister had done since 1688. He filled positions in the civil service with men of his personal choice, not with henchmen of his henchmen. He concentrated ruthlessly on a man's present usefulness; anyone who could plead only past services was likely to lose his pension or his place. This was political realism, because there were never enough plums to go around. For every one at the minister's disposal, three or four suppliants were clamoring in the lines outside his doors. He asked himself a single question — how much each gift would contribute to his power — and made his selection accordingly.

But even his machine, efficient as it was, could not function without support from the independent members of the Commons, and he wooed them assiduously throughout his years in office. Here his background had much to do with his success. He came of an old Norfolk family, country squires for generations, and was in some ways the epitome of his breed — hard-drinking, hard-riding, given to profanity and to wenching, with none of the graces that Chesterfield extolled or the aristocratic connections that most ministers had. He was of his class and made no bones about it, in fact made capital out of it. During debates in the House of Commons he would be nibbling on a Norfolk apple as if to emphasize his origins; and at the height of the South Sea Bubble he was more absorbed with buying land than stocks. He took care of his children as so many of the gentry tried to do, but of course with more success: for his eldest son he obtained a peerage and an extremely wealthy bride, and for his daughter the heir to an earldom. The independent backbenchers in the Commons might rail against him, and often did. But at bottom they understood him, and year after year they stuck with him.

He was far from a typical squire or he would not have got where he did. In many ways, such as his care for all the details of patronage and his systematic, single-minded pursuit of power, he was less like the gentry of his day than like a modern American political boss; in those ways he was a professional in an age of amateurs. But that was not the whole picture. For all his ostentation and coarseness, he was a connoisseur of wines and had a sure taste in art; the collection of paintings that he amassed was famous throughout Europe. On his Norfolk estate he built Houghton Hall, which is as much a monument to him as Blenheim is to Marlborough — not a palace but a country house, austere on the outside and magnificent within, embellished without thought of cost by the leading sculptors, plasterers, and furnituremakers of the day.[3] Sir Robert, in short, was an odd mixture of vulgarity and sophistication.

His strength as a politician lay in his common sense, his meticulous attention to detail, and the unerring judgment of people that is the *sine qua non* for manipulating them. His weakness lay in his incomprehension of the subtle, imponderable forces in domestic and foreign affairs. The system he built was singularly unresponsive to the public, even the narrow public of the electorate, except in moments of real or manufactured crisis; he himself was unable to gauge the tide of British opinion and often miscalculated how it was running. His foreign policy suffered from his inability to penetrate the hidden motives, the fear and ambition and prickly concern for national honor, that swayed the courts of Europe. He lacked the sixth sense, in other words, to be a creative statesman.

He did not pretend to be one, but conceived of himself as the defender of things as they were. Some one had to make the creaking governmental machinery work, foster commerce and lower taxes, and buttress a shaky throne; and he had supreme confidence that he was the only man who could do it. Perhaps he was right. Britain needed some years of quiet in which the new

---

[3] Plasterers may at first glance seem out of place among sculptors and furniture-makers; but English plasterwork, from the late Middle Ages through the eighteenth century, was one of the major decorative arts. For a fuller description of Houghton Hall and its contents see Plumb, *Walpole*, I, 81–87.

(*National Portrait Gallery*)

Robert Walpole, 1st Earl of Orford. From the studio of J.B. Van Loo.

dynasty could grow roots and a political system could emerge from the chaos of the past. Walpole, more than any single man, created the system, not so much by intent as because he needed it in order to survive. And this limited form of creativity may have been all that the age made possible.

Although his predominance was long-lasting, he could never take it for granted. The first challenge to it came out of the blue in the summer of 1727, when word arrived that George I had died suddenly in Hanover. The political wolves gathered for the kill: Sir Robert's days were numbered, they believed, because a new king meant a new minister. But they did not understand the odd little man who now took the throne. George II had led a wretched life, hated and bullied by his father and hating him in return, and had lost the self-confidence required of kings. He hid his loss behind a violent temper, a restlessness that kept him always in motion and always talking, and an almost insane preoccupation with the minutiae of his daily routine; even his mistress he saw at precisely the same hour each evening. He was a monumental bore to everyone around him, and if he had been a commoner he could have been ignored as a nonentity. On the throne he could not be; his weak, neurotic personality was a fact of politics.

Because he was weak he was profoundly dependent. But he was also that great rarity among his fellow monarchs, one who depended on his wife. Caroline of Anspach was a woman of some charm and much shrewdness; her manners were coarse, but her head was good enough to do her husband's thinking for him. He vented his temper on her, flaunted his infidelities in her face, bored her to distraction, and clung to her. She presumably did not love him as he, in his way, loved her. But she did love power, and through him she possessed it.

She was Walpole's opportunity. Soon after taking office under George I he had marked out the Princess of Wales as the friend he needed at court. He and Caroline, loving power in equal degree, understood each other. He had no intention of letting her get the upper hand; but he treated her, on almost Chesterfieldian lines, as if she had it: he consulted her assiduously and seemed to defer to her, and soon won her for his staunch ally. She helped him to survive the upheaval of her husband's accession, and before long to win a place in the heart of the new king second only to hers. For the next fifteen years, until his fall from office, Sir Robert was not only George II's servant and counselor but also, as nearly as anyone could be, his friend. Their relationship was closer than any between sovereign and subject since the days of Charles I and Buckingham a hundred years before.

The Years of Stability (1727–1738)

Sir Robert was now called "the Great Man," admiringly by his friends and mockingly by his enemies. The mockery rang hollow, for he exercised a kind of power that no minister had ever approximated. He seemed to have a hold on royal favor and on parliament that was unchallengeable, and to stand on an eminence from which only death could topple him. But the appearance was deceptive; the novelty of his position and his way of maintaining it made for insecurity. The oligarchs were unaccustomed to being dominated by anyone, particularly an upstart squire, and for every man he fed with a political plum he left three or four hungry and embittered. The longer his regime lasted and the more completely he controlled all patronage, the more rancorous his enemies became. They railed and mocked at him in the Commons and the Lords, and intrigued with undiscourageable hope to turn the King against him.[4] They also used the popular press, then in its brawling infancy, to whip up public excitement by satires, cartoons, ballads, and all the other arts that Grub Street could devise, and so bring outside pressure to bear on the closed world of parliament. Sir Robert, thanks to their efforts, lived from crisis to crisis.

In 1732 he himself, quite unwittingly, provoked one that proved to be more than he could handle. It originated in his attempt to improve the tax structure, one of the few areas in which he was a genuine reformer. He wanted to reduce the land tax, partly because he believed that it put an unfair burden on the country gentlemen, partly because he needed their support. But he could not reduce the chief source of revenue without finding a substitute, and the obvious area in which to look for one was that of customs and excise. This form of taxation not only increased with the growth of trade but bore on all consumers alike, rich and poor; and Sir Robert had a marked preference, natural in a man of property, for taxing the poor as against the rich.

He had long been alive to the need for encouraging trade. He had helped manufacturers by reducing export duties on their goods and import duties on their raw materials, and had simplified the process whereby imports destined for sale abroad passed through the country duty free. He had also experimented, in a few categories of goods imported for home consumption, with shifting from customs to excise — from a duty levied on goods when they entered the country to a tax levied on them when they were released for sale. Tea, cocoa, and chocolate had been admitted duty free and taxed instead through the retailer; and in Walpole's opinion the experiment had proved extremely advantageous.

The advantages of excise were of two sorts. In the first place, eliminating customs duties on the enumerated commodities took the profit out of smuggling them; and smuggling was a vast commerce that cheated the government out of hundreds of thousands of pounds a year. In the second place, collecting a tax from retailers required an army of excise men; and the more jobs Sir Robert could provide the greater would be his patronage. At the beginning of 1732 he decided to reduce the land tax to five percent of assessed value, to reimpose a salt tax that had recently been discontinued (thereby creating still more collectors' jobs), and to extend the excise to wine and tobacco. It would be hard to imagine a proposal that seemed less explosive and turned out to be more so.

In the popular mind customs and excise officers were corrupt tyrants.

[4] The best modern account of their activities is in Archibald S. Foord, *His Majesty's Opposition, 1714–1830* (1964), chaps. 1–5.

They had behind them some of the most savage laws on the statute book,
which the courts interpreted in their full severity: in one case a man was
hanged merely for blackening his face, which was a common precaution of
smugglers working at night. The officers themselves were venal and
brutal, and against them the citizen had no effective redress. They were
hated by high and low, in a society addicted to smuggling and excise-evasion,
and the hatred mounted as law-enforcement became more rigorous.
Walpole's scheme was a match to this combustible material, and his
opponents were ready and eager to fan the flame.

 For a year, while the measure took its slow way toward a vote
in the House of Commons, excitement rose to a frenzy. The press did
its full part; boroughs sent deputations to Westminster; riots broke out; the
country seethed as it had on the eve of the Fifteen. But now the pressure
was of a different kind: it was on parliament, to turn against its master and
throw out his bill. The Lords and Commons were discovering that they did
not always live in a closed world, where they could legislate without
regard to the public. Elections were impending in 1734. The members of
the lower house and the noble borough-mongers in the upper one dared
not presume too far on even the most docile constituents.

 Walpole had blundered in his timing, but he was unperturbed.
Vilification in parliament was an annoyance, like mosquitoes, that did not
deflect him; popular anger outside the halls of Westminster seemed to
him almost unconstitutional. He ignored the danger signals and held to his
course. He was overconfident, after a decade of successfully manipulating
kings and Commons, and blind to the fact that his system, unresponsive as
it was to the electorate, did rest upon that solid earth. Now the earth
was quaking, and others felt the tremors if he did not. When parliament
reconvened after the Easter recess of 1733, which its members had spent in
their constituencies, Sir Robert was amazed to find his majority melting
away. At the last minute he gave in and withdrew the bill. At that
price he survived, but his position was never the same again. His opponents
had demonstrated the limits of his power. Now that they had forced
him to retreat once, they were all the more eager for the next opportunity.

 He had survived largely because the King and the coterie of
royal advisers had never wavered in their support. The opposition had tried
to capture the court through some of the King's favorites in his household,
notably Lord Chesterfield, but had run up against the stone wall of
George and his Queen. Chesterfield had been dismissed from his post,
whereupon he and his friends had carried the struggle to the House of
Lords. They had come within an ace of winning it there, but the influence
of the crown had brought enough wavering peers into line to give the
administration a narrow victory.

 Walpole could no more take his sovereign for granted, however,
than he could the two houses. He lived under the constant danger that
the King would insist on a policy that parliament would not support, and

the danger was greatest in the area of foreign affairs. Here George II
had distinct and stubborn ideas of his own; he did not see eye to eye with
Sir Robert, let alone with the House of Commons. Any crisis in Europe,
consequently, might become a crisis at home, and the tumult over the
excise coincided with the beginning of just such a crisis — which culminated
in the first European war since the Treaty of Utrecht. The war jeopardized
Walpole's foreign policy, and his insistence on keeping Britain neutral
strained his relations with the King as they had never been strained before.

    Sir Robert's diplomacy was governed by a single-minded desire
for peace. His objections to war were, like everything else about him,
eminently practical: war would endanger the regime by creating the
opportunity for a Stuart restoration and by alienating the landed interest.
Walpole was almost obsessed by the threat from the Jacobites, with
whose schemings he kept in touch through a wide network of spies. He
had no fear that the Pretender, unaided, could raise a successful rebellion;
what he feared was rebellion encouraged and aided by France. Any
war in which Britain became involved would, he believed, soon bring in
France; the way to stop the Jacobites was therefore to keep the peace. Here
the future bore him out: Britain's first war did draw in France, and did
bring a Jacobite invasion with French support.

    As for the landed interest, the best way to ensure its loyalty to
the Hanoverians — and to Walpole himself — was to keep down the land tax.
The only way to do that was to economize, and the only way to economize
was to stay out of war. Sir Robert could well remember what had
happened in 1710, when disillusionment with a long and costly war had
brought a Tory triumph and the resurgence of Jacobitism. He had learned
the lesson and did not want to see it repeated.

    The core of his foreign policy, in consequence, was a rapprochement
with France; and he had the good luck to find circumstances propitious.
The death of Louis XIV in 1715 had left the throne to a boy of five, his
great-grandson Louis XV, and not until 1726 did French politics become
stabilized after the fluctuations of a regency. In that year the young King
called to power his tutor, Cardinal Fleury, a man of seventy-three, who
directed policy for the next sixteen years. This aged cynic — subtle, crafty, and
elusive — was poles apart from the squire of Houghton Hall, but they shared
the love of power and the desire to enjoy it in peace. Each was bent on setting
his nation's house in order after the wars of the previous generation.
Although both had to contend with, and eventually bow to, belligerent
factions at home, for more than a decade they worked together, in an
unavowed and uneasy partnership, to prevent a major European conflagration.

    One that threatened to be major broke out in 1733, the so-called
War of the Polish Succession. Poland, which was approaching dissolution as
a state, was a bone of contention among the great powers; and a dispute
over its elective kingship brought on a brief war between Austria and the
Bourbon monarchies, France and Spain. France had an interest in Poland,

where Louis XV's father-in-law was a candidate for the throne. Spain had no interest whatever, but hoped to regain control of the Italian principalities lost to Austria in the Utrecht settlement. Britain, as Walpole saw it, had no major concern with either Poland or Italy, and therefore no cause to intervene.

King George disagreed. For all his faults his viewpoint was more European, less insular, than Walpole's, and he recognized that a decisive defeat of Austria would upset the balance of power. He deeply distrusted France and, as a German prince, had an underlying loyalty to the Holy Roman Emperor, Charles VI, who was also ruler of Austria. For these reasons George wanted to intervene and dreamed of leading his armies himself to the emperor's rescue. But Walpole knew that he could not stir parliament to war even if he would. Its independent members might have kindled at the prospect of naval hostilities, to further British trade, but could see no more point than he could in fighting for Poland or Italy or even Vienna. He worked long and hard to convince his sovereign, who eventually, against his better judgment, gave way; Austria got no British aid. She was defeated in Italy, where she lost the south to a Spanish Bourbon prince; Louis XV's father-in-law gave up his claim to the Polish throne and received in compensation the Duchy of Lorraine, which was to revert to France at his death. The powers finally reached this settlement in 1733, without consulting or even informing the British government. Walpole had chosen isolation at the price of being ignored.

By 1738 his troubles were mounting at home and abroad. Frederick, Prince of Wales, who did what he could to justify his parents' loathing for him, had broken with them completely in 1736 and set up a court of his own, which became the focus of the opposition. In 1737 Sir Robert had lost his most valuable ally by the death of Queen Caroline. Many peers were his avowed enemies, and under their patronage a new generation of would-be Davids was being trained to use their oratorical slingshots on Goliath; the most brilliant of these "boy patriots" was William Pitt, the grandson of "Diamond" Pitt, a merchant who had made his fortune in India and put it to work in English politics. The technique of embarrassing Walpole was highly developed. At one moment a handsome allowance for the Prince of Wales was moved in the House of Commons, and the Minister barely managed to defeat this insult to the crown. At another the opposition forced him to fine the city of Edinburgh for a riot in which an English officer had been lynched; the Scottish members of the House of Commons, considering the fine an insult to Scotland's national pride, turned against Sir Robert. So it went. Now by taps and now by blows, now by leverage and now by pouring acid, his enemies were slowly undermining his position.

The International Crisis (1738–1739)

The opposition could not destroy "the Great Man," however, as long as the country remained prosperous and at peace. Only a war, if it was unpopular or mismanaged, would enable his foes to pull him down; they consequently worked for war as assiduously as he worked to prevent it. His survival came to depend more and more upon his ability to hold to the course he had mapped out in foreign policy, at a time when that course was becoming more difficult with every year that passed. New sources of friction with France were appearing in America and India. The delicate balance that the Utrecht settlement had established in Europe was endangered by the approach of a Habsburg dynastic crisis as menacing as that before the War of the Spanish Succession. A long-standing quarrel between Britain and Spain threatened to explode at any moment into war. Walpole for years had been careful, as he put it, to let sleeping dogs lie. Now all the dogs seemed to be waking at once, and they were growling ominously.

Friction between Britain and France in North America was grounded in geography. France possessed or claimed land to the north and west of the British colonies, extending in a vast arc from the Gulf of St. Lawrence, by way of Lakes Ontario and Erie and the valley of the Ohio and Mississippi, to the Gulf of Mexico. The British colonists on the Atlantic seaboard, as their population mounted, inevitably pressed westward across the Appalachians in search of land and furs, and trespassed increasingly on what the French considered their preserve. The struggle had already started, for the European wars of William's and Anne's reigns had had their colonial counterparts; but nothing had been settled, and year by year the pressures built up. Although they had little effect as yet upon the statecraft of Whitehall and Versailles, where colonial squabbles were still sideshows, the time for a final solution was approaching.

India was the scene of Anglo-French friction of a quite different sort. Here the British East India Company had long been jockeying for position against its Portuguese and Dutch rivals, not as empire-builders but as traders. The last thing that the directors of the Company wanted was to extend their territorial jurisdiction beyond Bombay, Madras, and Calcutta, the coastal cities that they controlled as centers for their trade with the interior. But profitable trading was possible only as long as the native government was able to maintain order. By the 1730s the great Mogul empire was falling to pieces, and the rulers of its former dependencies on the coast were struggling with each other for predominance. At the same time the French, with their newly organized Compagnie Perpetuelle des Indes, were beginning to make rapid inroads into the Indian market.

The next inevitable step for both the British and the French Companies was from trade to politics. No matter what the directors in London might say about keeping aloof from native affairs, the Englishmen on the spot knew better. They saw the local Indian rajah, to take a concrete but hypothetical example, demanding a higher price each year for maintaining the East India Company's trading privileges, and knew that the French were outbidding them at court. They also knew that the rajah's nephew claimed the throne, and with a small investment of British funds could probably get it. To retain the Company's trading position its agents were almost irresistibly tempted to invest in the pretender, install him as rajah, and then protect him, once he became their client, against French efforts to reinstate his predecessor. As long as the Indians were fighting among themselves for power and Europeans were vying for trade, the two forms of competition were bound to mesh, and the Europeans were bound to find themselves fighting through their protégés. The stage was set for one of the great struggles in the history of imperialism, a struggle that ended years later with the ousting of the French and the subordination of all the native states to a trading company that became, despite itself, the paramount power of India.

Neither Walpole nor anyone else, of course, understood the forces that were at work in India and in North America, because those forces were not yet clear; and the same was true of Europe, which was Sir Robert's chief concern. There he saw, as did the rest of the world, that a problem was impending for the House of Habsburg, one that promised to strain the resources of diplomacy as they had not been strained since 1701. But he could not guess that diplomacy would fail and the continent be plunged into a quarter-century of wars.

The Habsburgs were in dynastic trouble. The Emperor Charles VI faced a prospect almost as dismal as that of his Spanish cousin forty years earlier — this time not the extinction of his line but the accession of a woman. His only surviving children were daughters; a woman's inheriting a throne was always dangerous, as Henry Tudor had realized, and was particularly so when her possessions were surrounded by powerful and rapacious neighbors. Charles devoted his life to dealing with the danger. By a document known as the Pragmatic Sanction he arranged for all his hereditary dominions to go to his elder daughter, Maria Theresa. For years he peddled this document around the courts of Europe, offering a variety of concessions until he induced every great power to recognize Maria Theresa as his heir. He hoped that he was living in a world in which kings were gentlemen, even though it was pointed out to him that their promises did far less to guarantee his daughter's inheritance than could have been done by a full treasury and a strong army, neither of which he had. Europe waited for his death, to see which king would be first to forswear himself and plunder Maria Theresa's realm.

The Coming of War with Spain

These were some of the dangers to peace that confronted Walpole in the late 1730s, and all of them soon materialized. But the danger that first occasioned war came from quite a different quarter. While pressures were building up toward bloodshed in North America, India, and central Europe, Britain suddenly found herself fighting Spain. Anglo-Spanish antagonism, which was by then an old story, was so deep-rooted that it perhaps could not have been resolved in the long run by peaceful means; but the issues in the particular crisis of 1738–1739 could certainly have been. Walpole's diplomacy, however, was hamstrung by two factors: an opposition that was eager to bring him down through war, and the mutual suspicion engendered in London and Madrid by years of bickering. Both governments worked hard for compromise because neither wanted a conflict; Walpole lacked the will to fight, Spain the means. The way in which the efforts to keep peace were defeated is worth examining in some detail, partly because the crisis was a turning point in the history of the period, partly because it illustrates how economic and political forces can frustrate the best intentions of diplomats.

The ground of Anglo-Spanish friction was economic, and the war that resulted was more purely commercial than any Britain had fought since the Dutch wars. Then her goal had been the Dutch carrying trade; now it was the market of Latin America. Spain herself produced only a tiny fraction of the goods that her colonies demanded. Was the remainder to come from France or Britain? The government of Philip V, if only because he was a Bourbon, looked to France, whose merchants gained a greater and greater share of the legitimate trade between Spain and the Caribbean. Their British rivals responded in the only way they could, by illegitimate trade. They had lost the hopes that they had once pinned to the asiento; but it still served the traders of the South Sea Company as a cloak for smuggling, and the merchants of Jamaica and the other British islands smuggled on their own.

The situation was sure to breed trouble and grievances. Spanish authorities in the Caribbean had no way to prevent smuggling except to stop every British ship that came within range and search it for contraband. This right of search was hotly resented, and with reason. A merchant captain en route from London to Jamaica on legitimate business might find himself blown off course into Spanish waters, stopped, accused of being a smuggler bound for Cuba, and ruined by the confiscation of his ship. Worse still, Spanish officials did not have the money for a regular customs service and therefore licensed as a coastguard almost any one who was willing to work on commission; such men were out for all they could get and were more interested in the value of what they seized than in the legality of the seizure.

Legality, in fact, had little place in the Spanish Main, as the Caribbean was called. In a sea infested with pirates, the smugglers and coastguards who warred with each other were only a short remove from piracy themselves. When British sailors caught a Spanish patrol vessel at a

disadvantage, they often gave it rough handling; and the Spaniards replied
in kind. "It is without doubt irksome to every honest man to hear such
cruelties are committed in these seas," a disgusted British admiral wrote
home from Jamaica. "But give me leave to say that you only hear one side of
the question. And I can assure you the sloops that sail from this island,
manned and armed on that illicit trade, has [*sic*] more than once bragged to
me of their having murdered seven or eight Spaniards on their own shore.
. . . It is, I think, a little unreasonable for us to do injuries and not know how
to bear them. But villainy is inherent to this climate."

The innocent — or at least those who protested their innocence —
suffered along with the guilty. In June 1731 Captain Robert Jenkins arrived in
London with a cargo from Jamaica, and a story to tell that curled the hair.
Spanish coastguards had boarded his ship while it lay becalmed off Jamaica;
they had searched it for contraband, found none, and then begun to look
for cash. Three times they hanged him to his foreyard, Jenkins said, and each
time dropped him to the deck half dead and demanded to know where his
money was hidden. He kept protesting that he had none; they thereupon cut
off part of his ear with a cutlass and tried to scalp him, "but his head being
close shaven prevented the execution of it. They returned him the piece of
his ear again," Jenkins continued, "and bid him give it to King George,
uttering some scandalous words. They beat his mate, cut his boatswain, and
stripped him and his people of all their clothes, beds, and bedding, leaving
them nothing to wear or lay on." Then they let the ship go.

Such atrocity stories as this, repeated from year to year, began to do
their work. West Indian traders clamored for redress; the press took up their
cause, and by 1738 its campaign was as hot as in the days of the excise
crisis. Pamphleteers fanned John Bull's belligerence with talk of preventive
war. "No time can be more seasonable for a war with Spain than the
present," one of them argued, "since we have the strongest motives to think
every year will augment her revenues, her alliances, or territories." The
point about revenues was nonsense, and the point about territories trivial:
the British believed that Spain was about to claim their newly established
colony of Georgia as lying within the borders of Spanish Florida. The point
about alliances was more substantial: Spain was angling for a French alliance,
which was one of Walpole's chief reasons for not wanting to fight. He
feared — and events bore him out — that war against one Bourbon power
would sooner or later mean war against both.

Intent as he was on keeping the peace, he could not do it
singlehanded. The mounting popular pressure for war seemed to him an
impertinence, which he was ready to defy. "Are all desires," he asked the
House of Commons, "proper to be gratified? Is an inflamed populace to give
laws to the legislature?" But pressure from the legislature itself he could
not long resist. The opposition was pressing him hard and was raking over
the past for material with which to inflame parliament. Captain Jenkins
was called to tell his seven-year-old story, and in doing so immortalized

himself. When asked his thoughts while his ear was being cut off, he answered that "he recommended his soul to God and his cause to his country." As propaganda this magniloquent balderdash was worth its weight in gold.

The Captain's ear has an interesting resemblance to the U.S.S. *Maine,* sunk in Havana harbor in 1898. The loss of the ear served the same purpose for British agitators that the loss of the battleship did for American: both were concerned, not with the circumstances of the supposed atrocity, but with using it to bring on what they assumed would be an easy and profitable war. The Spaniards may have had nothing to do with separating Jenkins from his ear, just as they probably had nothing to do with the explosion that sent the *Maine* to the bottom. What they were accused of doing, not what they did, helped to determine history.

The opposition accused Walpole of having no care for the nation's honor. His only way of defending himself, short of war, was to win a tangible diplomatic victory and win it soon. This was difficult enough, because the Spaniards were past masters of evasion and delay. It was doubly difficult because victory had to be won under the watchful eyes of parliament, "which is in this country a terrible monster," the Spanish ambassador told his government, "and is ruled by private interests under the plausible name of the public good." The situation was too explosive, the ambassador warned, for long and delicate negotiations; parliament was demanding prompt results. Walpole's diplomacy was working against a deadline imposed upon it at Westminster.

The one fact in his favor was that Spain had no more desire for war than he had. The Spanish fleet was in even worse condition than the Spanish treasury, and Madrid was willing to pay a reasonable sum in compensation rather than become embroiled with the leading naval power of Europe. The British negotiators were also reasonable because they needed quick action. They started by demanding £340,000 damages for ships and cargoes illegally seized in the past by Spain, but finally settled for £95,000. On this basis the Convention of Pardo was drawn up and was ratified by both governments in February 1739. Peace seemed assured.

Walpole still had to weather a storm in parliament, where the opposition now spoke for an infuriated public. Hope had run high that the government would force Spain to pay munificent indemnities, punish guilty officials, formally abandon her claim to Georgia, and above all disavow her right of search in Spanish waters. Instead, all that the Convention provided was a pittance in cash. The settlement, William Pitt told the House of Commons, was "a stipulation for national ignominy, an illusory expedient to baffle the resentment of the nation. . . . The voice of your despairing merchants, the voice of England has condemned it; be the guilt upon the head of the adviser!" But the "adviser" still had the votes. Although many members of the opposition seceded from parliament in disgust, Walpole secured endorsement for his policy. It had been a close battle, in doubt until the last minute; but once more "the Great Man" had won.

It was his last triumph, and it was empty. By now he stood almost alone in his insistence on peace; key members of his own cabinet were against him, the King was wavering, the country was in a war fever, and the Prince of Wales came out as the champion of the "patriots." Sir Robert might have been able to beat down even this opposition, but the final blow came from Madrid. First the Spanish government refused to pay the damages agreed upon until it received compensation for a quite extraneous claim against the South Sea Company, and the Company responded with a counterclaim of its own. Then, while this altercation was heating the atmosphere, Madrid made a further condition: it would not pay until the British fleet was withdrawn from the Mediterranean. At that point hostilities became inevitable.

The developments that culminated in the second Spanish condition show how the fear of war can lead to war. While the Convention of Pardo was being negotiated, the British government had ordered a fleet to Minorca in order to put pressure on Spain; when the Convention was ratified, the ships were recalled. Almost immediately thereafter Whitehall began to doubt Spanish good faith and to suspect (wrongly, as it turned out) that Madrid was making an alliance with France. If the two Bourbon kingdoms joined forces, Gibraltar and Minorca would be doomed without naval protection; the Admiralty therefore reversed itself again and ordered the fleet to remain. The reaction in Madrid was immediate and understandable: Britain was acting in bad faith and meant war. If that were so, Spain would be demented to pay out £95,000, when she was already desperately short of cash, to the power that was about to attack her. She consequently made payment contingent on withdrawal of the fleet, and the small tragedy of misunderstandings was played out.

Spain, in British eyes, had willfully repudiated the Convention of Pardo. This was what the warmongers had been praying for, a *casus belli*. Even Walpole now had no alternative to war, for he was faced by a revolt within the cabinet led by his chief lieutenant, the Duke of Newcastle. All the work of Sir Robert's negotiators, all his arguments for compromise and dragooning of votes in parliament, had come to nothing. He did not want to fight any more than he had at the beginning; but he had to relinquish either his policy or his office, and he still loved power. On October 19, 1739, the royal heralds at Temple Bar announced Britain's declaration of war. "It is your war," the Minister told Newcastle, "and I wish you joy of it."

Walpole's Achievements

The beginning of the conflict that was christened the War of Jenkins' Ear marked not only the collapse of Walpole's policy but the end of his era. Although he held on to what was left of his power for more than two years, they were a shabby postscript to a proud career. War was not his element, and the period with which he is properly identified is the quarter-

century before 1739, during which Britain was at peace, except for the brief
flurry of the Fifteen, and consolidated and developed the gains of the past.
In that time the nation's financial system, once it survived the South Sea
Bubble, stimulated a prosperity that became the envy of Europe; the
parliamentary system took on a new form, with the cabinet recognized as its
central mechanism and patronage and influence replacing the old war of
parties. Although Walpole dominated these developments, he did so by virtue
of his personality and not his constitutional position. He left behind him no
tradition of one-man rule — quite the contrary. His power aroused deep and
continuous distrust, as witness the virulence of the opposition, and for the
rest of the century even the phrase "prime minister" continued to be suspect.

Sir Robert was not a prime minister in the modern sense; he was
both more and less. More, because no minister before or since has exercised
so much power for so long or put his stamp so deeply on his age. Less, because
he had behind him a machine, not a party, and so could never rely on a
majority in the House of Commons that would vote as instructed; less, also,
because his dependence on the king forced him to guard constantly against
intriguers at court and in the House of Lords. He kept his place only by
endless manipulation and compromise, and at two critical moments by
surrendering the policies for which he stood. If his power was great, so was
its price.

In manipulating his world he also served it. He gave it stability, kept
it at peace, furthered its prosperity. He has often been accused of debasing
its standards of political morality, but the best answer to this charge is to ask
which of his opponents had higher standards. They were as prosaic and
cynical as he was, with no greater dreams and much less shrewdness; the
most that can be said of them is that by the end of the period they sensed,
as he did not, the expansive forces in the nation that were urging it on to
adventure.

Walpole acted as a dam to these forces, and the Spanish war was
the breaking of the dam. From 1739 until 1815 Britain was involved in one
war after another, and never had more than a twelve-year interlude of peace;
she was also involved in economic changes at home, at a rapidly increasing
rate, that made her by 1815 the one industrial power of the world. The quiet
days were over, the rest period in which the country had gathered its strength
after the upheavals of the Stuart era. Now the strength was being called
into play, and tested as it had never been before.

4 The Winning of Empire

The Expansion of the Conflict (1739–1740)

In 1739 Britain found herself in a war for which she was unprepared. This was no accident of the moment; unpreparedness is a recurring theme throughout her history, just as it is in the history of the United States, and for the same underlying reason. Both nations have been island powers, strategically speaking, and as such have been immune from any massive invasion at the outbreak of war; both, therefore, have traditionally tended in peacetime to deny their armed services the equipment, training, and thought required to keep them ready for battle. Both have usually bungled and sometimes been defeated at the start of hostilities, and have then set to work to create a fighting machine. Geography has given them time, as it has not given a land power like France, to learn how to fight *after* the declaration of war.

At the outbreak of the Spanish conflict, Britain was in an even worse state than usual. The army was negligible, the navy in the doldrums, and Walpole's government inexperienced and inept at military planning. Of these shortcomings the first seemed the least important; everyone expected the war to be a return to the Elizabethan tradition of plundering the Spanish Main, and for that lucrative occupation no great number of troops was required. Even small expeditions, however, proved to be beyond the capacity of the War Office, which could neither organize nor supply them effectively; the soldiers sent to the Caribbean accomplished nothing and died like flies. This was bad enough, but the blundering of the navy was worse. Its officers were better at fighting each other and the generals with whom they were supposed to cooperate, than at fighting the Spaniards; and the Admiralty had no concept of how to use sea power. The nation, having embarked lightheartedly on what was assumed to be a small and easy struggle, lacked the capacity to win it.

This was a bad augury, for within a year a far greater struggle began in Europe. In 1740 the Habsburg Emperor, Charles VI, died; and the accession of his daughter, Maria Theresa, was the signal for neighboring powers to try to partition her territories. This attempt concerned Britain because it threatened to destroy the whole balance of European power. For two hundred years continental rivalries had centered in the antagonism between the Habsburgs and the reigning house in France, first Valois and then Bourbon; and for half a century Britain had found in the Habsburgs her counterweight to Bourbon aggression. Now that the troubles of Maria Theresa gave new scope to French ambition, the dictates of self-interest shifted British attention from the Caribbean to Europe.

France was not the first to tear up the Pragmatic Sanction and begin plundering Maria Theresa's dominions. That particular dishonor was reserved for a man known as Frederick the Great, the Hohenzollern who had just ascended the throne of Prussia. His small but relatively compact state in northern Germany, with Berlin for its capital, was emerging into the ranks of the great powers by virtue of its army; Prussia, as Napoleon once said, was hatched from a cannonball. Frederick well knew that he could increase his power only at the expense of the Habsburgs, who had long been the paramount German dynasty; and he found his opportunity in a woman's weak and impoverished inheritance, which he had promised to respect. In December 1740 his troops marched into Silesia, the Austrian province adjacent to his own dominions; and as the price of annexing it he offered Maria Theresa an alliance against the rest of the world. She scornfully refused, and war began.

Much more was at stake than Silesia. Frederick was beginning a struggle between Austria and Prussia for dominance of the German states, and it went on until 1866. This new theme in the power politics of Europe drowned out before long the old theme of Austro-French rivalry. For the next fifty years, until the coming of the French Revolution, Austria and Prussia were opposed; and until 1763 their opposition was a major factor in Britain's policy. She ended by conquering India and Canada, in large measure because Frederick began by conquering Silesia.

The connection between wars in Europe and wars outside was almost inevitable. The Austro-Prussian quarrel touched off by the Silesian issue in 1740 developed into a struggle for central Europe, just as the Anglo-Spanish quarrel of 1739 developed into a struggle between Britain and the Bourbon powers for empire overseas. These two conflicts, going on at the same time, became the constants around which alliances arranged and rearranged themselves. France was lured by her old ambition of expanding in Europe, and aligned herself with either Prussia or Austria in attacking the other; Britain almost automatically took the opposite side, partly to guard Hanover and partly to have a continental ally while fighting the Bourbons at sea and overseas. The two wars of the midcentury were not, like those of Louis XIV, between France and a European coalition led by Britain; they were between coalitions of fluctuating membership. But the fluctuations, however bewildering on the surface, preserved the two fundamental antagonisms: in both wars the Habsburg fought the Hohenzollern, and Britain fought the Bourbon states.

The Nature of Eighteenth-Century Warfare

Conflicts were conducted like business operations. The wars of religion were things of the past, and the wars of nation against nation were things of the future; calculation and reasons of state took the place of passion. Each belligerent entered on hostilities in the hope of profit, whether in terms of trade or territory, and fought as long as fighting served its ends; then it made peace on the best terms possible and awaited another opportunity. An agrarian state like Prussia coveted new provines, the revenues and population of which could be translated into additional army corps; a maritime state like Britain coveted new naval bases and lucrative colonies, which could be translated into dominion of the seas. Alliances were based on expediency and might shift with circumstances, for allies that were concerned entirely with their own interests were unreliable comrades-in-arms. The aims of each were flexible, and expanded or contracted as the war went well or badly; but they were always realistic and limited aims.

Land warfare could not be carried to extremes. The officer class of every European state, including Britain, was virtually synonymous with the aristocracy, and had to be as long as the old regimes survived; for only men dependent upon the crown for their privileges and loyal to it through long tradition could be trusted to command the force on which the social order depended. But no country had enough aristocrats in its population to officer a mass army, any more than it had enough money in its treasury to equip and feed such an army. For social and financial reasons, in other words, the military establishment of even a great power was by modern standards extremely small. The result was that no government had the means, even if it had had the will, to push a war to total victory — to annihilate the enemy's army, seize his capital, and dictate terms of peace. The social system imposed moderation even upon war-making, man's most immoderate activity.

Campaigns were not only limited in their aims but also, for the most part, inconclusive in their results. A principal reason was that the armies were composed of soldiers who served for pay, not love of their country. Many of the small states hired out their troops to the highest bidder, and even in the national monarchies the enlisted man knew little of nationalism. Such loyalty as he had was to his regiment, a loyalty that was the first meaning of the phrase *esprit de corps*. He came from the lower classes and was often in service because the civil authorities had wanted to get rid of him —

> The youth whose most opprobrious fame
> And clear convicted crimes have stamped him soldier.

Only an iron discipline made troops out of such material, which the Duke of Wellington later described as "the scum of the earth." An officer could not trust his men out of his sight for fear they would desert, and consequently could not send them to scout and forage on their own; the army, instead of living off the countryside, had to carry with it virtually everything it needed. It therefore moved at a snail's pace, always concerned for its supply lines, rarely daring to leave an enemy fortress in its rear. Campaigns were largely matters of maneuver, of threat and counterthreat, sieges begun and raised; even the winning of battles might bring victory no nearer.

Commanders had good reason to dread a battle because of the way it was fought. The muskets of the day were not accurate beyond fifty yards; infantrymen were therefore trained to advance in precise and rigid line until they came within range, then fire a volley from the entire line, then charge with the bayonet — while their opponents, in turn, were firing at them point blank. The effect was murderous. Casualty rates often ran between thirty and fifty percent of the troops engaged. If those who were left won a victory, in the sense of driving the enemy from the field, they could rarely exploit it by rapid pursuit, which would disorder their line and expose them to counterattack. Most actions, in consequence, produced no gain commensurate with the slaughter involved, and the slaughter in itself was a defeat. The men lost were specialists, hardened by long and rigorous training, and could not be readily replaced; squandering them to no purpose was lunacy. For the orthodox commander a battle, in the words of a German military writer, was "the remedy of the desperate"; and, when both sides were anxious to avoid fighting, campaigns produced results as modest as the casualty lists.

The upshot was that land warfare was slow and inconclusive. Between 1740 and 1763 the great powers were fighting for fifteen years, and almost the only effect on the map of Europe was to transfer the province of Silesia from Austria to Prussia. While Britain continued to concentrate her efforts on this continental conflict she achieved nothing, except the protection of Hanover; not until she shifted her main effort to the ocean, and concentrated on a naval war for the expansion of trade and empire, did she find the road to victory.

Naval war had, in some ways, much in common with war on land. Neither a navy nor an army could be improvised. The square-rigged sailing vessels that were the warships of the period were costly and slow to build; sailors and naval gunners, like soldiers, were the product of long training; and the backbone of the fleet, the three-decked ship of the line that was the precursor of the later battleship, was too highly specialized and too valuable a unit of firepower to be lightly risked. Actions at sea were commonly fought between two lines, sailing on parallel or opposite courses and firing broadsides at each other like the volleys of soldiers, and the immediate results were likely to be as inconclusive as those of land battles. But there the resemblances ended.

War at sea was different in kind from war on land. A fleet, unlike an army, did not have to stop to besiege a fortress in its path or fritter away its strength in guarding supply lines; it carried with it what it needed and could go wherever there was blue water. Every enemy ship disabled, every base captured or put out of commission, shifted the balance in some degree and prepared the way for the next advance. Naval war was cumulative in its effect, if intelligently directed, and therefore led in the long run to decisive results.

Its final objective, as the British slowly learned, was not merely to defeat the opposing battle fleet but to drive it from the sea. Ships bottled up in port were at a disadvantage: their crews grew slack from want of practice, and their captains lost their skill in maneuvering with other ships. A blockading squadron, on the other hand, because it had to keep the sea in every kind of wind and weather, tended to increase in efficiency even at the cost of damage to the ships. Hence the longer a blockade was maintained, the greater the disparity was likely to be between the passive and the active navy, and the more complete the predominance of the latter. The fruit of that predominance could be the acquistion of every enemy possession overseas.

So much for the theory of sea power. But theory in war evolves from practice, which is a slow teacher. The British Admiralty, even when it learned the practice of blockade, had little understanding of the theory behind it. The practice was not learned until twenty years after the outbreak of hostilities in 1739, and was forgotten again in the War of American Independence and relearned in the 1790s. Another century elapsed before the theory was formulated — and then by an American.[1]

The War of the Austrian Succession (1740–1748)

In the long evolution of British strategy the War of the Austrian Succession was a mere preliminary, a process of trial and error in which error predominated. Britain had not yet realized the potentialities of sea power, and two factors were chiefly responsible for delaying her realization. One was the traditional emphasis, inherited from the days of Marlborough, upon land warfare in Europe, an emphasis now heightened by the need for defending Hanover; the other was developments at home that culminated in a Jacobite rising. These two factors, accentuated by governmental ineptitude, produced one of the most inconclusive struggles in British history.

The war was slow in getting started. France began to intervene on the side of Prussia as early as 1741, and Spain revived her old dream of

---

[1] By Alfred T. Mahan in his famous trilogy, *The Influence of Sea Power upon History, 1660–1783* (1890), *The Influence of Sea Power upon the French Revolution and Empire, 1793–1812* (1892), and *The Life of Nelson* (1897). These classics, which are still eminently readable, were among the most influential historical works of the nineteenth century. Mahan's purpose was to demonstrate, in terms of Britain's past, the ways in which a great navy serves the national interest. The doctrines that he enunciated have so deeply affected naval thinking throughout the world that he might be called the Charles Darwin of sea power.

ousting the Austrians from Italy; but several years elapsed before the Bourbon powers revealed clearly that their aim, like that of Frederick, was to partition Maria Theresa's inheritance. This aim deeply affected Britain, partly because Spain was her open enemy and much more because France intended to conquer the Austrian Netherlands, in which British interests were as closely involved as they had been at the time of the Utrecht settlement. Not until the spring of 1744, however, did the nation formally enter the war.

The reason was in great part the political currents and crosscurrents in London. Early in 1742 the mismanagement of the Spanish war drove Walpole from office at long last, as his opponents had calculated. The departure of his dominating figure left a political vacuum, and the little men who squabbled for his place had neither the vision nor the support in parliament to create effective policy. They hired German troops to assist Maria Theresa and safeguard Hanover; George II, acting as a German prince while Britain was still technically neutral, assumed command of this army, and in 1743 had the satisfaction of leading it to a quite inadvertent victory over the French — the last time, fortunately, that a British sovereign ever commanded in the field. But the King's triumph did not still the parliamentary outcry that he was sacrificing British interests to Hanoverian; he was turning the nation, said William Pitt, into "a province to a despicable Electorate."

The King's ministers did not have the wit to devise a coherent offensive strategy, and France saved them the trouble by seizing the initiative. The government of Louis XV, just as Walpole had expected, revived the cause of the Stuarts and massed troops and ships for an invasion of England to coincide with a Jacobite rising. When the plan was abandoned in the face of British naval preparations, the Jacobites decided to go ahead on their own in the hope of forcing the hand of Versailles.

Their leader was no longer James, by now an aging failure, but his son the Young Pretender. Charles Edward Stuart, "Bonnie Prince Charlie," was in some respects the ideal romantic hero: he was strikingly handsome, and had a magnetism and charm that recalled the Duke of Marlborough; he lacked Marlborough's other gifts as politician and soldier, but he did have courage and a sense of dedication. When he set off from France in a small ship in July 1745, bound for London by way of Scotland to topple King George off his throne, the venture seemed utterly hopeless. Perhaps it was, but in the next few months the Stuart cause came closer to success than at any time since the Battle of the Boyne in 1690.

The Forty-Five, like the Fifteen, began with a Highland rising. Soon after Charles landed on the west coast of Scotland with only seven companions, he had an army of clansmen at his back. He made straight for Edinburgh, and by mid-September was installed in his ancestors' palace of Holyrood. Four days later he defeated the only force of British regulars in the country. Meanwhile, far to the south, the cold wind of panic began to blow through Whitehall; the government hastily recalled troops from the Low Countries and summoned King George from Hanover. If the Pretender had been strong enough to invade England at once, he might have had a chance; but he waited for reinforcements until the end of October, and by that time armies were massing to bar his road. He eluded them all and marched south to Derby, little more than a hundred miles from London. There he stopped, hesitated, and after bitter argument yielded to his advisers and turned back. Retreat, as he knew, was the end of his bid for a crown.

Yet by then he had no other course but retreat, for events were demonstrating that the name of Stuart, outside the Highlands, no longer had any magic. The years of Walpole had done their work of reconciling the English, and even the lowland Scots, to the Hanoverian regime. Men would not turn out to fight for that regime, because it did not command a fighting loyalty; but neither would they turn out to fight against it. Without their support the Stuart cause was doomed. Prince Charles and his advisers cared less about the presence of hostile armies than about the absence of the recruits they had hoped for, and when they found the populace watching their march with indifference they knew that the game was up. A rabble of kilts and the skirl of bagpipes and a cause from the distant past made no impression on the Whig magnates or the peasants of Derbyshire, and their apathy was as strong a defense for King George as his soldiers were.

The Jacobite army retreated across the border and into the Highlands, where it starved through the winter. The end came in April 1746 when the King's younger son, the Duke of Cumberland, destroyed the ragged Highlanders in a battle on Culloden Moor. The Pretender, with a price of £30,000 on his head, wandered between Jacobite households on the mainland and in the Hebrides for the next five months, sometimes disguised as a woman, until in September he finally found a ship to take him to France. He left his followers to the ferocious vengeance of Cumberland, who was known thenceforth as the Butcher; and the government also took punitive measures. Many Highland chiefs saved themselves by exile, while the old clan organization was broken up by act of parliament and the clansmen were disarmed. In the years that followed, the Highlands slowly emerged from their backwardness and became, at the price of much suffering, an integral part of Scotland.

As for Bonnie Prince Charlie, he soon ceased to be bonnie. His wanderings after Culloden had driven him to drink, and the remainder of his long life was devoted more and more singlemindedly to women and alcohol. When he died in 1788 his shadowy claim passed to his younger brother Henry, a cardinal in the Roman Church; and with Henry's death in 1807 the male line of James II was finally extinguished. Its hopes had died in the Forty-Five, and thereafter its exiled followers flitted through the capitals of Europe with nothing to do but play the game of might-have-been. "It is to no sort of purpose to talk to those people," Lord Chesterfield warned his son, "of the natural rights of mankind and the particular constitution of this country. Blinded by prejudices, soured by misfortunes, and tempted by their necessities, they are as incapable of reasoning rightly as they have hitherto been of acting wisely."

Their action in precipitating the Forty-Five was from their point of view unwise, at least by hindsight, because it doomed their cause; but from the viewpoint of Versailles it was a godsend. It gave France the initiative in the war. When the British government withdrew its troops from the Low Countries, the French moved into the Austrian Netherlands and part of Holland; and all the efforts of the British and Dutch failed to dislodge them. The Austrians were no help, even when Frederick, with Silesia for his prize, withdrew Prussia from the conflict. France, like Prussia, had won a substantial gain on the continent; but overseas her position was precarious. Although in India she had captured Madras, in America she had lost the fortress of Louisbourg, on Cape Breton Island, which was the key to the St. Lawrence. It had been captured by an expedition from Massachusetts, supported by a squadron of the Royal Navy; and the whole of French Canada lay open to attack. This was the threat by which the British, in the peace negotiations, pried loose the French hold on the Low Countries.

All the belligerents by now were weary. The business of war offered no assurance of further profit for any of them, and they were ready to bargain. The peace treaty that they hammered out, signed at Aix-la-Chapelle in 1748, was by modern standards fantastic. Spain made minor gains in Italy, but the only major change was that the powers agreed to Frederick's acquisition of Silesia. He alone emerged as a clear-cut victor. Elsewhere the prewar status quo was reestablished — the French back in Louisbourg, the British in Madras, the Austrians in their part of the Netherlands, the Dutch in the border fortresses that they had acquired at Utrecht. Britain made an almost casual peace with Spain: the asiento would lapse in the near future, and the chief issue that had brought on war in 1739, the Spanish right of search, was passed over in diplomatic silence. Walpole was dead by now, but his ghost might have chuckled. Nine years of fighting and spending money — to the tune of some £80 million — had brought his country nothing.

Reversal of Alliances and Renewal of War (1748–1757)

The Treaty of Aix-la-Chapelle left all the basic questions open. In India and America the Anglo-French rivalry was as intense and explosive as ever. In Europe Austria and Prussia were not reconciled, but only resting; France was ready to fight again whenever a promising opportunity offered. Before long Maria Theresa provided one. She had no intention of accepting the loss of Silesia as final, and to get it back she needed a more stalwart champion than Britain had proved to be. She began to make overtures at Versailles, to which the British government had only one possible answer — overtures at Berlin. While Austria and France had been at loggerheads, Austria and Britain had been friendly; now that Austria and France were drawing together, Britain had no recourse but to turn to Prussia. This realignment of the powers, particularly in the years 1754–1756, is known as the Diplomatic Revolution.

There was in fact nothing revolutionary about it. The War of the Austrian Succession had grown out of two rivalries and had resolved neither one; they continued through a period of uneasy truce. In India the French and British companies encouraged little wars between their client rajahs, while in America the French strengthened their line of forts and trading posts from the Great Lakes to the lower Mississippi. In Europe the Austrian desire for Silesia gradually led to a much more grandiose project, a coalition of powers to dismember Prussia. To settle the issues left unsettled at Aix-la-Chapelle a new and greater war was in the making, and the only question was where it would first erupt.

The answer proved to be in North America, where the French and British claims overlapped in the great forests of the Alleghenies, and both sides were determined to assert what they considered their rights. In 1754 an ex-surveyor and colonel of Virginia militia by the name of George Washington led a small expedition of volunteers to the Forks of the Ohio, the site of modern Pittsburgh, only to find the French established there in Fort Duquesne; Washington and his whole force were captured. News of this small debacle stirred the British government to act. In 1755 it sent troops under General Braddock to seize Fort Duquesne, and a naval squadron to the mouth of the St. Lawrence to intercept reinforcements for Canada. Braddock was ambushed and killed; most of the French reinforcements got through, but some were captured. This was war, real if undeclared, and within a few months it spread to Europe.

There the opening of hostilities was as much the result of fear as of intent. Britain, drifting into a conflict with France, feared for the safety of Hanover; France feared a coalition of continental powers against her; Prussia feared that Maria Theresa would succeed in finding confederates. The old alliance system was breaking apart, and no one knew what kind of realignment would succeed it. Frederick of Prussia was not one to wait on events; as dangers gathered about him, he acted. In January 1756 he formed an alliance with Britain; in September he invaded Saxony, which he intended to add to his dominions. These moves raised against him a ring of enemies. France, whom he had deserted for Britain, turned to Austria; and this Franco-Austrian combination was promptly joined by Russia. The Romanov Empress, Elizabeth, detested Frederick and saw an opportunity to possess herself of eastern Prussia; for these reasons she projected Russia for the first time into the power politics of western Europe. The Seven Years War was beginning, and it was once more a war of intended partition. Russia, Austria, and France expected to make the Prussian state, which had been the sole gainer from the previous conflict, the victim of the new one.

France immediately seized the initiative. In the spring of 1756, before any formal declaration of war had been issued, she had attacked and captured Minorca with its British garrison; now her armies poured into the

Germanies, and in 1757 overran Hanover. For the planners at Versailles the
Electorate was crucial. They accepted Britain's naval superiority as irreversible,
and realized that it would in all likelihood cost them a good part of their
colonies; but they expected to redeem this loss at the war's end in the way that
France had recovered Louisbourg in 1748, by surrendering gains in Europe.
Hanover, they calculated, would serve them in the peace negotiations as the
Austrian Netherlands had served them at Aix-la-Chapelle: by returning it
they would win back their overseas empire. They would then be left in
possession of whatever other European conquests their armes might make, and
Maria Theresa promised them the Austrian Netherlands if she recovered
Silesia. Their strategy, in other words, was based upon the lesson of the
previous war, that Europe was the crucial theater and that gains there would
recoup any losses elsewhere.

The Rise of William Pitt

What the French did not take into account, because they did not yet
know it, was that they were pitted against the two greatest strategists in the
period between Marlborough and Napoleon. One was King Frederick. The
crisis that he had helped bring on himself challenged his powers as never
before, and he rose to the challenge. Although his army was the best fighting
machine in Europe, it faced odds so overwhelming that a lesser man would
have succumbed; even he thought at times of suicide. He lost battles and even
campaigns; he saw his troops melt away, and the Russians occupy Berlin.
But he held on, always fighting, always formidable, and in the end managed
to preserve — unfortunately, perhaps, for the world of the future — the Prussia
that was hatching from a cannonball.

Pitt, like Churchill, might never have achieved leadership if the
war had not begun with calamitous British defeats. The "boy patriot" who
had opposed Walpole had made a name for himself by his oratory and, after
Sir Robert's fall, a place for himself by his abilities. But King George,
remembering Pitt's stigmatizing Hanover as "a despicable Electorate," had
kept him from high office and forced him to bide his time for years in a
minor position. During those years two brothers, Henry Pelham and Walpole's

old lieutenant the Duke of Newcastle, had carried on Sir Robert's system and bungled their way through the War of the Austrian Succession and the uneasy peace that followed. The world of the Pelhams felt no need of inspiring leadership.

Henry Pelham's death in 1754 deprived the administration of its manager in the House of Commons, and was the beginning of Pitt's opportunity. For two more years Newcastle stumbled on by himself as head of the government, a position for which he was wholly unfit. He had the disadvantage of sitting in the House of Lords, but what principally disqualified him for leardership was his personality. He was a timid, fussy little man, always chattering and fidgeting; and even King George held him in supreme contempt. The Duke stayed in office for thirty years, nevertheless, because he knew more about the arts of political manipulation, thanks to Walpole, than anyone else in the kingdom; but he was no man to galvanize the nation in a crisis. As a minister he was indispensable; as first minister he was impossible.

The war opened with defeats, not only on Minorca but in North America and India; and under these blows Newcastle was driven from office in November 1756. Pitt came to power on his own terms, to the King's fury; but in the spring of 1757 George dismissed him and tried to form a ministry of his own choosing. For more than two months the battle raged. Pitt had enormous popularity outside parliament; and once more, as in 1733 and 1739, the pressure of an aroused electorate was brought to bear on Westminster. Yet no amount of pressure could create the political machine that was prerequisite for conducting the business of government; the only man with such a machine was Newcastle, and place had to be made for him. In June 1757 the King, grumbling ferociously, accepted a Pitt-Newcastle coalition; and it remained in office for the next four years. The Duke managed the patronage and votes; Pitt managed the war.

They were an odd pair. "The Duke of Newcastle and Mr. Pitt," said Chesterfield, "jog on like man and wife, that is, seldom agreeing, often quarreling, but by mutual interest . . . not parting." They could not afford to part, because both loved power and neither could have it alone; and their views on the war, although widely divergent in theory, were much less so in practice. The focus of Newcastle's interest had always been European, and in particular Hanoverian. Pitt cared no more than he ever had about Hanover in itself; his focus was trade and empire overseas. But he cared a great deal about keeping the French busy with an inconclusive German war, and it would not be inconclusive unless they were kept out of the Electorate. Hence he was as much concerned as his colleague with Hanoverian defense; in the closing phase of the conflict he made his famous remark that "America had been conquered in Germany."

During his first year in office with Newcastle, Pitt was unable to conquer anything. In North America an attempt to take Louisbourg failed, and the French advanced south from the St. Lawrence to threaten the Hudson Valley. From India came news that in June 1756 the native ruler of

Bengal had captured the British post at Calcutta; after the surrender some of the garrison had been stifled in the notorious Black Hole, the punishment cell of the fortress. In Europe, during 1757, a massive British raid on the French coast, costing £1 million, achieved nothing; the Austrians defeated Frederick in Bohemia, and an Austro-Russian force raided Berlin; the French occupied Hanover. Only at the end of the year did the tide turn in Germany, when the King of Prussia defeated in quick succession the French at Rossbach, in Saxony, and the Austrians in Silesia. The Austrians recovered, but the French never did; Rossbach blunted their offensive and broke their hold on Hanover. For the next five years they tried to regain the initiative in Germany, and their failure to do so subverted their whole strategy. Rossbach, Napoleon said years later, was the battle that started the Bourbon regime toward its collapse in revolution.

The Years of Victory (1758–1760)

Prussia's crisis did not end at Rossbach — far from it. In the ensuing campaigns her enemies pressed harder and harder upon her, until Pitt recognized that British interests required large-scale intervention. He steadfastly refused to commit the bulk of the British army to the continent; but he did send a contingent, which at its peak came to 20,000 men, and he poured out money for hiring Germans. He furnished Frederick a yearly subsidy of £670,000 for his campaigns against the Austrians and Russians in the east, and employed some 55,000 mercenaries to cooperate with the British contingent in guarding Hanover and Prussia on the west. This Anglo-German army on the Rhine, commanded by Frederick's chief lieutenant, Prince Ferdinand of Brunswick, carried on the work begun at Rossbach, and was the means of rendering the German war completely inconclusive for France.

In 1759 Prince Ferdinand won a battle. Out of it came a controversy that had long repercussions in Britain, and that illustrates the complex interplay between war-making and politics. George II was aging rapidly. His son Frederick had died in 1751, and the heir to the throne was the King's twenty-one-year-old grandson, George, Prince of Wales, who according to family custom was on bad terms with his grandfather. The commander of the British expeditionary force serving under Ferdinand of Brunswick was Lord George Sackville, a favorite of the Prince of Wales and consequently *persona non grata* to the king. Sackville was equally unpopular with his chief, Prince Ferdinand, whom he showered with advice in public and criticized in private. This was the setting for the Battle of Minden.

In the battle, after the Anglo-German infantry had driven the French into retreat, Brunswick ordered Sackville to deliver the *coup de grace* by a cavalry attack. Nothing happened; the moment was lost. Prince Ferdinand, furious, charged his subordinate with disobedience. Lord George answered that the orders had not been clear, but he was relieved of his command and ordered home. The fat was in the fire: Pitt had to choose between turning on Sackville and offending the Prince of Wales, or supporting Lord George and offending the King and Brunswick. He took the former course and sided with the King. Sackville, ostracized, demanded a court-martial, a demand that at least showed courage. A famous court-martial two years before, of an admiral who had helped to lose Minorca, had resulted in his being shot on his quarterdeck. Sackville fared better, but not much. He was found guilty of disobeying orders, declared unfit to serve in any military capacity, and disgraced before the whole army. If ever a career seemed to be blasted, it was his. Yet this was the man to whom the Prince of Wales, as king in later years, entrusted chief responsibility for suppressing the American rebellion.

Minden was more than an occasion of controversy. It was also a significant victory, even if incomplete, and one of a constellation that made 1759 a year long remembered. "I know that I can save this country," Pitt had said in 1756, "and that no one else can." Now he was making good his words by implementing well-laid plans. He saw the war as an integrated whole and had evolved for it an integrated strategy. The parts were not new but had all been tried before in slipshod fashion; his achievement was to bring them together into a system, much as Walpole, a generation earlier, had created a political system out of ingredients ready at hand. But Pitt's system, unlike Walpole's, produced sensational results.

The new strategy derived from one geographical fact, that Britain was an island and France was not. An insular state can concentrate upon its navy, whereas a state with exposed frontiers must divide its energies between sea and land; Pitt exploited this advantage. He raised an army, it is true, of almost 150,000 men, but broke with tradition by sending only a small fraction of it to Europe; for that phase of the struggle he relied primarily on subsidies and mercenaries to contain France, wear down her strength, and prevent her taking the offensive at sea. There he intended to defeat her and, when he had done so, to use the army to gather in her empire.

Sea power and its concomitant, blockading the Mediterranean and Atlantic coasts of France, were the core of his strategy. The test came in 1759, when the French projected an invasion of the British Isles. To cover it the Toulon squadron broke out of the Mediterranean for a junction with the main fleet at Brest, but was destroyed in a battle off Portugal; the ships at Brest then put to sea for a rendezvous with the transports, only to be annihilated in a second battle. Thereafter the remaining units of the French fleet stayed prudently in port, where the long months of inactivity undermined their crews' morale and seamanship. France lost access to the Atlantic and so to her overseas colonies.

The effect was soon felt from the Ganges to the St. Lawrence. Pitt himself had little interest in India, where the Anglo-French struggle was ostensibly between two commercial companies rather than two governments. But the companies were becoming in effect governments; they had learned to recruit sepoys, Indian troops who served under European officers, and to use them for making full-scale war. Both sides depended on support from home, and the turning point came when Pitt detached a few warships to the scene. The French government, thanks to the British blockade, could send nothing equivalent, and before long the Royal Navy commanded Indian waters. This was the opportunity for Robert Clive, the first of the great proconsuls who served the East India Company. He and his lieutenants reconquered Calcutta, seized the enemy's posts in Bengal, and by 1761 had destroyed French power in India.

Success in America was even more dramatic. In 1758 Louisbourg fell, and Braddock was avenged by the capture of Fort Duquesne; in 1759 General Wolfe won Quebec in a brilliant campaign that cost him his life; in 1760 a fleet and converging armies took Montreal and finished the conquest of Canada. Meanwhile, far to the south in the West Indies, the British were gathering French islands like ripe plums; by 1762 they had Dominica, Martinique, Guadeloupe, and St. Lucia. This surfeit of riches from all parts of the world, which surpassed men's fondest hopes and seemed miraculous, was the result of the blockading squadrons that rode the sea in all weather off the coast of France.

But blockade, even though it produced such victories, did so at the price of alienating the neutral maritime states. Ships of those states could not be permitted to carry French goods under their flags and so maintain the trade between France and her empire. At the start of the war, accordingly, the British government enunciated the Rule of 1756: trade that had been closed to neutrals in time of peace was also closed to them in time of war. Because France had not hitherto permitted them to participate in the commerce with her colonies, in other words, they might not do so now. The rule was enforced not only by the British navy but by swarms of privateers, licensed by the government to search neutral shipping for contraband and appropriate for their own profit whatever they found. The right of search, which had so infuriated British merchants when exercised by Spain in Spanish waters, was now being exercised under the Union Jack on a vastly larger scale. The neutrals were too weak to fight and could only bide their time for revenge.

Britain's victories were costing her not only goodwill but also vast sums in cash. The subsidies to Prussia; the cost of the troops that guarded western Germany, of the more than four hundred ships in the navy, of combined operations overseas; the £1 million given the American colonies for raising their own military forces — these and other outlays strained the financial resources of the country to the breaking point. By 1760 the revenue had climbed to £15 million, more than double the figure for 1756; but expenses were still soaring above income and had to be met by loans. The national debt rose between 1756 and 1763 from less than £75 million to almost £133 million. To Newcastle and other conservatives such figures spelled ruin. Even Pitt realized that a nation of roughly seven million, masses of whom were desperately poor, could not pour out gold forever. But he would not make peace until he had led the nation to victory, complete and final.

Whether he could continue to lead it was another question. His colleagues no longer followed him as unquestioningly as they had in the dark days of the war and were beginning to tire of his arrogance. The public, grown almost blasé about victories, was beginning to tire of his unrelenting demands. Most important of all, he was now serving a new king and could not count on his support. George II, who had begun by detesting his great minister but had fallen under his spell like everyone else, had died in the autumn of 1760, and the accession of his grandson changed the whole face of politics.

George III and the Fall of Pitt (1760–1761)

The young King was a man to be reckoned with. His personality stamped his reign, at least in its first quarter-century, more deeply than those of George I and George II had ever stamped theirs. Part of the reason was that he was not Hanoverian at heart: he cared little for his Electorate and, as he said, "gloried in the name of Briton." The rest of the reason was that he came to the throne at a much younger age than his grandfather or great-grandfather, was far more energetic and intelligent, and had a higher notion of what a king should be. He did not dream of subverting the constitution to exalt his own power, but neither did he intend to be a figurehead. He would take back into his own hands the means of political influence that had hitherto been largely deputed to the ministry of the moment, and be a king who ruled, through loyal servants in the cabinet and parliament, for the good of the nation at large.[2] This was far from an ignoble aim; indeed it was almost like constitutional poetry after the dreary prose of Walpole and the Pelhams. But in the long run the effects were catastrophic.

The reason was that the King could not achieve his aim without diminishing oligarchical power. For half a century the Whigs had been

[2] The role of George III has received a great deal of attention from historians, and they are still far from agreed. The traditional and highly unfavorable Whig interpretation is exemplified in the numerous writings of Sir George O. Trevelyan: *The Early History of Charles James Fox* (1904); *The American Revolution* (2nd ed., 4 vols., 1905–12); and *George the Third and Charles Fox* (2nd ed., 2 vols., 1914–15). The pioneer work of reevaluation was done by Sir Lewis B. Namier in *The Structure of Politics at the Accession of George III* (2 vols., 1929) and *England in the Age of the American Revolution* (1933). See also Richard Pares, *King George and the Politicians* (1953), and Herbert Butterfield, *George III and the Historians* (1957). A brief but excellent summary of this historiographical controversy is in Dorothy Marshall, *Eighteenth Century England*, pp. 322–28.

(*National Portrait Gallery*)

George III. Portrait from the studio of Alan Ramsay, ca. 1767.

governing, on condition that they deferred as far as feasible to the sovereign's wishes and prejudices, likes and dislikes; they and not he had been the essential policy-makers. The accession of a monarch determined to guide policy himself was profoundly threatening to them, so threatening that conservatives thought the King's intention unconstitutional. But they could not fight him on that ground, for constitutional theory, as distinct from previous practice, was more on his side than on theirs. Neither could they fight him effectively by manipulating votes in parliament, for the main sources of influence and patronage were rightfully his. The means by which they had hitherto governed, with tacit royal consent, were precisely the means by which the new King expected to reduce them to the status of servants in fact as well as name. The only legal way to stop him would have been to abolish the rotten boroughs and placemen, in order to remove the principal sources of royal influence over the House of Commons. But this would have meant destroying the system that the Whigs themselves had constructed and by which they exercised power; such reform they would not consider. Neither would they, for the most part, acquiesce and give the King his way. The result was a period of tension and instability that lasted for more than two decades.

The period opened with the fall of Pitt. George could not begin to free himself from subordination to his ministers while the Great Commoner towered over him. Pitt was loyal, but not cut out to be a servant; he would either rule or go. The King and his advisers were in somewhat the same position as the Tories fifty years before: again the nation was wearying of a long war, and the man who dominated the scene was committed to fighting on to victory. That man was as vulnerable by 1761 as Marlborough had been by 1711. Many politicians, Newcastle among them, had ceased to believe that the kind of victory for which Pitt stood was feasible or even desirable. If France were destroyed as a great power, the whole state system of Europe would be disjointed, and no one could calculate the effect. A compromise settlement would be far better, these conservatives believed, than a triumph that would shatter the traditional balance of power. Getting rid of Pitt would be politically dangerous, but giving him his head would be worse.

In 1761 the government learned that Spain was preparing to intervene on the side of France. Intervention, at a time when the Spanish navy was in its usual doldrums and the French navy had been chased from the sea, was such stupidity that some members of the cabinet could not fully credit the news; they hoped that at the last minute Madrid would reconsider. Pitt insisted on immediate attack before Spanish preparations were complete. His colleagues refused, and for once would not be bullied. By now he was too autocratic to accept their refusal; he was accustomed to directing every aspect of the war effort and to riding roughshod over the susceptibilities of every department, and would not brook even the united opposition of the cabinet. "Being responsible," he said, "I will direct, and will be responsible for nothing I do not direct." This was the end. He was no longer permitted to direct, and in October 1761 he resigned.

The next few months saw a rush of events. In January 1762 the Empress of Russia died; her successor, an ardent admirer of Frederick, not only stopped fighting but threatened to ally with him. Almost at the same moment Spain declared war, and the measures that Pitt had concerted were carried out: British forces seized Cuba and the Philippines. Thus in Europe Frederick was saved from the ring of his enemies and given a chance to triumph over Austria, while overseas the Bourbon powers were surfeited with defeats. The final victory that Pitt had worked for seemed to be in hand.

The Peace of Paris

But the British government, like the courts of Madrid and Versailles, had had enough. In May 1762 the old Duke of Newcastle was forced from office, and the King installed as first minister his close friend and former tutor, the Scotsman Lord Bute. George and Bute were determined to make peace. They cared little about the German war and less about safeguarding the interests of their Prussian ally, whom they left to shift for himself as best he could. Frederick, thus unceremoniously deserted, was furious; and in the long run Britain paid a heavy price for his anger. She also paid a price for Bute's hurry to settle with France, whom he handled as ineptly as he handled his ally. He showed such eagerness for peace that the French raised their terms and extracted concessions to which their defeats did not entitle them. The Peace of Paris of 1763, it is fair to say, was the first good news that France had had since 1757.

Even Bute, however, could not squander all the results of Pitt's strategy, and in the peace Britain made enormous gains. France ceded to her Canada, Cape Breton Island with its fortress of Louisbourg, and all French holdings between the Alleghenies and the Mississippi except New Orleans; in the whole of North America France retained only her rights in the Newfoundland fishery (supposedly worth £1 million a year) and two small islands in the St. Lawrence for drying the fish. Spain received from France New Orleans and the rest of the vast province of Louisiana, as a sop for Madrid's ill-starred intervention, and got back from Britain Cuba and the Philippines in exchange for ceding Florida and returning Minorca. Britain restored to France Guadeloupe, Martinique, and St. Lucia in the West Indies; the French also returned to India, but with only a shadow of their former power. Thus the treaty, on the surface, was a typical eighteenth-century compromise: everyone got something and no one got enough to upset the equilibrium.

But the balance of concession and counterconcession was more apparent than real. The war that ended in the Peace of Paris was unlike any other in the century between 1688 and 1792, for one power emerged

as the incontestable victor in the world outside Europe; and in the
peace settlement Britain, for all Bute's errors, clinched her victory. In the
West Indies, it is true, she sacrificed the strategic position she had won:
her returning three islands to France left the whole question of predominance
to be fought out again. But in North America and India that question was
settled. France lost her empire on the American continent, for which she
had struggled since the early seventeenth century; and her ceding Louisiana
to Spain showed that her hopes were gone. In India her position was little
better: even though her traders returned, the most they could do — and did
for years to come — was to stir up local rulers against the British and so
contribute to the series of wars through which the East India Company
became the paramount power in the subcontinent. The old French empire
was finished, and a century elapsed before France gained another of equivalent importance.

The Peace of Paris, in retrospect, was the decisive moment in the
second Hundred Years War. At that moment Britain acquired predominance
over France, her only serious rival, in the struggle for dominion of the overseas
world; and subsequent French attempts to reverse the verdict never came close
to success. That verdict determined the future. The Pax Britannica, the oceanic
peace enforced by the Royal Navy during the century between the fall of
Napoleon and the outbreak of the First World War, was the logical and
almost inevitable outgrowth of Britain's triumph in 1763.

Triumph came from sea power, intelligently harnessed and directed
for the first time. King Frederick, the greatest soldier of his age, had
fought for seven years on land and came out where he started, with
Silesia and nothing more. Britain had taken to the sea, gathered in the
richest plums of the mercantile world, and then almost contemptuously
tossed some of them back to their former owners. This sudden revelation
of strength impressed Europe in general and France in particular. Montesquieu,
Voltaire, and other French writers had long admired British society in contrast
to their own; and now the hardheaded realists at Versailles tried to appropriate
the secret of British power. After 1760 they began, for the first time in the
century, a major effort to build up their navy. The effort was too belated
to affect the outcome of the war, but it did affect the future. When the day
came for revenge, France had the wherewithal.

The Price of Victory

In 1763 Britain was on a pinnacle of her history, and the prospects
seemed bright. But a thoughtful observer, looking back over the recent past
and studying the example of Prussia, might have wondered whether Britain's
very success was not dangerous. Frederick had triumphed in the War of the
Austrian Succession, and his disgruntled neighbors had then joined hands
to partition his territory. They had not succeeded, and he had not succeeded

in defeating them; no one had won the Seven Years War on the continent, whereas Britain had won it overseas in a way that made her the envy of all the maritime powers. Victory bred trouble for the victor, to judge by Frederick's experience, and the British empire was now as tempting an object of partition as Prussia had been a decade earlier. France and Spain were awaiting their opportunity, and it would come whenever the British government began to blunder.

To have avoided blundering entirely would have taxed the wisdom of Solomon, for in the aftermath of war Britain confronted a host of problems. The most immediately pressing was financial. The national debt was staggering, and the recent acquisitions in America promised to increase it; the annual cost of protecting and administering Canada and Florida alone, it was estimated, would come to a quarter of the entire prewar budget. New sources of revenue had to be found, but where? Not by increasing taxes or customs and excise duties at home; these had already been exploited to the limits of public patience, and further demands would be political suicide for any administration. Not by levying internal taxes in the American colonies; only the colonial legislatures could legally do that. Not by asking those legislatures to tax themselves, for experience had shown that they would not respond. The only possible answer was some system of taxing the colonies indirectly, by customs duties and the like, to make them carry their share of the imperial burden. The rudiments of such a system had long existed, but it had never been effective; to make it so, new methods would have to be devised by the British government and rigorously enforced by its agents in America. Increasing the revenue, in short, meant tightening imperial control from London.

There was the rub. The Americans had always been hard to control, and the situation in which they now found themselves encouraged them to be headstrong. Hitherto, if they had lost no love on the mother country, they had been unable to afford an open breach. They were divided among themselves, culturally and economically as much as geographically; and this lack of cohesion had made them keenly aware of the danger from the French on their frontiers. Protection had been their first necessity, and it had induced them to put up grudgingly with the arrogance of British officers and the demands of British governors. Now the whole picture had changed. During the war the colonists had learned a little about cooperating with each other, and more about quarreling with British regulars; and the Peace of Paris had freed them from their need of the mother country. Few of them, if any, yet dreamed of independence; but for the first time the possibility was there. If Pitt conquered Canada in Germany, he helped to lose the American colonies in Canada.

This generalization, like most in history, much oversimplifies the intricacies of cause and effect. Britain's conquest of Canada was one factor in the American problem, and her financial needs were another; but the two in conjunction are not enough to explain what followed. To turn American resentment into rebellion something more was required, and that was ineptitude in Whitehall. If wise counsels had prevailed there, the government might conceivably have found an acceptable method of raising colonial revenue without raising colonial tempers; or it could certainly have forgone the hope of revenue for the sake of loyalty, because events proved that the mother country was still a long way from bankruptcy. But in the years after 1763 no wise counsels were heard. A series of short-lived ministries alternated between concession and coercion in America and, instead of producing a consistent policy, wobbled toward disaster.

The wobbling was the outcome of the political instability that had set in with Pitt's resignation. The King could not find ministers who were both competent and amenable to his guidance. The strong-willed did not remain long in his service; the weak-willed did not have the capacity to serve him well. His struggle against the entrenched forces of Whiggism produced frustration on both sides, and distracted both from giving the colonial issue the hard-headed scrutiny it required. That issue was explosive because it brought together a complex of forces. A King determined to have his way against politicians accustomed to ruling, fiscal pressure that came out in ill-considered measures, colonies no longer held by self-interest to the mother country, Europe hostile and the Bourbons yearning for revenge — these factors were the ingredients of trouble. Trouble came, and grew rapidly worse. Within twenty years of Britain's greatest imperial triumph she suffered her greatest imperial defeat.

5 The Loss of Empire

The American Problem

The American colonies in general, and New England in particular, had always been difficult to govern. They had quarreled with British officials, civilian and military, and above all had resented British efforts to regulate their commerce. As early as the 1670s Whitehall was complaining to the king that the New Englanders "do not conform themselves to the laws, but take a liberty of trading where they think fit," and that the question to be faced was "what degree of dependency that government will acknowledge to his Majesty." Ninety years later the question was still unanswered.

During those years it had scarcely been confronted. The mother country had been too much absorbed in domestic and European affairs to pay much attention to the colonies, or to notice that they were growing enormously in population, wealth, and self-confidence. Most of the king's ministers, from the days of Danby to the days of Pitt, cared little about America and knew less; and they had few experts to advise them. The Colonial Office did not yet exist, and until 1768 no single member of the cabinet was charged with American affairs. The only knowledgeable body was the Board of Trade, created in the reign of William III to supervise colonial commerce and the relationship of the various governors with their legislatures; but the board could not act except by recommendations to the cabinet or parliament. The British government, although it reserved to itself the right to decide imperial policy, was not organized in a way to make statesmanlike decisions.

Neither was it able to implement effectively the decisions that it did make, for its agents in America were unreliable. Customs collectors were notoriously lax, and the few who disapproved of smuggling enough to bring cases to court were likely to see them thrown out by local juries. Governors were in no position to exert royal authority. Most of them were pulled between the need to obey the crown, which appointed them, and the need to placate their assemblies, which paid their salaries. When royal policy and local opinion were at odds, the governor was in a dilemma; but the assemblymen had the whip hand. "I must," said a governor of New York in the 1740s, "either come into their measures — which by doing it may forfeit my governorship — or starve." The constitutional problem was analogous with that in England before the evolution of the cabinet: the various colonial executives were not responsible to their legislatures but depended on them for money, and no legal mechanism existed for resolving a quarrel between the two branches of government. As long as this situation endured, real reform of the imperial system was out of the question.

Ideas of reform had long been under discussion in London, and by 1763 had cohered into something approximating a program. It was never precisely defined during the next twelve years, as a sequence of rapidly changing ministries blundered down the road toward Lexington. But behind the alternating ministerial experiments with coercion and conciliation is discernible the dim outlines of policy, applied in different ways to two very different areas. One was the wilderness west of the Alleghenies, still populated only by Indian tribes, that France had ceded in 1763; the other was the settled colonies of the seaboard. In the first the essential problem was how to keep the peace, in the second how to raise the money required for keeping the peace.[1]

The British government was convinced that strict limits had to be imposed, if possible from London, on white settlement of the wilderness. Otherwise colonial land hunger would continually stir up the hornets' nest of Indian wars, niggardly and irresponsible colonial assemblies would give no help in restoring order, and the resultant demands on the British army and exchequer would be prohibitive. The remedy was to close the frontiers to settlers and police the area with British garrisons at strategic points. The need for such policing was demonstrated in 1763–1764 by a widespread Indian rising known as Pontiac's Rebellion. It was suppressed, the military posts were strengthened, and a royal proclamation forbad white settlement in the wilderness. What remained to be seen was whether the seaboard colonies could be made to pay for the garrisons and respect the proclamation.

They would clearly do neither of their own free will. To secure a fixed revenue from them, Whitehall had to devise some form of indirect taxation that was both legal and enforceable. The question of legality was an open one even in Britain, where many men shared Pitt's opinion that the powers of the imperial parliament over the colonists did not include "that of taking their money out of their pockets without their consent." Even if this could be done legally, it could not be done safely; for an enforceable system was necessarily one controlled from London, and any tightening of imperial authority was dangerous. It meant curtailing what the colonists had come through long usage to regard as their rights. If the British used the navy to strengthen the hand of the customs collector, they would be attacking the colonial "right" to smuggle; and if they transferred the prosecution of smugglers from colonial courts to their own Admiralty courts — the only way in which they could secure convictions — they would be assailing the American

---

[1] For the most recent study of this problem see Jack M. Sosin, *Whitehall and the Wilderness: the Middle West in British Colonial Policy, 1760–1775* (1961).

idea of judicial process. If they found the means to give each royal governor the financial independence that he had to have to carry out the king's commands, they would deprive the colonial assemblies of one of their most cherished weapons. Money could not be raised, in other words, without raising a host of issues — economic, legal, and political. Once those issues came to the fore, as they did in the 1760s, they proved impossible to resolve by peaceful means.

The Decade of Wobbling (1761–1770)

Consistent pressure on the colonies might conceivably have been effective, but the administrations of the 1760s could not be consistent. Ministers did not stay in office long enough to learn from experience how ignorant they were of colonial realities, let alone to become knowledgeable; they came and went as the Whig old guard struggled to resist royal influence and the King struggled to assert it by choosing his own servants. In this conflict the American issue was a factor, but one that was more often exploited for partisan purposes than considered on its merits.

The King's one experiment in governing through a favorite was as brief as it was inglorious, for the incompetent Lord Bute fell from office almost as soon as he had negotiated the Peace of Paris. He was followed for two years (1763–1765) by an unbending Whig of the old school, George Grenville, and then for a year by the Marquis of Rockingham. King George lost no love on either man, and in the summer of 1766 he tried the experiment of bringing back the one great figure of British politics. William Pitt was not cut out to be the kind of servant the King was looking for, but he did have a chance of steering the government out of its doldrums. He was the greatest orator of his age, who whenever he spoke "carried with him unpremeditated," in Chesterfield's phrase, "the strength of thunder and the splendor of lightning." He was enormously popular in the country, and even the Americans looked up to him. The new empire was in great part his creation and he, if anyone, might be expected to solve its problems.

But he did nothing. At the moment he returned to office he undercut his position by accepting a peerage and becoming Earl of Chatham. Chesterfield expressed the amazement of the political world that any consideration could have induced Pitt to withdraw from the House of Commons, "which procured him his power and which could alone insure it to him, and to go into that hospital of incurables, the House of Lords." Greater wonders were to come. By December 1766 the new Lord Chatham was in the grip of a severe depression, which for the next two and a half years kept him a recluse; and in his absence the cabinet disintegrated into quarreling factions. In 1768 he resigned to his erstwhile lieutenant, the Duke of Grafton, who proved to be little more of a leader than Chatham had been; but until the beginning of 1770 the government floundered on. Then at long last King George found the man he had been looking for, Lord North, from whom he could expect unconditional loyalty; and the decade of shifting ministries came to an end.

But that decade had fatal effects in the empire. During the 1760s the question of imperial revenue was gradually converted into a constitutional issue, in which the colonists' appeal to their rights and liberties as the King's subjects became an overt challenge to the authority of the crown in parliament. Grenville took the first steps toward raising this issue, first by readjusting import duties in America and tightening the methods of collecting them, then by the famous Stamp Act of 1765. The act required the purchase of government stamps for a variety of paper articles, from newspapers to legal documents; the money so raised was to go toward defraying the expenses of the military garrisons. The best political forecasters, in America as well as in the mother country, had no inkling of the storm that ensued — resolutions from colonial assemblies, a general congress to petition for redress, mobbing of those who distributed the stamps, a boycott of British goods. The American issue was at the forefront of British politics when Grenville fell, and the Rockingham ministry had to decide whether to retract or face the threat of civil war. British opinion was as much aroused as American, but far more divided; and the division expressed itself in Rockingham's solution. He repealed the act but, to muster the votes for repeal, added a declaratory act that proclaimed the right of parliament to tax the colonies. The ministers, as a critic drily remarked, "have relinquished the revenue but judiciously taken care to preserve the contention."

This was the situation that Chatham inherited and, in the two years that he left the government leaderless, matters went from bad to worse. His Chancellor of the Exchequer, Charles Townshend, followed a policy of his own, which was designed to buttress royal authority by a series of integrated measures — strengthening customs collection, adding new duties on imports into America, and using the resultant revenue to free governors and other officials from dependence on the colonial assemblies. The Americans regarded this as a revival of the policy behind the Stamp Act, in a more effective and therefore more dangerous guise, and reacted accordingly. The Massachusetts assembly took the lead in denouncing the Townshend duties as taxation without representation, and was promptly dissolved by the Governor. But the Boston mob, not he, had effective power; and soon he could no longer govern. Whitehall took the only possible course short of evacuating the province: it ordered in troops. Then, as if to cloud the whole issue, in 1769 Grafton's ministry retreated on the financial question and repealed all the Townshend duties except a symbolic levy on tea. Again, as in 1766, parliament relinquished the revenue and preserved the contention.

How it could have ended the contention at that stage is difficult to see. The argument about money had been transformed into an argument about the right of the mother country to exercise any control over the colonies; and that point could not be resolved by argument. Few men on either side of the Atlantic were yet thinking of the extreme solution, independence, or were ready to go to the other extreme and hold the empire together by force.

But the quarrel had grown so far by the time North took office in 1770 that a mutually acceptable compromise between the extremes was probably out of the question. This was the fruit of the decade of wobbling.

Wilkes and Reform

The 1760s were notable for another development, which aroused much more attention in Britain than colonial discontent and had almost as great significance for the future. The ineptitude of successive ministries was bringing the whole parliamentary system into disrepute and, for the first time since the seventeenth century, was awakening the force of political radicalism. The leader of this movement was a remarkable if not estimable man, John Wilkes, who for many years kept the world of Westminster in turmoil. He was ugly in appearance; he was also charming and witty, and even in a period of lax morals and little faith was notorious as a rake and blasphemer. If the fear of God was not in him, neither was the fear of man. He began by attacking the King and ended by attacking the whole constitutional structure that gave the King his power.

Wilkes first achieved notoriety in 1763. He was then a member of the House of Commons and the owner and editor of a newspaper, the *North Briton,* which acidly criticized first Bute, then Grenville, and through them their royal master. The King had Wilkes arrested on a general warrant, an order issued by a secretary of state and naming no names; this exercise of executive power was reserved for emergencies, and its legality was doubtful. Wilkes was committed to prison on a charge of seditious libel, but he did not stay there. He secured his release through the courts on the ground that a member of parliament was privileged against arrest for libel; he then brought suit against the responsible secretary of state, alleging that general warrants were illegal. The court eventually so decided, and the Minister was fined.

This attack on the Goliath of officialdom made Wilkes such a popular hero that the Grenville ministry dared not leave him alone. It counterattacked, induced the House of Commons to deny that its privilege covered libel, and exposed in the House of Lords an obscene parody of Pope that Wilkes had been printing for private circulation. He was now open to prosecution both for obscenity and for his earlier libel in the *North Briton.* Early in 1764 he fled to France, whereupon he was expelled from the House of Commons, convicted *in absentia* of libel, and outlawed. Four years later he returned, unrepentant and unafraid, and was promptly elected to parliament from Middlesex. Just as promptly he was imprisoned under his old sentence for libel.

He was more dangerous in prison than at liberty. Mobs rioted outside his windows; troops were called in, fired on the crowd, and killed several; coroners' juries brought verdicts of murder against the military. The threat of revolution was in the air, and moderate opinion rallied to the government, now headed by the Duke of Grafton. In 1769 the House of Commons quashed Wilkes's election, only to see him reelected from Middlesex. Time after time the farce of expulsion and reelection was repeated, until at last the Commons declared his opponent, who had received a fifth of the votes, to be the legal member. The house was openly flouting the will of the electorate.

By now a radical program of reform was taking shape. Its demands were all political: shorter parliaments, the abolition of rotten boroughs, a broader franchise, protection of the individual against executive or legislative persecution. For the time being this program got nowhere because it horrified conservative Whigs. They were eager to defeat the King by cutting off his means of parliamentary influence, but had no desire to change the traditional nature of parliament; and they proved to be strong enough to resist any major reform for another sixty years. The agitation personified by Wilkes, nevertheless, was the first significant sign of revolt. The unenfranchised were grumbling at their betters, who were responding by high-handed and sometimes illegal actions; the effect was to call into question the whole idea of an exclusive governing club, composed of a sovereign, his ministers, and the Lords and Commons, that could ignore the will of even the few who voted in elections. The King's threat to the constitution of the club proved transitory, but the threat from below grew stronger over the years until it produced the upheaval of 1832.

The Coming of War (1770–1775)

By 1770, when Lord North took office, the two threats were fused; and rebellion at home seemed as likely as rebellion in the colonies. North had no thought of yielding to the reformers. His central purpose was to allow the crown to exercise the powers that it rightfully possessed according to his concept of Whig theory — to permit the King to guide policy through ministers who were dependent upon his favor. At the price of alienating many old-guard politicians, North intended to found his administration on the support of a group known as the King's Friends, those members of parliament whose loyalty or self-interest made them willing to give the sovereign his way. At a time when the whole parliamentary system was in bad odor with the public, this was a dangerous course.

A critic of the government, who signed himself with the pen name of Junius, pointed out the danger in no uncertain terms. "One particular class of men," he wrote, "are permitted to call themselves the King's Friends, as if the body of the people were the King's enemies. . . . Edward and Richard the Second made the same distinction between the collective body of the people and a contemptible party who surrounded the throne. The event of their mistaken conduct might have been a warning to their successors." If his readers had forgotten the deposition and murder of those two Plantagenets, he reminded them of the more recent past. Now that the royal prerogative was being exercised *through* parliament, he declared, it was even more dangerous than when the Stuarts had exercised it against parliament; and the remedy was the same. King George, "while he plumes himself upon the security of his title to the crown, should remember that, as it was acquired by one revolution, it may be lost by another."

Junius, like so many who use the past for predicting the future, was disappointed in his expectation; George did not provoke revolution at home. But he did provoke a bitter struggle there, and one that affected the coming revolution in America. His attempt to control parliament and his ministers' attempt to retain parliament's control over the colonies were necessarily interrelated; those who opposed one tended to oppose the other and to see in American resistance the best hope of maintaining the traditional British constitution. Chatham subsequently expressed this point in his famous comparison of the colonies with Samson: "America, if she falls, will fall like the strong man; she will embrace the pillars of the state, and pull down the constitution along with her."

North had no more intention of subverting the constitution than he had of reforming it. He looked on himself as a conservative, and the last thing he wanted to do was to rouse popular passions on either side of the Atlantic. He was a seasoned politician although not yet in his forties, a superb debater, and deft in managing the House of Commons.[2] He resembled Wilkes in his startling ugliness, and in his charm and wit; but he had none of that demagogue's strength. Under his polished surface the Minister was neurotically self-distrustful; decisions were agony for him, and leadership was beyond him. The King's search for a servant had brought him more than he had bargained for, a man who turned to him in crisis not only for guidance but for willpower.

At the start of North's administration the coming crisis in America was only a small cloud on the horizon. Grafton's repeal of the Townshend duties appeared to have soothed contention with the colonies, but the appearance was deceptive. Both the troops that still garrisoned Boston and the one remaining duty, that on tea, were symbols of the basic issue that had been raised; and it was an issue that no government could ignore for long. North soon persuaded himself that he had found a way to resolve it, and to the satisfaction of all concerned. The East India Company was compelled by law to ship its tea to England for reexport to America; if it were permitted instead to ship directly from the Orient, the reduced cost of transportation

[2] To find *Lord* North in the lower house instead of the upper is confusing, but so are British titles. North was not a peer, or he would have sat in the House of Lords. He was the heir to a title, and such an eldest son was — and still is — often called a lord by courtesy during his father's lifetime. To complicate matters further, under the Act of Union of 1801 an Irish peer who was not chosen by his fellows to represent them in the House of Lords might be elected to the Commons from a British constituency. See below, p. 154, n. 5.

would more than offset the surviving and symbolic duty on tea. The Americans would then buy cheaper tea and in the process be painlessly taxed. This seemed to be the way to kill three birds with one stone — to make a profit for the East India Company, to conciliate the colonists by lowering the price of tea, and to induce them to accept the principle of indirect taxation. The proposal was well meant, and it led straight to war.

North, like most of his predecessors, was ignorant of colonial realities. Cheaper tea threatened not only the powerful American smuggling interest but also legitimate dealers, who would have to dispose of their unsold stocks at a loss. Far more important, the colonists were quite able to recognize Greeks even when bearing gifts — to discern the principle of a tax, no matter what saving it might bring. Tea had become a symbol in Whitehall. It now became a symbol in Boston, when raiders dressed as Indians boarded the East India Company ships and dumped their cargoes into the harbor. The Boston Tea Party was open defiance, and the quarrel entered a new phase. Few had foreseen the challenge, fewer still had desired it; but, once it was made, Lord North's government had no alternative to meeting it.

Events marched fast to a climax. What the Americans called the Intolerable Acts closed the port of Boston until compensation was paid for the tea and remodeled the charter of Massachusetts. These actions had to be backed by force, and the only available troops were those that had been garrisoning the wilderness. Ever since 1768 they had been moving eastward to curb the growing discontent on the seaboard, and now Whitehall had to find another way of keeping peace among the Indians and — the other side of the same coin — excluding the land-hungry colonists. Its solution was the Quebec Act of 1774, which had a dual purpose: to detach the French Canadians from their southern neighbors by concessions to Roman Catholicism, and to give control of the wilderness to the only auhority on the spot that had shown some aptitude for the job, the government of Quebec. The effect was to intensify antagonism in the thirteen colonies, which again felt themselves encircled on the north and west by their old enemies, the French.

The Intolerable and Quebec Acts, like so many measures that came out of London in those years, constituted a policy that looked well on paper but had no solid foundation. A realistic policy is one that can be implemented, and the means of implementation did not exist. The French Canadians, even if they had the will, lacked the power to police the wilderness, just as the handful of British troops in Boston lacked the power to coerce Massachusetts. And Massachusetts, it soon became clear, was not alone. In September 1774 representatives of all the colonies except Georgia met in the First Continental Congress to concert means of resistance. Now that North's government had taken the strong line in words, the logic of events forced it to back up the words.

That logic the cabinet would not see. General Gage, Commander in Chief in America and Governor of Massachusetts, was insisting that he needed an army. He was in a panic, the ministers concluded, and really needed only a few stalwart subordinates to strengthen his nerve. Consequently they sent him, along with a handful of reinforcements, three major generals — William Howe, John Burgoyne, and Henry Clinton — who were destined to play crucial parts in losing the war that London still hoped to avoid. When the three landed at Boston in May 1775, that war had already begun. Gage's unsuccessful attempt to seize American supplies at Lexington and Concord had raised an impromptu army against him, and he was cooped up in the peninsula of Boston. In June the rebels occupied an adjacent peninsula, from which their guns could have made the town untenable. General Howe, sent to dislodge them, showed as much courage as stupidity in leading his troops directly against their breastworks; by the time he won the Battle of Bunker Hill it had cost him almost half his force. These "banditti," as British officers called the enemy, knew how to shoot.[3]

The Civil War (1775–1778)

In the aftermath of Bunker Hill royal authority crumbled throughout the colonies; royal governors either took refuge on shipboard, where the navy could protect them, or fled home to England. The war thus opened with a massive British defeat, much as the American Civil War, eighty-six years later, opened with a massive Union defeat: in both cases the rebels secured at a stroke control of virtually the entire area of rebellion. Lord North's government, like President Lincoln's, had to reverse a verdict already rendered, by attacking the enemy on their own ground, evoking support from those who were loyal but cowed, splitting the rebellion into parts and extinguishing it piecemeal. The only possible British road to victory was to take the offensive and drive it home.

Britain began with some great advantages. Her available army, although small, was an effective fighting machine; the notion that rebel Minute Men and militia, fired by the Spirit of '76, could stand up to British regulars in a pitched battle in the open is one of the myths about the war. Britain had vastly greater financial resources than the colonists, and a functioning governmental system in contrast to their improvised and discordant authorities in the states and the Continental Congress. Last and perhaps most important, for the first three years the Royal Navy had unchallenged command of the coast. The British were consequently able to

---

[3] The most recent studies of the British side of the struggle that began at Lexington and Bunker Hill are Piers Mackesy, *The War for America, 1775–1783* (1964); my biography of the commander who was saddled with the blame for losing it, *Portrait of a General: Sir Henry Clinton in the War of Independence* (1964); and Franklin and Mary Wickwire, *Cornwallis: The American Adventure* (Boston, 1970). For a full history of military operations see Christopher Ward, *The War of the Revolution,* John R. Alden, ed. (2 vols., 1952), and for a briefer and more readable account Willard M. Wallace, *Appeal to Arms: a Military History of the American Revolution* (1951).

blockade, to move their troops by sea faster than the rebels could move theirs by land, and to attack when and where they pleased; exploiting this advantage might well have won them the war.

But they were also laboring under a host of difficulties. The most insidious was the fact that they had no logical war aim. Military victory in itself is not such an aim, because the only reason to win a war is to produce a more favorable postwar situation; and here the British had little hope. If they suppressed the rebellion, what then? Garrisoning the colonies in perpetuity promised intolerable and purposeless expense; an empire held by force would not be worth holding. Whitehall was therefore compelled to seek some form of compromise peace, and hence to combine military pressure with conciliation. But a general instructed to fight with one hand and to negotiate with the other was unlikely to succeed with either, for the aims were incompatible. There was, furthermore, no real basis for negotiating. If Britain gave up her claim to authority she would give up what she was fighting for; George III would then, as a contemporary put it, cease to be "one jot more substantially King of America than King of France." On the other hand, if Britain refused to surrender effective authority she would preclude any compromise. The outbreak of hostilities, in short, plunged the government into a dilemma that was logically insoluble.

The way to wage the war was almost as hard to determine as the purpose of waging it. The effort to relieve the British taxpayer's burden by increasing colonial revenue had brought on the rebellion, which could not be quickly suppressed without adding greatly to the tax burden to support a large army and navy. The various groups of the opposition in parliament were either against the war or lukewarm about it, and the surest way to weld them together and provide them with allies was to demand new taxes; hence the ministry, in order to survive, had to make war economically. But economy meant at best a slow decision, which was dangerous for quite another reason: the likelihood of foreign intervention increased with every month that hostilities lasted, for France and Spain were waiting to learn whether the rebellion was serious enough to offer them a reasonable chance of revenge on Britain. With a restive parliament on the one hand, and the menace of the Bourbon powers on the other, the government was caught between the devil and the deep blue sea.

A strong cabinet, strongly led, might have silenced the peace-mongers and rallied the waverers at home, as President Lincoln's administration did in 1861, and steeled the country to fight a civil war. But Lord North was too timid and self-deprecating to keep his subordinates in hand; they went their own ways, while he begged repeatedly and in vain for the King's permission to resign. George, rather than North, held the government together; and he knew even less than his Minister about how to run a war. Responsibility for its conduct therefore devolved largely upon two officials, the Earl of Sandwich and Lord George Germain. Sandwich was the First Lord of the Admiralty, in other words the civilian head of the navy; Germain, in the recently created post of Secretary of State for the American Colonies, made himself the civilian head of the army. Between them they were a gift without price to the American cause.

Lord Sandwich, a rake and a former friend of John Wilkes, had had long experience of naval administration. But it had taught him neither strategic sense nor how to discover and promote fighting admirals; he was content with humdrum ideas and timorous commanders. Germain, the American Secretary, had taken a new name since the Seven Years War; he was the Lord George Sackville who had been court-martialed and cashiered from the army after the Battle of Minden.[4] The officers who now served under him remembered his past disgrace, and he did little to earn their respect. His principal talent in directing military operations was that of evading responsibility for those he suggested. He had slightly more taste than Sandwich for aggressive strategy, but no more gift for finding aggressive commanders. Both men played favorites and contributed to spreading the factionalism of Whitehall throughout the armed services.

Generals and admirals were gentlemen even before they were officers, and many of them did not scruple to put their dignity or political opinions ahead of their professional duty. Some refused to serve, because they disapproved of the ministry or the war or both; others served so halfheartedly that they were suspected of "opposition principles," which meant sympathizing with the enemy. Commanders frequently asked to resign; if the government felt compelled to let them do so, they were likely to reappear at home, often as members of parliament, to air their caustic criticisms. The oligarchy was a house divided, and the division ran from London to the army's headquarters and the admiral's quarterdeck.

By the spring of 1776 the administration had at last realized that it faced a full-scale war, and had made preparations accordingly. British troops were inadequate in numbers for the job ahead; they had been augmented by mercenaries from various German states, whom the Americans lumped together under the hated name of Hessians. General Howe had replaced Gage as commander in chief in the autumn of 1775; he was now provided with a force of some 30,000 men, the largest that Britain had ever sent overseas, and was supported by a strong fleet under his older brother, Viscount Howe. The objective was New York. Boston, threatened by artillery that the Americans had captured at Fort Ticonderoga and carried across New England, had already been evacuated; in the coming campaign the Howes intended to seize Manhattan as a base for controlling the lower Hudson, while General Carleton, the Governor of Canada, advanced south from the St. Lawrence by way of Lake Champlain to the upper Hudson. New England would thus be cut off from the rest of the rebel colonies.

General Washington, the new American Commander in Chief, decided to defend Manhattan by immuring his army on it. The decision

---

[4] For Germain's disgrace see above, pp. 77–78.

should have been fatal to him: his troops were hopelessly inferior to their opponents in quality and numbers, and Lord Howe's ships commanded the surrounding waters. But General Howe was a slave to orthodoxy. After the lesson of Bunker Hill he dreaded risking his precious regulars in battle, and in any case he was much more interested in gaining territory at low cost than in destroying the enemy force. He did destroy a part of it in August 1776 in the Battle of Long Island; but a subordinate had planned the action, and Howe had only grudgingly fallen in with the plan. He then maneuvered Washington out of New York, into Westchester, and eventually across the Hudson, all without serious bloodshed. Meanwhile a small American flotilla on Lake Champlain, improvised by the energy of Benedict Arnold, had turned back Carleton's advance from Canada. This was scarcely the way to achieve a quick decision.

The rebel army, almost in spite of its commander, remained intact; the King's army, thanks primarily to its commander, won an island and lost the best chance it was ever to have of winning the war. The results of the campaign reflected little glory on either side, and bore out the acid comment of a British observer: "Any other general in the world than General Howe would have beaten General Washington, and any other general in the world than General Washington would have beaten General Howe." [5]

Yet in the week before Christmas 1776 British victory seemed only a matter of time. Washington's army, even though it still existed, had been driven into Pennsylvania, surrendering to the enemy New Jersey and lower New York; and to protect his new gains Howe had established posts, manned by Hessians, along the Jersey shore of the Delaware. He was too confident to be cautious, and it never occurred to him that Washington could be dangerous. The American himself thought that the game might well be up, but he had one more play. On Christmas night he ferried his ragged troops across the Delaware and captured the Hessian garrison of Trenton. On January 2, 1777, the British counterattacked and pinned him against the river, but during the night he slipped away to Princeton, destroyed a British force there, and vanished into the New Jersey hills. This was a different Washington from the general of the previous summer. In little more than a week he had revived a dying cause, and so changed the face of the war.

But the British were undeterred by their small taste of defeat. Their main forces were unimpaired, and for the summer campaign of 1777 they planned an even greater effort. It would, the government confidently believed, crush the rebellion once and for all. The campaign as projected had two parts. One was an advance from Canada to the upper Hudson by the route that Carleton had attempted in 1776; the command of this invasion was given to General Burgoyne, the dapper soldier-playwright known as

---

[5] This famous and anonymous quip seems to have appeared first in *Lloyd's Evening Post* (August 14–17, 1778), where it is imputed to Lafayette. But the young Frenchman, even if he had had the wit to make it, would scarcely have had the will; he was a great admirer of Washington.

Gentleman Johnny. The other part should have been, according to all the dictates of common sense, a move by Howe with the main army from New York up the Hudson to meet Burgoyne; but it was nothing of the sort. Sir William (the Commander in Chief had recently been knighted) determined instead to leave only a small detachment on Manhattan under his second in command, Sir Henry Clinton, and take the rest of the army by sea to the Chesapeake for an attack on Philadelphia. Burgoyne, he airily supposed, could look after himself. Germain agreed; instead of listening to those who tried to warn him that such disperson of force was stupid, he adopted Howe's and Burgoyne's mismatched plans without a thought for their incongruity.

Howe's campaign was a thorough success. Washington tried to defend Philadelphia, to no better effect than when he had tried to defend New York; by late autumn his army, soundly defeated, was forced into winter quarters at Valley Forge. But meanwhile the British suffered a disaster on the Hudson that outweighed their gains in Pennsylvania. Burgoyne's invasion ignored the fundamental requirements of supply: as he advanced southward his communications with Canada were stretched to the breaking point, and he could not establish communication with New York by way of the Hudson; an American army stood in his path, and American forts barred the river. By early October he was marooned at Saratoga, unable to continue, to retreat through the wilderness, or to exist where he was. Sir Henry Clinton, on Manhattan, learned of his plight and made a desperate effort to fight his way up river to save him. But the odds were insuperable, and Burgoyne was by then beyond help. On October 17 he surrendered.

Saratoga was decisive, not in America but in Europe. For some time the Court of Versailles had been giving the rebellion surreptitious aid and watching its progress with calculating eyes; did it or did it not provide the opportunity for revenge that the French had been craving since 1763? Even if it did, would intervention be wise? "The spirit of revolt, wherever it breaks out," said one of Louis XVI's chief ministers, "is always of dangerous example." But Burgoyne's surrender was proof that the rebels were able to maintain themselves, and the chance of recouping French prestige by helping them seemed to outweigh the menace of their ideas. In March 1778 Versailles announced the signing of a treaty with the infant United States.

The World War (1778–1783)

French intervention changed the whole character of the struggle. What had been a civil war fought on the American seaboard became a world war, fought from India to the Caribbean. Spain was expected to join France, and did so in 1779; thereafter Britain, for the first time, faced a coalition without an ally of her own. The crux of the fighting was no longer on land but at sea. There the British, thanks to the revival of the French navy, faced formidable opposition in their task of guarding the outposts of empire and supporting the armies in America. Their best chance of victory was to revive Pitt's earlier strategy of blockade in European waters, but the numerical odds made this far more difficult to do than it had been twenty years before. Everything hinged on whether daring and skill could compensate for too few ships of the line.

The first months after the French announcement proved that daring, and even clear thinking, were in short supply at Whitehall. The Admiralty permitted the French Mediterranean fleet to sail from Toulon, pass the Straits of Gibraltar unopposed, and make for North America; the British commanders there were not sent timely reinforcement or even timely warning. Instead the cabinet made two moves: it dispatched a commission to America to negotiate peace at almost any price short of independence; it commanded the army to evacuate Pennsylvania and retreat to New York by sea, and did not bother to alter this plan when it learned that a French fleet was arriving off the coast. The government did everything possible, in short, to arrange for failure. It told the Americans, by the retreat from Pennsylvania, that its peace overture was based on weakness; it ordered the army to sea, in vulnerable transports, when enemy ships of the line were in the offing; it did nothing to forewarn, let alone forearm, the responsible commanders.

Sir William Howe had recently resigned, and the army was in the hands of Sir Henry Clinton. Although he was a far more contentious and difficult person than the easy-going Howe, Clinton was fully his equal as a tactician and far abler as a strategist. Sir Henry's naval colleague was still Lord Howe, who was waiting for his successor's arrival from England before following his brother into retirement. The Admiral's presence was a lucky accident; he was the one competent naval chief who served in America during the war, and he and Clinton between them saved what was left of the British position.

Sir Henry took liberties with his instructions. He marched the army overland to New York, engaging Washington en route in an inconclusive battle, and joined Howe and the fleet at New York just when the French arrived off the harbor. The enemy commander refused to attack in the face of Howe's naval dispositions, and sailed off instead to capture a British post in Rhode Island. Howe thwarted him there, by a mixture of determination and good luck; and soon afterward the French left for the West Indies. The campaign had produced no gain for either side, but the British were left in possession of New York and Rhode Island. Their peace overture was contemptuously rejected; and the commissioners, with such little dignity as they could muster, sailed home from their fool's errand.

The next year, 1779, was equally inconclusive. Clinton planned an elaborate campaign around Manhattan, which came to nothing because his promised reinforcements did not arrive from England in time; the French fleet reappeared, this time off Georgia, which the British had recently garrisoned, and was repulsed in an attack on Savannah. Meanwhile Clinton was gathering his meager strength for a new move. He was convinced that the war could be won only by organizing support from the American loyalists, or Tories; and every effort to find such support in New England and the middle colonies had failed. The one area where loyalist sentiment had not yet been seriously tested was the south, and there he decided to go. In order to obtain the necessary troops he evacuated Rhode Island, leaving the British nothing in the north except Manhattan; and on Christmas Day he sailed with his army for South Carolina. He thereby opened the phase of the war that ended at Yorktown.

His decision to go south was a dangerous gamble. It meant dividing his forces between New York and the Carolinas at a time when enemy sea power might cut his water-borne communications. He knew that the Admiralty could not or would not confine the French to European waters and prevent their sending fleets overseas. The most it would do, when such a fleet sailed, was to detach what it hoped was an equivalent squadron, in what it hoped would be sufficient time, to what it hoped was the point of danger. This slapdash method of defense had failed to protect New York in 1778 or Savannah in 1779. Whether it could protect armies that were now being separated by hundreds of miles of seaboard remained to be seen.

Clinton opened his campaign for South Carolina with a brilliant victory in May 1780, when he surrounded and captured Charleston and the American army defending it. But immediately afterward he learned that another French squadron, this time accompanied by troops, was about to establish a base in Rhode Island. The news, which came to him from Benedict Arnold, who was already planning to betray the American cause, necessitated Sir Henry's returning at once to New York. He had to turn over the southern operations to his second in command, Earl Cornwallis, whom he neither liked nor trusted. The Earl was popular in the army, and as brave as he was ambitious. But he was also headstrong and had no more strategic sense than a charging bull, so that to leave him in virtually independent command was an invitation to trouble.

Clinton and the naval chief who had succeeded Howe, Admiral Arbuthnot, returned to a summer of frustration at New York. First they learned that the French had landed troops in Rhode Island, commanded by the Comte de Rochambeau. Then, when the Admiral left to reconnoiter the enemy position in Narragansett Bay, he and Sir Henry spent two months in quarreling about what they were going to do; in the end they did nothing. Next came the climax of Benedict Arnold's conspiracy to betray West Point, the new American fortress guarding the Hudson. The Americans discovered the plot by accident and captured and hanged Clinton's emissary and close friend, John André; Arnold escaped to New York and was commissioned a British brigadier general. Although Clinton thus acquired one of the ablest commanders on either side, he could never make good use of him because Arnold was distrusted. British regular officers had little love for American loyalists as colleagues, and none at all for a turncoat.

In December, nevertheless, Clinton gave Arnold command of an expedition to the Chesapeake. The progress of the southern campaign necessitated establishing a post on the bay, where a small body of troops supported from the sea could cut overland communication between Washington's army in the north and American forces in the Carolinas. Arnold established himself at Portsmouth, Virginia; and in March 1781 he was almost captured there in a combined attack by Washington and the French fleet from Rhode Island. The latter was defeated at sea by Admiral Arbuthnot, and the Franco-American operation collapsed. But seven months later it was repeated on a larger scale against Cornwallis.

By the spring of 1781 Cornwallis was turning his eyes toward Virginia, for he had had more than enough of campaigning to the southward. After securing what he thought was control of South Carolina in 1780, he had embarked on an offensive through the back country of North Carolina — where he was out of touch with the sea, had to live off the countryside, and hence had to move his army from place to place; he could never stop long enough in any one area to organize loyalist support and so consolidate his gains. He could only strike blows in the air, like Burgoyne on his march to Saratoga; and the Earl was pitted against a far abler opponent than Gentleman Johnny had met. Nathanael Greene, the American commander in the south, had a gift for winning campaigns by retreating. Cornwallis chased him to the border of Virginia, defeated him in battle in March 1781, and then, desperate for supplies, fled to the coast. His retreat left Greene free to move against South Carolina, which he promptly did. The Earl, instead of following him, marched with the wreck of his army to join Arnold in Virginia.

This move was foolhardy. It endangered all that the British had won in the south, greatly increased their commitment to the Chesapeake, and for the first time brought Cornwallis within striking distance of the Franco-American forces in the north. The Earl insisted that Virginia was the key to the war, and he made it so. He did it without even consulting his chief, who was furious but dared do nothing. The government, Clinton believed, was grooming Cornwallis to succeed him, and the prospect paralyzed Sir Henry's will; he would neither resign to the man he detested nor exert authority over him. This failure of leadership, like Pitt's in 1766, had serious consequences. For the remainder of the campaign, which was the crisis of the war, the army had no unity of command and therefore no unity of purpose.

In August 1781 Cornwallis grudgingly obeyed an order from Clinton to establish a post at Yorktown. By that time the British forces were divided into three widely separated contingents: in South Carolina, at Yorktown, and on Manhattan; Greene was threatening the first, and Washington and his French ally, Rochambeau, had the choice of attacking the second or the third. They chose Yorktown, and proceeded to capture it by one of the most brilliant combined operations of the eighteenth century.

The operation rested on French sea power. Admiral de Grasse had recently reached the West Indies from France with a fleet that outnumbered

CANADA

Boston

WASHINGTON &
ROCHAMBEAU
Newport

Philadelphia
New York

Charlottesville
GRAVES & HOOD
DE BARRAS
Richmond
CORNWALLIS Petersburg
Guilford Court House 1781 York-
town
Charlotte 1780
Winnsboro
Camden
Charleston Wilmington
Savannah

ATLANTIC
OCEAN

HOOD

DE GRASSE

BAHAMA
ISLANDS

THE CAMPAIGN OF 1781

American forces
French forces
British forces

CUBA

HAITI

the British West Indian squadron; and he now offered to bring his entire line
of battle to the Chesapeake. Washington and Rochambeau eagerly accepted.
They prepared to march overland to Virginia, while the small French
squadron at Rhode Island sailed to join de Grasse and give him an
overwhelming superiority. French ships would close the mouth of the
Chesapeake, cut off Cornwallis from the army at New York, and so seal his
fate.

De Grasse sailed from the West Indies at the beginning of August.
Admiral Sir Samuel Hood followed him with what he thought — quite
mistakenly — was an equivalent force, to join the much smaller British
squadron at New York. The commander of that squadron was no longer
Arbuthnot, who had recently sailed for home, but Admiral Graves, a pleasant
nonentity who was senior to Hood and therefore outranked him. At the end of
August, when Hood arrived at New York, he persuaded Graves to sail with
him at once for the Chesapeake. The two admirals reached the entrance to the
bay, and there they had a nasty shock: French ships came out to meet them in
a seemingly endless line. Graves nevertheless attacked. Even though he was
badly outnumbered, the battle was tactically no more decisive than most
engagements of the period; but its strategic effect was momentous. The British
fleet fell back on New York and left Cornwallis to his fate.

The Earl had still several weeks of grace before the enemy army
arrived from the north to besiege him. In that time he might have escaped,
but instead he did nothing except appeal to Clinton for help. At the beginning
of October the siege began. Cornwallis thereupon made one abortive effort to
break out, and then on the 17th — four years to the day since Burgoyne's
capitulation — asked for terms; on the 19th he surrendered. After all his
activity in marching and countermarching through the Carolinas and Virginia
he had allowed himself to be caught in a trap; and his behavior in it had been,
as Washington said, "passive beyond conception." That passivity brought the
American war to a close.

The reason was not that Britain no longer had the means to fight, but
that she no longer had the will. For many months before Yorktown
war-weariness had been growing at home. Not since the news of Charleston
had there been any real taste of victory, and troubles were pressing in from
every side: Ireland was in turmoil; neutral maritime states had formed an
armed league to enforce against the Royal Navy their right to trade where
they pleased; Britain's old friend the Netherlands had been goaded into
entering the war against her; the King's prestige was sinking, and his
adamant refusal to consider American independence was coming to be more
and more widely regarded as folly. The news of Yorktown was the last straw.
North's government staggered on for a few more months, with the opposition
in full cry. In March 1782 the House of Commons resolved that offensive war
in America should end; a few weeks later North resigned. The King prepared
to abdicate, but then thought better of it. His policy was repudiated, however,

and with it his dream of governing by manipulation. At the cost of her American colonies Britain regained her traditional political system.

The Peace Settlement

In September 1783 the peace treaties were signed at Paris and Versailles. Britain acknowledged the independence of the United States and its sovereignty as far west as the Mississippi; she ceded Florida and Minorca to Spain, and minor possessions in the West Indies and Africa to France. From the viewpoint of Versailles these gains were little to show for five years of fighting; but the Anglo-French war had been indecisive, and France was in a weak bargaining position. Her strategy had been inept. Instead of providing just enough assistance to keep the American war going, and to distract the British with it until she had gathered in conquests of her own, she had brought it to an end before she had anything to show for her efforts. The result was triumph for the United States but not for her. She acquired little prestige, a burden of debt, and the virus of revolutionary ideas.

The acknowledgment of American independence was of course a schism in the old British empire, but it was not such a complete break with the mother country as it appeared to be at the time. In the fifteen years after the peace treaty, 1783–1798, Anglo-American trade doubled. The tradition of hostility between the two countries, born of the war and soon to be nourished by a second war in 1812, lasted for another century. Yet during that time the United States grew to nationhood within a framework of British power. The Royal Navy, after the War of Independence even more than before, controlled the egress from Europe and discouraged European states from gaining new footholds on the American continent. The United States was consequently free to expand westward without hindrance and to acquire, when the time became ripe, land from Florida to Louisiana, from Texas to California, that had formerly been claimed by France and Spain. Expanding northward was another matter. Canada long remained a temptation to the growing republic and after 1814 produced periodic crises in Anglo-American relations. But the very fact that the crises did not produce war indicates that they were no more than surface turbulence.

Underneath that turbulence the United States and Britain had more in common than either one cared to acknowledge. Between the Canadian frontier and the West Indies Britain had no vital interest. She never seriously considered reconquering her former colonies, or encircling them on the west as France had once tried to do; and she had no intention of permitting a rival to subjugate them in her stead. Her command of the Atlantic acted as an effective, if often inadvertent, barrier against European interference in America, and insulated the United States from outside dangers so effectively that it grew into a great power without possessing, except in its Civil War, the large army and navy that were the hallmarks of all other great powers. The British not only acknowledged a new republic in 1783; they also took on its protection, quite unintentionally, while it steadily inched its way westward into the empty space that stretched to the Pacific. Just as the failures of the Royal Navy contributed to the birth of the new nation, so the power of that navy was its mainstay in childhood and adolescence.

6 Pause between Storms

The Oligarchy

The brief interlude between the War of American Independence and the last and greatest struggle of the century, the war against the French Revolution, was on the surface a period of relative calm. The great issues of the past were settled: the Bourbon powers had tried and failed to regain what they had lost overseas in 1763; the problem of how to govern the thirteen American colonies no longer existed; the King's attempt to dominate the ministry had ended with North's resignation, and the balance of power between the sovereign and the oligarchy had been in essence restored. The Whigs were able to set their house in order again; and it stood, like the country palaces of the magnates, as if it would last forever.

For the few who had money and position, life was a delight. Society moved with a seasonal rhythm from town to country and back again, congregating in London for the winter when parliament met, dispersing in summer to its members' country estates. In the dog days of July and August no one of fashion wanted to be in town, and least of all in parliament; men's light summer clothing had not yet been dreamed of, and the heat of Westminster could be intolerable. In winter, on the other hand, the great country houses were likely to be frigid; most of them were designed for grandeur rather than warmth, and the wood that burned in their monumental fireplaces made little impression on the chill of the rooms. Town houses, being smaller and more compact, were better suited to cold weather. Political and social life, which served the comfort of the oligarchs, consequently moved through a yearly cycle of urban and rural; and the cycle continued until modern times. Lord Byron, who was a product of the Georgian aristocracy, satirized the exodus from London with which the country season began. His lines, written in the 1820s but describing what had been happening for generation after generation, are worth quoting.

> 'Tis perhaps a pity
> When nature wears the gown that doth become her
> To lose those best months in a sweaty city,
> And wait until the nightingale grows dumber,

> Listening debates not very wise or witty,
> Ere patriots their true *country* can remember; —
> But there's no shooting (save grouse) till September.

Comfort and hunting were not the only reasons for the exodus from London. The rulers of Britain were still as deeply rooted in the countryside as their grandfathers had been; but they were also more urbane, both figuratively and in the literal sense of being habituated to the city. Their social position as magnates in their localities was intimately connected with their parliamentary position as boroughmongers and manipulators of county elections and with their economic position as landlords; their influence on the national scene derived from their rural power. Yet they were much less earthy than the blue-blooded country bumpkins of Walpole's day, for time had eroded their provincialism. Many of them had been polished in youth by the Grand Tour, kept up their knowledge of Europe through frequent travel, and spoke and read French as a second language. They might regard foreigners with the scorn of Samuel Johnson or the humor of Laurence Sterne; but their opinions were likely to be based on firsthand experience, and they were achieving a level of sophistication that would have delighted Lord Chesterfield. At heart they were still uncompromisingly British; on the surface they were cosmopolitan.

Their taste had improved, and the change shows most clearly in the monuments that they were building to their own grandeur. A typical example, just as Blenheim Palace was typical of an earlier period, is Kedleston Hall in Derbyshire, which is largely the work of a famous Scottish architect and decorator, Robert Adam. A comparison of the façades of the two structures shows that they have much in common: they are symmetrical, in that the flanking wings are balanced on each side of the central building; and there is a rhythmic alternation of such decorative motives as columns and pilasters, round-arched and square-headed windows. But there the resemblance ends. Vanbrugh's work at Blenheim reveals an almost obsessive concern with variety and mass. The design has so many constituent parts that it is a busy jumble, with no surfaces of plain wall on which the eye can rest; and the elaboration of obelisks on the skyline looks like the headgear of a crowd of overdressed dowagers. Adam, by contrast, achieves his effect through restraint. The flanking wings are subordinated to the central block, though tied to it by the repetition of window motives; the columns are concentrated on a single point of emphasis, and the moldings of doors and windows and stringcourses are set off against unadorned stonework; the silhouette is clean against the sky. Kedleston, though on a smaller scale than Blenheim, is equally monumental but much quieter. It is self-assured, where the other is self-assertive.

A great house such as Kedleston was a hub of county society. Guests were constantly coming and going, to stay for a meal or a weekend or a

Blenheim Palace. Engraving by Colin Campbell. Vitruvius Britanicus, 1715 Edition, Volume I.

(*Columbia University*)

Kedleston Hall. Engraving by Colin Campbell. Vitruvius Britanicus, 1715 Edition, Volume IV.

(*Columbia University*)

month; hospitality was mixed with business. The selection of local candidates
for parliament, the choice of a new vicar or justice of the peace, the planning
of an enclosure act or of how to pull down a cabinet minister, were discussed
and often settled over the after-dinner port and madeira. The country house,
in other words, was more than a building or even a way of life; it was a
political institution, which endured as long as the governing class endured.
The leaders of that class were not, like their counterparts in eighteenth-century
France, drawn away from the countryside to the court in order to win favors
from the king. Courtiers they were in season, and adept at scrambling for
governmental plums; but they were never mere courtiers. The sources of their
power and the centers of their lives were in their counties, and above all in
their estates.

The Lower Classes

No estate of any size could be maintained without a vast number
of servants. Horses and carriages, the only means of conveyance, required
an army of stable boys and grooms; a similar army of parlor maids wielded
the dusters and polishing cloths and brooms that were the only means of
housecleaning. The formal gardens that were coming into vogue needed a
staff of their own. A kitchen large enough to serve twenty or thirty guests,
and body servants to attend to their needs, meant an additional horde of cooks,
scullery maids, footmen, valets, lady's maids, each with status and functions
strictly defined by custom, and all presided over by the head butler and
housekeeper, the monarchs of the world below stairs. It was a world that
the gentry took for granted, but on which their whole way of life depended.
These servants were by modern standards incredibly ill-housed,
overworked, and underpaid; yet they were among the most fortunate members
of the working class. They at least had some measure of security, whereas
the farm families from which many of them came were increasingly exposed
to the winds of change. The standards of living in rural England had been
rising steadily throughout the century, thanks in large measure to improved
methods of producing foodstuffs.[1] But one of the principal techniques for
increasing production, the enclosure of open fields, was now bringing serious
trouble to the countryside. Since the middle of the century the enclosure
movement, particularly in the southern counties, had greatly accelerated. The
principal method employed was private acts of parliament which empowered
commissioners to cut through the tangle of property rights involved, and the
resultant division of the open fields tended to favor the important local citizens.
For the small men, enclosure could be a disaster. In many cases they were
left with holdings too meager to be farmed, and simultaneously lost their

---

[1] For these agricultural improvements see above, pp. 39–41.

age-old right to pasture cows and geese on the common land of the manor, which the lord now took for his own.

> The law locks up both man and woman
> Who steals the goose from off the common,
> But lets the greater felon loose
> Who steals the common from the goose.

The long-term effect of enclosure was to increase the size of land-holdings and concentrate them in fewer hands, as many peasants sold out and became either tenant farmers or landless laborers. For the laborer existence was bleak. Population was increasing, particularly after 1780; hired hands were consequently plentiful and wages low. The laborer, lacking a cow, lacked butter and milk in his diet and was already turning perforce to tea, the mainstay of the lower classes from that day to this. He worked long hours for little return and with little hope of improving his lot, and the threat of the workhouse always hung over him. He was probably no worse off in material goods than his ancestors had been; but he was more dependent on those above him in the social scale and, with the destruction of the old manorial community, more open to the impersonal forces of supply and demand.

The lives of the rural poor were often, in Thomas Hobbes's phrase, "nasty, brutish, and short." Those of their urban counterparts were even more so. In the country the squires and magistrates, lazy or indifferent as many of them were, could at least identify their local paupers and had some vestigial sense of responsibility for them. In the large cities most paupers were unknown to the authorities, who lacked the resources to help even if they wanted to. The mass of the urban poor lived on the edge of subsistence, in conditions that would have made a modern slum seem like paradise. The houses had no plumbing, and the sewers were the gutters outside. Overcrowding eliminated privacy and almost assured sexual promiscuity. Such employment as there was varied with the seasons, and when there was none thieving took its place. Punishments for crime were savage, but the chance of getting caught was slight; even London did not have a police force worth the name until the nineteenth century.

The inhabitants of the dark, foul-smelling alleys of the capital were lawless not only as individuals but in the mass; one of their few ways to force themselves on the attention of their betters was to riot. The mobs that screamed against Walpole's Excise Bill in 1733 reappeared throughout the century, and even the king's ministers went in constant fear of having their windows smashed and perhaps their skulls as well. In 1780 a mild parliamentary effort to soften the penal laws against Roman Catholics touched off an explosion of mass bigotry known as the Gordon Riots. For a week London was in the grip of the mob, which soon turned to destruction for its own

Gin Lane. Engraving by William Hogarth. A caption at the bottom of the print reads:

Gin cursed Fiend, with Fury fraught,
Makes human Race a Prey;
It enters by a deadly Draught,
And steals our Life away.

Virtue and Truth, driv'n to Despair,
It's Rage compells to fly,
But cherishes, with hellish Care,
Theft, Murder, Perjury.

Damn'd Cup! that on the Vitals preys,
That liquid Fire contains
Which Madness to the Heart conveys,
And rolls it thro' the Veins.

sake, burned and looted and broke into prisons, and even attacked the Bank of England. At last the army restored order and saved the ruling class from what many of its members considered incipient revolution. But the danger remained, and would remain as long as the slums spawned violence and the city magistrates lacked the force to restrain it.

The poor, in addition to threatening public order, were also a major and increasing drain on the taxpayer. The system of poor relief was by now almost two hundred years old, dating from the end of Elizabeth's reign, and was as variegated as the system of borough representation in parliament. Responsibility for relief lay with the individual parish, the smallest unit of civil as well as ecclesiastical government; in each parish a tax was levied, called the poor rate, which was then disbursed to the needy. The neighboring justices of the peace supposedly supervised the distribution of these funds, but in practice the parochial officers had a large measure of autonomy. They used it, understandably enough, in the interests of the rate-payer more than of the poor, and were primarily concerned with providing relief at minimum cost.

The most popular method, because it seemed to be economical, was the workhouse. Here all the paupers were brought together, given food and shelter of a sort, and put to work. In the century after 1660 workhouses spread through the country, and the results were appalling. Children and aged, sick and well, virtuous and vicious, sane and lunatic, were jammed together in filthy buildings that bred disease and despair. The workhouse, furthermore, did not prove to be economical; for the costs of poor relief rose alarmingly. Parliament grew disillusioned with a system that was both in-efficient and inhumane, and in 1782 authorized a new departure. Thenceforth a parish might replace its workhouse with a poorhouse, to shelter only the aged and infirm, and might relieve its able-bodied paupers in their own homes by giving them either work to do there or money to supplement inadequate wages.

The second alternative, supplementing wages, appealed to the parish employer. He could pay his laborers less than a living wage and be sure that they went on living, for they would receive enough from the parish rate to keep them from starvation. In the 1790s some ingenious justices of the peace, meeting at the village of Speenhamland in Berkshire, worked out a sliding scale for supplementing wages from rates according to the price of bread, and this so-called Speenhamland system spread through the country and remained in effect until 1834. It was extremely costly, and tended to depress the general wage scale at the expense of the rate-payer. But it did provide the working poor with some measure of protection in a period of critical economic change, and by doing so helped to assuage what might otherwise have been explosive discontent. At a time when much of Europe was torn by the revolution spreading outward from France, British laborers remained loyal to a society that, for all its shortcomings, did at least keep them alive.

The Religious Revival

A force of a quite different kind was also immunizing the laborers against the ideas of the French Revolution. In the late 1730s a new outburst of Christian faith had come from a small group of Anglican clergymen, and by the 1780s their work was having a profound impact on the working classes. No movement could have been more unexpected, either in its origin or its impact. The eighteenth-century Church of England was an institution in the doldrums; its gospel was rationalized and diluted to fit a secular age, and its clergy were more concerned with teaching how to be good than how to be saved. Although they preached that charity to the poor was part of Christian duty, with the poor themselves they had little concern. Neither, for that matter, had the dissenters, for the Puritan tradition had never been involved with the mass of the people. Organized Christianity was of and for the propertied classes, as it had been since the Restoration, and did not dirty its vestments in the poorhouse and the slum, whose inhabitants consequently had little more contact with religion than if they had been living in the Dark Continent.

But the Church of England was not completely absorbed with being respectable. A few of its members still held to the concept expressed by its last famous archbishop, William Laud. The Church, as Laud had envisaged it, was the whole of society, in St. Paul's phrase the Body of Christ, of which rich and poor alike were parts; and salvation through Christ was open to all the faithful rather than limited, as the Calvinists held, to a narrow circle of the elect. This Anglican concept survived, if dimly, in the intellectual torpor of what had once been the stronghold of Laudianism, the colleges of Oxford; and out of Oxford came the beginnings of a spiritual revolution.

On a May evening in 1738 John Wesley, a former fellow of an Oxford college and a high-church Anglican priest, had an overwhelming experience. "I felt my heart strangely warmed, I felt I did trust in Christ, Christ alone, for salvation; and an assurance was given me that he had taken away *my* sins, even mine, and saved me from the law of sin and death." Wesley became convinced that every one to whom this experience of conversion came was saved, and that every one to whom it did not come, no matter how good or pious, was in a state of damnation. His duty, therefore, was to open the hearts of men so that God might invade them — to preach hell fire on the one hand, repentance and salvation on the other. This was a startling message to a rationalistic age, for it meant that God was not a set of precepts or an abstraction, but a Person concerned with redeeming every one of His creatures.

Wesley and his companions, a small group called Methodists, began to carry their gospel to all who would listen. They went from parish to parish, asking and sometimes demanding to be heard from the pulpit. They held out to their listeners the choice of heaven or hell, Christ or Satan, and denied them the comfortable middle ground between belief and unbelief;

they preached with a passion and crude power that left some convulsed with repentance, some with anger. The workings of grace, which the Methodists hailed, more skeptical Christians stigmatized as mania; and this clash of views could not be arbitrated. The parish clergy, understandably enough, resented the itinerant missionaries who troubled their peace, and began to bar them from their pulpits. The Methodists then took to the highways and byways, speaking wherever they could gather a crowd. They still considered themselves Anglican priests, but when their church excluded them they found their congregations out of doors.

Their greatest preacher was George Whitefield. He struck fire from the humble, and they gathered in the hundreds, thousands, and even tens of thousands to listen to him. He was a man of passion and intuition, not logic, and cared as little for theological niceties as for the disapproval of his bishop. His one overmastering purpose was to save souls, wherever and however he could reach them; and he, more than anyone else, was responsible for transforming Methodism from a revival within the established church into a mass movement outside it. John Wesley was deeply reluctant to accept this transformation. He had an almost superstitious reverence for Anglican ritual and usages, and if he could have had his way would never have left the ecclesiastical fold. But that fold was not for him and his followers, and they were inexorably forced out of it.

Two worlds were in conflict. One was the cool and decorous world of the established clergy and the society to which they ministered; the other was the primitive, stormy world of the lower classes, steeped in superstition and half-believing in witchcraft, which the Methodists were kindling with their talk of miracles and demonic possession and redemption open to all. These ardent spiritual egalitarians took at face value Christ's teaching about rich and poor, and they therefore seemed to the rich to be social as well as religious firebrands. "Their doctrines," wrote an irate duchess, "are most repulsive and strongly tinctured with impertinence and disrespect towards their superiors, in perpetually endeavoring to level all ranks and do away with all distinctions. It is monstrous to be told that you have a heart as sinful as the common wretches that crawl the earth." The duchess and her ilk would have nothing to do with the new movement for the very reason that the common wretches embraced it.

By the 1780s Methodism was to all intents and purposes a separate denomination. Wesley, in many ways the most conservative of revolutionaries, was being forced against his will to ordain his own clergy and even consecrate his own bishops; and in organizing his flock he showed an administrative genius at least equal to his power of touching men's hearts. His followers were mostly uneducated, drunk with what the period called "enthusiasm," and convinced that they were inspired by the Holy Ghost; hence they were in danger of falling apart, like the Puritans before them, into numberless splinter groups. But Wesley held them together. Tactfully and patiently and firmly he imposed upon them an ecclesiastical structure, and so gave them

the cohesion and corporate discipline that the Puritan sects had lacked.
By the time he died in 1791, Methodism was a force to be reckoned with.

The institution that had cast out the Methodists was soon affected by
them. The Church of England, unreceptive as it was to change, still considered
itself Christian; and it could not remain impervious to the new evangelism.
Before the end of the century a leaven was working in many Anglican rectories
and even some episcopal palaces. It showed itself in a heightened stress upon
the experience of conversion, upon Bible-reading, upon the social implications
of the Gospel, and upon a variety of good works that ranged from the
establishment of Sunday schools to agitation against the slave trade. This
so-called evangelical movement gained ground within the established church,
just as Methodism gained ground outside it; and in the next sixty years
the two in conjunction helped to alter the whole tone of British society.
Gradually the aristocratic code of the Georgian era, with its emphasis on
reason and detachment and the Chesterfieldian graces, gave place to the
earnest and muscular Christianity of the Victorians.

The religious revival, it has been argued, contributed in two ways
to strengthening Britain for the coming wars against France. One was by
turning the workers against the atheism of the French Revolution, the other
by inculcating in them a sense of order and discipline that was antithetical
to the spirit of revolutionary violence.[2] This argument, like most generalizations from history, cannot be proved. The only proof would be written
testimony, from innumerable workingmen who professed themselves Christian,
on how they regarded the social order; and the testimony does not exist.
"The short and simple annals of the poor" are in fact neither short nor
simple, but neither are they written; few laborers knew how to write, and
still fewer did. Hence the historian lacks the evidence to clinch his case,
and can at best advance conclusions that are plausible but not demonstrable.

Industrialization

Whether or not religion helped to sustain the British people
through the coming duel with France, the growth of new industries un-
questionably did; on this point the evidence is abundant enough to warrant
a firm conclusion. Industrialization did not have entirely beneficial effects —

[2] William E. H. Lecky, *A History of England in the Eighteenth Century* (7
vols., 1892), III, 145–46; Elie Halévy, *England in 1815* (vol. I of *A History of
the English People in the Nineteenth Century*, 2nd ed., 6 vols., 1949), p. 424–
26. Lecky's monumental work, which first appeared in 1877, is by now antiquated. But he was a talented historian writing in a leisurely age, and his
volumes contain a wealth of information, lucidly presented, on every aspect
of the period. Halévy was a French scholar who knew British history better
than most Englishmen. His treatment of the nineteenth century is as exhaustive
as Lecky's treatment of the eighteenth, and his judgments are always interesting
and often provocative.

far from it — but did create vast new economic resources, out of which
Britain financed more than two decades of war and grew stronger in the
process, until she emerged in 1815 with a power felt throughout the world.
That power, on which she founded the Pax Britannica of the nineteenth
century, had its source in the eighteenth, in the mills and furnaces and mines
of the Georgian age.

The Industrial Revolution, unlike most revolutions, did not begin
at any one moment; nothing in it corresponds to the Battle of Lexington
or the fall of the Bastille.[3] Ever since the opening of the Hanoverian era
the pace of development had been accelerating in many interdependent areas
of the national economy, and change in each stimulated change in the others.
One such area was commerce. As the British merchant marine outstripped
its European rivals, the profits of the carrying trade swelled the supply of
available capital. Another area was agriculture. As the spread of enclosure
and improvements in stockbreeding produced more food with a smaller
labor force, the great landholders, like the great commercial magnates, acquired
surplus wealth to invest. A third area was banking and credit. The financial
system established after the Glorious Revolution not only maintained the
confidence of the business community but provided the mechanisms for
attracting capital to new ventures. Without the fluid wealth generated by
commerce and agriculture and made available through the bankers, factories
could not have been built or mines dug; without a surplus food supply the
factories and mines could not have been manned, for a working class divorced from the land would have starved. The sudden industrialization
that marked the reign of George III, in other words, was not the result of
accident or of a few crucial inventions, but of the fact that for the first time
in her history Britain had arrived at a point where large-scale manufacturing
was possible.

The complex process of industrialization is difficult to grasp, because
almost every change influenced and was influenced by every other. Take
coal and iron and steam, for example. In mid-century an effective way was
found to use coal, instead of wood, for smelting iron; until then depletion of
the forests had threatened to extinguish the iron industry. Coal mining also
was threatened by water that leaked into the mines; and the deeper they
went the worse the problem became. The solution, as will soon be seen, proved
to be steam pumps, which were eventually developed into steam engines.
Thus steam helped to provide coal for the iron foundries, which in turn
provided the metal for steam engines, while the coal mines provided fuel
for the foundries and engines alike. The three industries grew in such

---

[3] The classical treatment of early industrialization is Paul Mantoux, *The
Industrial Revolution in the Eighteenth Century* (1928). See also John H.
Clapham, *An Economic History of Modern Britain* (3 vols., 1930–38); Gilbert
Slater, *The Growth of Modern England* (1932); Abbot P. Usher, *An Introduction
to the Industrial History of England* (1920); and Henry Hamilton,
England: a History of the Homeland (1948).

intimate relationship with each other that describing any one by itself is meaningless.

The process of change, nevertheless, can be most easily understood by focusing upon a single industry. The best focus is not coal or iron or steam engines or even the wool trade, which had so long been at the center of the nation's economy, but an upstart, the manufacture of cotton cloth. Largely because it was an upstart, the cotton trade took an early lead in the race to industrialize and kept it for generations.

Cotton cloth of a sort had been manufactured by hand since the late seventeenth century in Lancashire, on the western slope of the Pennines. The primary reason why the industry grew up in that backward part of England was water: the prevailing winds from the Atlantic with their burden of rain, which make the west coast one of the wettest parts of the island, ensured both a reliable source of waterpower in the Pennine streams and a moist atmosphere in which the fragile cotton threads could be worked without breaking. Lancashire therefore became the cotton kingdom, with Manchester for its capital and Liverpool for its port.

The earliest incentive to cotton manufacture was cloth imported by the East India Company, which caught the fancy of the British public. The Company, intent on protecting its market from domestic competition, had the alliance of the wool trade, which wanted no rival textile industry. Early in the century these powerful vested interests secured legislation to discourage domestic cotton manufacture; but the industry throve in spite of laws that soon became dead letters. The early years of the cotton trade went far to determine its character. It attracted men of daring, who were tough and unconventional and ready to seize every opportunity for increasing their output. They had to be adventurers to make headway against the conservative woolen interest, which the state had controlled and cherished for centuries. They were self-made men, nurtured on open and even cutthroat competition, and wanted from the government neither regulation nor protection. By the 1780s they were already showing the spirit, though not yet the theory, of what became Victorian free enterprise.

They were also beginning to challenge the economic predominance of wool. By now they had most of what they needed to increase production — an expanding market, capital to build factories and a labor force to man them, food to feed their workers. The principal difficulty in their way was technological: machines were not available for the entire manufacturing process, which at some stages was held to the snail's pace of the hand laborer. Just as a chain is no stronger than its weakest link, so the output of cloth is no faster than the slowest operation involved.

The revolution in the cotton trade was the progressive mechanizing of four main operations in producing cloth. The operations are harvesting and transporting the cotton, combing its matted fibers and spinning them into thread, weaving the thread into cloth, and lastly finishing and bleaching and dyeing the cloth for market. The first major improvements were made in weaving, and their introduction there revealed a basic characteristic of industrialization: accelerating what has been the slowest operation removes that bottleneck and accelerates the whole manufacturing process, but only up to the point where some other operation becomes a new bottleneck. The focus of improvement therefore shifts from one to another and back again, in a never-ending battle for more output.

At the accession of George II, when the cotton trade had still been confined to the workers' houses, the bottleneck had been weaving. The invention of an improved shuttle by John Kay in 1733 increased the productivity of the looms until four spinners were required to keep one weaver in thread. Spinning then became the bottleneck, and inventors tackled the problem of a spinning machine; by the time of the American Revolution two such machines driven by water power, one the brain child of James Hargreaves and the other of Richard Arkwright, were in common use. They were far too expensive for domestic workers, and even the capitalist could afford them only if he kept them in continuous operation; he therefore put them in a factory to which the workers came in shifts. Before the end of the century hand laborers were an anachronism in cotton-spinning, and the factory system was well established.

Weaving again became the bottleneck, but here progress was much slower. The hand loom, as improved by Kay, was vastly more complex than the spinning wheel; and years passed before an effective machine was devised to replace the loom. In the interim the hand weavers were the aristocrats of the trade; for the very reason that they could not keep up with the output of the new spinning mills, their services were everywhere in demand. But their days were numbered. Manufacturers were becoming more clamorous for inventions, and inventors were becoming more adept. Before the end of the Napoleonic Wars the power loom was in operation for all but the finest cloths, and weaving was in transformation as spinning had been.

Mechanizing these two operations stimulated change elsewhere. Bleaching the cloth was temporarily a bottleneck, but by 1800 chemists had managed to reduce the time needed for bleaching from several months to a few days. The demand for raw cotton exceeded the supply, bcause the old methods of harvesting were inadequate, until the New England inventor Eli Whitney provided the answer with his cotton gin. Thus by the strange ramifications of cause and effect the needs of Lancashire mills in the 1790s contributed to an American invention, which in turn contributed to the spread of cotton-growing in the southern states and the concomitant strengthening of slavery — and so to the Civil War of 1861.

In Britain the transformation of the cotton trade was intimately associated with other changes in industry, of which the most dramatic was the harnessing of power. Until the reign of George III man's sources of power for work and travel had not increased since the Middle Ages. The sources were three: animal or human muscles; the wind, operating on sail or windmill; and running water. Only the last of these was suited at all to the continuous operating of machines, and it had great disadvantages. Streams flowed where nature intended them to, and factories had to be located on their banks, whether or not the location was desirable for other reasons; even the most reliable waterpower, furthermore, varied with the seasons and disappeared in a drought. The new age of machinery, in short, could not have come into being without a new source of power that was both movable and constant.

The source had long been known but not exploited. Early in the century a pump had come into use in which expanding steam raised a piston in a cylinder, and atmospheric pressure brought it down again when the steam condensed inside the cylinder to form a vacuum. This "atmospheric engine," invented by Thomas Savery and vastly improved by his partner, Thomas Newcomen, embodied revolutionary principles; but it was so slow and wasteful of fuel that it could not be employed outside the mines for which it had been designed. In the 1760s James Watt perfected a separate condenser for the steam, so that the cylinder did not have to be cooled at every stroke; then he devised a way to make the piston turn a wheel and thus to convert reciprocating into rotary motion. He thereby transformed an inefficient pump of limited use into a steam engine of a thousand uses. The final step came when steam was introduced into the cylinder to drive the piston backward as well as forward, thereby increasing the speed of the engine and cutting its fuel consumption. At long last the new source of power was fully harnessed.

Watt's steam engine was soon showing what it could do. It was liberating industry from dependence on running water; the factories did not have to go to the streams when power could come to the factories. The engine was eliminating water in the mines by driving efficient pumps, which made possible deeper and deeper mining. Iron manufacture, which had been starving for fuel while it depended on charcoal, now fed upon a wealth of coal; and blast furnaces with steam-powered bellows were turning out more steel and iron for the new machinery. Steam was the motive force of revolution, as coal and iron ore were the raw materials. Matthew Boulton, Watt's partner in manufacturing steam engines at the great Soho Works near Birmingham, well understood the importance of his product. "I sell here, Sir," he proudly remarked to James Boswell, "what all the world desires to have — *power.*"

Power alone, however, did not solve all the problems of industry; growth required not only coal and iron and steam but new means of transport. Although Britain was singularly fortunate in having an abundance of high-quality coal and iron ore in close proximity, bringing them together over even short distances was impossible on the roads of the period. The typical eighteenth-century main road was impressive only in its name — the king's highway; it was usually no more than a narrow strip of cobblestone flanked on each side by dirt tracks, which in wet weather degenerated into seas of mud. Such tracks were not passable for carriages, let alone for heavily

laden wagons. As routes of supply for the machinery, the food, and above
all the coal that the factory system required, they were out of the question.

Something better had to be found, and the earliest answer was
canals. In 1761 the Duke of Bridgewater opened a short canal from his colliery
to Manchester and thereby cut in half the cost of transporting his coal.
Other capitalists followed his example and soon laced Britain with a system of
artificial waterways. Still others took to the road and formed turnpike trusts
for maintaining stretches of causeway on which tolls were charged. These
roads were a boon to the traveler for years to come, and Lord Byron cele-
brated them in *Don Juan*.

> What a delightful thing's a turnpike road!
>   So smooth, so level, such a mode of shaving
> The earth, as scarce the eagle in the broad
>   Air can accomplish, with his wide wings waving.

Shaving the earth and cutting waterways in it were all well and good;
neither improvement, however, could solve the manufacturer's problem, which
was how to carry heavy weights to and from the points of industrial
concentration. Canal boats could carry the weights, but canals could not
cross hilly terrain; turnpikes could cross the hills, but would not stand up
under great weights. Still another solution was needed.

The ingredients for it lay ready to hand. In some industrial regions
heavily laden wagons, with flanged wheels, were being hauled by horses along
metal rails; and the stationary steam engine was puffing in the factory and
mine. Another generation passed before inventors succeeded in combining
these ingredients, by putting the engine on wheels and the wheels on the rails,
so as to provide a machine to take the place of the horse. But the railroad
age was a logical, almost an inevitable, result of what had already happened
in the eighteenth century.

At the close of that century industrialization was in no more than its
initial stages. Canals were being built and roads improved; coal-mining, iron
manufacture, and the cotton trade were booming; and in some industrial
processes, such as cotton-spinning, machines were replacing hand labor,
steam engines were replacing waterpower, and the factory system was firmly
established. But only certain areas of the economy were affected as yet, and
much of what the Victorians took for granted was still undreamed of in 1800.
Steel, in contrast to iron, was a luxury because it could not yet be cheaply
produced. The stationary steam engine was of limited efficiency, and the
locomotive and steamship were unknown. Weaving, even in cotton, was
done on the hand loom. Last but not least, the wool trade was scarcely
touched by machinery and steam for a generation to come. Throughout the
Napoleonic Wars, with bustling innovation on all sides — in the furnaces of
the Midlands, the collieries of South Wales and Northumberland, the mills of
Lancashire — wool-spinners and weavers of Yorkshire and East Anglia

went their old ways undisturbed. They had almost as little to do with the industrial world rising around them as the gentry of Jane Austen's novels.

To say that the wool trade was conservative is not to say that its leaders were indifferent to the increasingly serious competition from cotton. They were, on the contrary, gravely worried, and clamored for the kind of statutory protection that parliament had afforded them earlier in the century. Stamping out the cotton trade, wrote one of their pamphleteers in 1782, would be beneficial to all concerned. Manufacturers who abandoned cotton for wool would "employ more hands, get more money, and at the same time enrich their country . . . while we all join with loyal hearts and ready hands in the support of government, and by encouraging our woolen manufactures extend our commerce, the *life* of naval war, the *existence* of our floating castles, the grand PALLADIUM of the *BRITISH EMPIRE*."

This pompous howl in the name of patriotism had as little effect on parliament as on the mill owners of Lancashire. The government had traditionally been attentive to big business, for not even the most aristocratic administration imagined that land was the unique source of the nation's wealth; and the wishes of the business community had been reflected in the statute book. But now a split was appearing in that community. On the one hand the leaders of the old established industries, such as wool, clung to the familiar ways and demanded protection from domestic and foreign competitors; on the other hand the iron and coal and cotton magnates were coming to favor unregulated competition at home and a liberalizing of commercial restrictions in order to encourage British exports. The revolutionizing of industry was generating a movement to reform the nation's economic policy.

Pitt and Reform

The reformers were fortunate in their prime minister. Lord North's fall in the spring of 1782 had led to a year and a half of political turmoil, which ended in what proved to be the longest-lived ministry since Walpole's. In December 1783 the King called on William Pitt, the second son of the Earl of Chatham, to head his government. The young man was already a seasoned politician at the age of twenty-four; he was also a superb administrator, who had as shrewd a head for finance as Walpole himself, and a greater taste for experimenting. The experiments were primarily of two sorts, attempts to liberalize commercial policy and measures to improve Britain's antiquated fiscal system.

In his commercial policy Pitt was influenced by Adam Smith, the famous Scottish economist whose *Wealth of Nations,* in 1776, had first preached the doctrine that unfettered private enterprise operates to the public good. Governmental control of the economy, according to Smith, was an artificial and therefore undesirable interference with the natural laws of supply and demand; what was needed was not control but freedom for

(*National Portrait Gallery*)

William Pitt the Younger by J. Hoppner.

every man to follow the dictates of self-interest. That interest was assumed to
be enlightened and intelligent, so that the conflict of individual interests
in open competition would redound to the benefit of all. The wealth of a
nation rested upon the production of consumable goods, Smith argued, and
the way to increase production was to leave each producer of goods or services
"free to pursue his own interest his own way." The machinery of governmental regulation created over the years ought to be dismantled; and state
interference be limited to those areas, such as education and public works, that
cannot be supported by private capital. Because Smith put great stress on
national defense and hence on sea power, he commended the navigation acts
that were designed to encourage the British merchant marine at the cost
of foreign competitors; but with this exception he believed that the rule in
commerce, as in industry, should be uninhibited competition. He was thus the
chief source of the later classical economists, who preached laissez-faire, or
free enterprise, at home and free trade abroad.

William Pitt, said Smith, "understands my ideas better than I do
myself." The compliment was not only exaggerated but irrelevant, for Pitt
as a politician was much less interested in theory than in what would work.
Although he was willing to lower tariffs if he could thereby increase trade, and
let industry manage itself unless he saw good reason to interfere, he
was even less of a doctrinaire believer in free trade and laissez-faire than
was Adam Smith. The young prime minister's tentative experiments in the
1780s, nevertheless, did foreshadow those two sacred principles of Victorian
economics.

The first experiment was with reducing tariffs between Britain and
Ireland. The American Revolution had stirred the Irish to consciousness
that they too had rights, and had given them a rare opportunity for self-
assertion. After the intervention of France in 1778 an army of volunteers
had been raised in Ireland, ostensibly to defend the island against invasion,
and in the last years of the war this force had become a powerful threat
to Britain. Lord North and his successor, negotiating at the cannon's mouth,
had made substantial trade concessions and withdrawn the control that the
British government had exercised for centuries over the legislation of the
Dublin parliament. Pitt wanted to continue the conciliatory process in a
friendlier atmosphere, by mutual economic agreements that would amount
to a commercial union. But a complex of forces was working against him.
Now that Irish manufactures were recovering from the doldrums of the early
Hanoverian era, conservative British industrial interests dreaded to see
the domestic market flooded with Irish goods. Pitt's political opponents made
the most of these fears, and also stirred the fears of the Irish that commercial
union would subvert their newly won political autonomy. The Prime
Minister abandoned his measure, and one more chance was lost of a rap-
prochement between the two countries.

Pitt was undiscouraged. In the following year, 1786, he opened
negotiations for a treaty with France to effect a mutual reduction of tariffs.

This overture to Britain's oldest, most inveterate rival showed both his
courage and his clear-sightedness. "To suppose that any nation can be un-
alterably the enemy of another," he said, "is weak and childish. . . . It is a
libel on the constitution of political societies, and supposes the existence of
diabolical malice in the original frame of man." He had to contend with
the "weak and childish" not only in parliament but among leaders of the
older industries. The latter formed a pressure group, known as the General
Chamber of Manufacturers, to impress upon the business world that the
principle behind the treaty was one of "serious and awful importance . . .
comprehending a prodigious change in the commercial system of this
country."

But Pitt found influential allies among men in the new industries.
They believed, as he did, that the treaty would benefit both sides. France ex-
ported primarily such products as wine, they argued, which did not
compete with British manufactured goods; an agreement between the two
nations would be mutually profitable and would usher in an era of good
feeling. Here again was a foretaste of the future, of the Victorian faith that
free trade would in the long run eliminate wars and establish utopia; the
faith was still embryonic, but the point was already being made that a lowering
of tariffs meant a lowering of tensions. When Pitt succeeded in concluding
the agreement, known from the name of his chief negotiator as the Eden
Treaty of 1786, the point was clearly put in a jingle celebrating the occasion.

> May kingdom 'gainst kingdom no more be at spite;
> For both 'twere much better to trade than to fight;
> And whilst mutual friendship and harmony reign
> Our buttons we'll barter for pipes of champagne.[4]

Pitt's economic reforms were not confined to the Eden Treaty, and
those he made at home proved to be more important because they were more
lasting. He attacked smuggling by reducing and simplifying import duties
and by extending the excise (as Walpole had tried and failed to do) to
tobacco, wines, and other articles on which smugglers had hitherto made their
profit.[5] He improved the tax structure, abolished numerous sinecures, established
a Consolidated Fund in which all revenues were deposited and from which
all governmental expenses were paid, and created a Sinking Fund, from the
accruing interest of which he hoped eventually to pay off the public debt.
This last experiment was not a success, but the others were. Pitt did more

[4] Between 1785 and 1793 Pitt made numerous but unsuccessful attempts to
secure similar treaties with other powers; see John Ehrman, *The British Government and Commercial Negotiations with Europe, 1783–1793* (1962). The
Eden Treaty vanished, like most of the rest of the eighteenth-century world,
in the explosion of the French Revolution.
[5] For Walpole's failure to extend the excise see above, pp. 55–56.

than anyone else in the eighteenth century to curb bureaucratic peculation and bring order and efficiency into the finances of the state, and he accomplished his work in the nick of time. Although his reforms bore little relation to the work of the new manufacturers, he, like them, was strengthening the nation for the ordeal to come.

In other areas his efforts at improvement were halfhearted and unsuccessful. In 1785 he proposed reforming the House of Commons by gradually abolishing a number of rotten boroughs; but, when he encountered strong parliamentary opposition and found that even his eloquence could not kindle a lethargic public, he abandoned his measure. Three years later he championed the campaign led by William Wilberforce, an evangelical Anglican who was one of his closest friends, to wipe out the slave trade throughout the empire, and continued to sponsor the cause intermittently until 1792; then he let it drop. The opposition was strong, from the King as well as the West Indian merchants and shipping interests, and the Prime Minister was no crusader. He was liberal by temperament more than by deep conviction. When his own career was at stake he would fight hard; when a worthy cause was at stake he would espouse it and press it up to a point, but would not hazard his position on it.

Pitt's character was squarely at odds with that of his great rival, Charles James Fox. The two men had much in common: they believed that the American war had been a mistake; they wanted to reform parliament and end the slave trade and conciliate the Irish; they were experts in the thrust and parry of debate, and powerful orators. But as people they were poles apart. Pitt wrapped himself in a lofty and chilling virtue, and never unbent except to a few intimates; he was a Puritan of politics, hardworking and incorruptible, who won from his contemporaries vast respect and little love. Fox was just the opposite. He embraced great causes, often with more passion than wisdom; he drank and gambled excessively and with gusto; he threw himself into political battling with everything he had, and yet retained enough sense of humor to be unembittered when victory time and again eluded him. Although in his long career he never achieved more than momentary power, he was probably better loved than any other man in the history of parliament. He was big, both in girth and in personality, and what a friend called his "negligent grandeur" left its mark upon the age.

Empire in India

One of Pitt's major achievements was to find an answer to the question of how to govern India. Ever since the Seven Years War that question had played an increasing role in British politics, as the East India Company had become more and more deeply involved in the affairs of the native princes. Political involvement was as far removed as ever from the intent of India House, the Company's headquarters in London, for the

directors were still interested in trading, not governing. But their hands were
forced by their own servants. The men on the spot realized that the only
way to safeguard trade was to assume political power, and they carried
on the process begun during the Seven Years War of transforming the
Company into a sovereign state. By the time Robert Clive left India in 1767,
the Company had establishments at Bombay on the west coast and Madras
and its environs on the southeast coast and, far more important, was the
paramount power in Bengal. There the British held extensive territory and
controlled, through native puppets, the revenue of the entire province.
Bengal was the cornerstone of the empire that India House was inadvertently
acquiring.

The government at home could not long remain indifferent to what
was happening. Company officials, Clive among them, were returning with
great wealth gained by dubious means; and these "nabobs" strutting their
way through British society aroused both anger and envy. Anger, because
they were accused, often with good reason, of having shamelessly exploited
the natives; envy, because the golden fruits of exploitation were not open to
all the greedy but only to those with influence at India House. Two factors
combined, in other words, to attract the attention of parliament: the moralist's
desire to ensure at least some minimal standards of good government in
Bengal, and the politician's desire to share in the Company's vast and growing
patronage.

Lord North attacked the problem in his Regulating Act of 1773,
which was the first clear assertion of parliament's supremacy over India
House. The act created a governor general in Bengal, gave him authority
over Bombay and Madras, provided him with a council, stipulated who he
and the councilors were to be for the next five years, and settled upon them
handsome salaries to be paid by the Company. This attempt to solve the
problem had serious drawbacks. It made the directors of the Company
responsible for agents whom they had not chosen and over whom they had
at best an exiguous control. It established the position of governor general
only to circumscribe its occupant. His supremacy over Bombay and Madras
was ill defined; he could not override his council, in which he had only a
single vote, and the councilors did not have clearly demarcated powers of their
own. The resultant system was so cumbersome that only a man of genius
could have made it work at all.

The Company's service produced such a man. For the next twelve
years the governor general was Warren Hastings, one of the great proconsuls in the history of empire. During the crisis occasioned by the War of
Independence, when Britain was fighting with her back to the wall and
the French were stirring up trouble throughout India, Hastings almost
single-handed saved the Company and extended its power. His chief enemy
was neither French nor Hindu but one of his own councilors, Philip Francis,
a man with vast ambition and a program of his own. The Company should
continue to rule Bengal, Francis believed, without responsibility for justice

or effective administration or anything but moneymaking, and should leave the rest of India to its own devices. Hastings, in contrast, was convinced that the Company must become the paramount power in the whole subcontinent, ruling directly in Bengal through a governor general in whose hands authority was centralized, indirectly elsewhere through princely dependents and allies, and must slowly permeate the whole complex of native institutions with British concepts of justice and good government. Francis worked to perpetuate the old order, Hastings to create a new one.[6]

The Governor General won by a narrow margin, by means that were sometimes none too scrupulous, and in 1780 Francis left for home to engineer his revenge. By then Hastings was at war against a coalition of princes in central India, who had been induced by French intrigue and their growing fear of the Company to do what they had never done before, unite to drive out the British. They almost succeeded. Hasting's small armies of sepoys were overwhelmingly outnumbered, and he was so desperate for money that he resorted to what his enemies regarded as high-handed extortion. But by a mixture of hard fighting and shrewd diplomacy he managed to break up the coalition, and the advent of peace in Europe saved him in the nick of time from a French naval threat. By 1784 his work was done, and in India the position of the Company was stronger than ever before.

But in Britain its position was under attack. Recent events had made clear that North's Regulating Act left room for great irregularities, and rumor painted Hastings as a monster of rapacity. India House was split by factions, each of which had parliamentary support; and the quarrels in London were reflected in Bombay, Madras, and Calcutta, the capital of Bengal. Both the Company and its governor general needed surveillance by the state, but how was this to be achieved? If the Company lost all power to appoint officials in India, who would appoint them? The obvious answer was the crown. But Whig politicians like Fox, who had long fought the King's influence, had no intention of giving him such a vast increase in patronage. For parliament itself to appoint, as it had in 1773, would turn the Company's service into a grab bag for politicians. There was no feasible alternative to leaving India House autonomous in selecting its personnel.

Nor was there any alternative to an autonomous governor general. The Whigs were opposed by long tradition to the concentration of power in the executive, but the realization was slowly dawning on them that their tradition made no sense in the alien world of Bengal. London could not in

[6] Even Hastings was far from envisaging the way in which the new order would develop. For a vivid modern sketch of him see Philip Woodruff, *The Men Who Ruled India: the Founders* (1954), pp. 122–32. This volume, the first of two, deals with the period from 1600 to 1858; it is an unorthodox collection of portraits of men who served the Company, famous and obscure, good and bad, by an author who himself had a distinguished career in the Indian civil service. He is familiar at first hand with the kinds of problems that his predecessors faced, and describes them with a freshness and professional appreciation that most historians lack.

any case exert effective control over a governor general in Calcutta. The attempt to circumscribe him by a council had not worked, and he could not be circumscribed directly from Britain if only because of communications: to send him a dispatch and receive his answer might take as much as a year. He had to be given great leeway in order to function at all; Hastings himself might deserve to be called to account, but the power of his office could not be impaired.

Pitt met the problem by dividing authority at home between the Company and the government, and demarcating the relationship between London and Calcutta. His India Act of 1784 created the pattern of British rule for the next seventy-four years, and was as much a constitutional landmark as Hasting's governorship had been a political landmark. The essence of the new system was a partnership between the Company and the state: the former continued to direct commercial affairs, and the latter took responsibility for governmental affairs. A board of control, composed in part of cabinet ministers, was set up in London; to it the Company directors submitted proposals for political or military action, and from it they received their orders. The Company appointed all officials except the highest, but the board had power to remove them. The crown appointed the governor general, to whom Bombay and Madras were subordinated; and he was soon made commander in chief and empowered to override his council. Thus was established a mixed authority. The Company retained a sphere of action and its patronage, the government assumed responsibility for Indian administration, and the governor general acquired the free hand that he needed.

While the India Act was creating the future, it also tried to perpetuate the past by condemning territorial conquest and intervention in the affairs of the native states. Hastings correctly interpreted these provisions as reflecting on his policy, and in 1785 he resigned and came home. Three years later he was impeached for misconduct as governor general. Philip Francis had poisoned the minds of Edmund Burke and others in parliament, until they saw in Hastings the epitome of all the evil, extortion, and ruthlessness that had stained British rule for generations. He was the scapegoat more than the epitome, for he had committed fewer and more venial sins than most of his predecessors while fighting against heavier odds; but even he was not above reproach. For seven years his trial dragged on, draining his fortune, until at last he was acquitted on every count.

He deserved vindication, but his impeachment was more significant than the rights and wrongs of the charges against him. For many years the conduct of the Company's servants had troubled even the tough consciences of British politicians, who were coming to realize slowly and grudgingly that political authority in India meant responsibilities to the governed. The state, now that it had assumed the authority, could not in honor shirk the responsibilities and join in the game of exploitation. Burke persuaded himself that Hastings had done exactly that, and should be called to account for it. "I impeach him," he said in closing his indictment, "in the name of all the commons of Great Britain, whose national character he has dishonored. I impeach him in the name of the people of India, whose laws, rights, and liberties he has subverted. . . . I impeach him in the name and by the virtue of those eternal laws of justice which he has violated."

The charge was as intemperate as the oratory suggests, and the victim was unfairly selected; but the underlying idea was valid. A principle cannot be judged by the use to which it is put, for good causes frequently lead to mistaken persecutions. So with Warren Hastings: his ordeal was unmerited, but it did serve notice on the future that Britain was concerned with justice in her eastern empire. She had to be, if only in self-interest; continuing exploitation would have corrupted the governors as well as brought tragedy to the governed. Burke, for all his partisan blindness, could at least see that the crown, in taking upon itself a new role, had also acquired a new duty — to provide a framework of order within which the Indians could enjoy their "laws, rights, and liberties."

The India of the nineteenth century was already beginning to take form. Britain, on the way to being the major power of the subcontinent, was developing a form of rule that was paternalistic and in essence dictatorial. Hastings's successors governed in what seemed by their lights to be the best interests of the governed, but remained as aloof from them as the early Stuart kings had been from their people. A governor general, in fact, might well have said of his subjects what Charles I said of his: "Their liberty and freedom consists in having government, those laws by which their lives and goods may be most their own. It is not their having a share in the government; that is nothing appertaining to them. A subject and a sovereign are clear different things."

This concept of sovereignty, anachronistic as it may seem at the end of the eighteenth century, was the only one on which the British could have operated, because it was the only one applicable to India. The Hindu and Moslem knew nothing of representative institutions or curbs on executive power. To them, from time out of mind, power had been the unfettered will of the sovereign, which had expressed itself for the most part in oppression, inefficiency, corruption, and bloodshed. British rule at its worst, by comparison with that of their own princes, meant an improvement of their lot. What they needed was to have orderly government, not to have a share in the government.

As Indians adapted to the British and the British to them, the effect on both sides was profound. The new rulers from the west had to break out of the constitutional traditions that had long been bred into them and learn the kind of autocratic paternalism that would work in an alien culture. Throughout the nineteenth century they continued to learn by trial and error, while the Indians began to learn from them novel ideas of liberty and parliament and nationhood. The system that Hastings had foreshadowed, the British Raj or government of India, began in response to the country's needs, much as the strong Tudor monarchy had begun in England three centuries before; it ended, as that monarchy had done, by educating its subjects to the point where they could dispense with it.

British dominion rested from beginning to end upon the Indians themselves. They provided the sepoys, the soldiers of the army by which first the Company, then the British crown, gained military predominance — thereby making India the outstanding example in modern history of a country brought by its own inhabitants under the rule of a foreign state. But the importance of the sepoys did not end there. They eventually became the means of British expansion outside India, and even a factor in the power politics of Europe. Until the First World War Britain never maintained at home a military force comparable with those of her rivals, but in India she did; and the Indian army strengthened her hand in international affairs. Danger to India or to the sea routes to India always touched a sensitive nerve at Whitehall, for a threat to the Raj threatened the heart of Britain's imperial position.

When Hastings was acquitted, the fantastic growth of tha Raj was still hidden in the future. But the elimination of the French and the weakening of the princes had prepared the way. Even though those old enemies were not yet ready to admit defeat and crises aplenty lay ahead, the means of weathering crises were at hand in the sepoys and in a workable system of government; and a new sense of responsibility, in London and Calcutta, ensured that the worst exploitation was over and that power in future would be soberly used. The foundations of the nineteenth-century empire were securely laid.

Conclusion

Britain was also preparing at home for her nineteenth-century role. The nature of government was changing: Pitt was modernizing the fiscal system and experimenting with new economic policies; and the King, as his Prime Minister gained firmer control, was almost imperceptibly moving away from the center of the political stage. Great aristocrats still dominated local and national affairs from their country palaces and the House of Lords, and were at the peak of their sophistication and splendor; but it was the splendor of approaching sunset. Landholding was no longer the sole hallmark of the wealthy. Iron and coal and steam and cotton textiles were creating a new class of plutocrats who would soon demand political and even social recognition, and who were already challenging the traditional concepts of what economic policy should be. The old cohesiveness of the ruling class was beginning to give way, and a growing tension between landed and industrial magnates presaged a struggle for power that eventuated, a half-century later, in a vast readjustment.

The chief reason why this struggle took another fifty years to work out was Britain's wars against the French Revolution and Napoleon. For the better part of a generation, a continuous military crisis distracted the nation from the need for domestic reform, whether of parliament, the poor law, or trade policy; and the need grew steadily more urgent. Industrialization developed with enormous speed under the pressure of war, but the development was so lopsided that it spawned problems and tensions; when the country emerged from twenty-two years of fighting in 1815, its economy and society were badly askew. The traditional ruling class was unable to find remedies and, after leading the country to victory abroad, went down to defeat before the forces of change at home.

7 The Struggle against the French Revolution

French Revolutionaries and British Liberals

On the afternoon of May 6, 1789, King Louis XVI opened the first session of the French Estates General that had been held in a hundred and seventy-five years. Events thereafter moved rapidly. The *ancien régime* was literally and metaphorically bankrupt, but the nation was not; France had the resources of money, manpower, and ideas to fashion a new order for itself and for much of the continent. By the autumn of 1789 the medieval Estates had been converted into the National Assembly; and Paris, the center of radicalism, had captured from Versailles the legislature and the royal family. Three years later France was a republic; she was at war against Austria and Prussia, had thrown back their armies, and was pouring her own into Savoy, central Germany, and the Low Countries. The Revolution had Europe in its grip.

The British were slow to realize what this upheaval meant. At its start different observers read different things into it: patriots predicted the disintegration of Britain's most dangerous rival; liberals saw the conversion of absolutism into a parliamentary system modeled upon that at Westminster; and both groups looked on in complacent approval. Only the radicals were enthusiastic, for they dreamed that the collapse of one regime of privilege would usher in a new day of freedom for all men. This dream was given enduring expression by the young William Wordsworth, for whom the French were the heroes of humanity:

> a people from the depth
> Of shameful imbecility uprisen,
> Fresh as the morning star. Elate we looked
> Upon their virtues; saw, in rudest men,
> Self-sacrifice the firmest; generous love,
> And continence of mind, and sense of right,
> Uppermost in the midst of fiercest strife. . . .
> Bliss was it in that dawn to be alive,
> But to be young was very Heaven!

The poet was voicing, in his exclamatory way, a sense of human kinship that was widespread among intellectuals of the period. They were interested in the rights of all men, not merely Englishmen or Frenchmen or Germans; and it was this cosmopolitan interest, reflected in the acts and words of the National Assembly, that gave the early phase of the Revolution its appeal outside France. The Assembly spoke of the powers inherent in one particular people, as Thomas Jefferson had spoken earlier in the Declaration of Independence; but both used terms so ultimate that they could apply to every people. The American proclamation of popular sovereignty had been a faint and distant challenge to the privileged orders of Europe; the French proclamation was a trumpet at the gates.

The supranational character of the ideas enunciated by the National Assembly can be seen most clearly by contrasting them with the ideas enunciated by parliament in the Glorious Revolution. The contrast lies in the language of two constitutional documents exactly a hundred years apart, the English Bill of Rights of 1689 and the French Declaration of the Rights of Man and the Citizen of 1789. The Bill of Rights opens with a recitation of past history, then declares illegal certain practices of King James that have violated the "undoubted rights and liberties" of his subjects and of parliament; it then settles the crown upon William and Mary. The document is a terse, prosaic bit of lawmaking, intended to remedy specific grievances of Englishmen and provide for the future of the monarchy, not to theorize about the nature of mankind. The French Declaration, on the other hand, speaks to the world in sweeping terms. "The ignorance, neglect, or contempt of the rights of man," it begins, "are the sole cause of public calamities and of the corruption of governments." Those rights, which are liberty, property, security, and resistance to oppression, belong to all men by virtue of being citizens, and can be limited only by law that is applicable to everyone and is made by the citizens through their representatives; without such law society has no constitution. The Declaration is not primarily legislative, like the Bill of Rights, but a statement of political philosophy that has no limits of time or place.

Wordsworth was not alone in believing that the Revolution was the dawn of universal freedom. Men prominent in many walks of life shared the young poet's enthusiasm. It was widespread among the new industrial leaders, such as James Watt and his partner, Matthew Boulton; Charles James Fox hailed the fall of the Bastille as the greatest and best event in history; Joseph Priestley, a famous chemist and freethinking theologian, wrote to a friend that "I feel myself becoming all French, both in chemistry and politics." Priestley, a nonconformist, detested the established Church of England and consequently applauded the revolutionaries' assault on the French equivalent, the Roman Catholic Church; he believed that "the time is approaching when an end will be put to all usurpation in things civil or religious, first in Europe and then in other countries." Many dissenters shared his views and saw in the Revolution their best hope of full religious emancipation.

In the autumn of 1789 Richard Price, a well-known nonconformist minister, published a sermon in which he adapted the philosophy of the

Declaration of the Rights of Man to the British scene. "A king," he declared, "is no more than the first servant of the public, created by it, maintained by it, and responsible to it. . . . His authority is the authority of the community; and the term *Majesty,* which it is usual to apply to him, is by no means *his own* majesty, but the *Majesty of the People."* King George and those who governed under his aegis derived their power from the people, to whom they were answerable and by whom they could be ousted for misconduct. This was the logic of the Declaration of Independence, of the National Assembly, and, Price believed, of the future: the light of liberty that had first appeared in the freeing of the United States was now "reflected to *France,* and there kindled into a blaze that lays despotism in ashes, and warms and illuminates *Europe!* Tremble, all ye oppressors of the world! . . . Restore to mankind their rights; and consent to the correction of abuses before they and you are destroyed together."

Burke and the New Conservatism

Such fire-breathing made the oligarchs uneasy. Many of them did not know precisely why, because as Whigs they considered themselves friends of liberty; but they were soon given reasons, when Price's sermon evoked an answer from the leading political theorist of the day. Edmund Burke had been strongly opposed to coercing the American colonies, but he refused to agree that the French Revolution was an extension of the American. To his mind France was busily subverting everything on which social order depended, and Price's implication that Britain should follow suit drove him to answer. His rebuttal was more than mere polemic, more even than is suggested by its title, *Reflections on the Revolution in France.* He went beyond reflecting upon a particular revolution to considering the basic questions that it raised about the relationship of the citizen to the state; and his treatise left its mark on all later conservative thinking.

Burke was no slave to the status quo. He recognized the truth of the old adage that times change and we change with them, and he had made his name as a reformer; but he insisted that reform must not be the means of eliminating the good with the bad. He was too much pervaded by a sense of the past to be a revolutionary. The social organism was for him not a thing of the moment, to be reconstituted according to the dictates of abstract philosophy; it was the product of a slow and infinitely complex process of historical development, "a partnership not only between those who are living, but between those who are living, those who are dead, and those who are to be born." The revolutionary would dissolve the partnership and destroy the organism in the hope of creating something better in its place. The French, to take the immediate example, were denying their past for the sake of an untried future, and their faith that reason alone could create utopia struck Burke as madness.

Their watchwords, liberty and equality, left him unmoved. Liberty in itself was no virtue: as he dryly pointed out, if we permit individuals to do as they please "we ought to see what it will please them to do before we risk congratulations. . . ." The liberties of Englishmen were not their abstract rights as members of the human race, but special privileges acquired and passed down to them by their forebears; and these privileges did not include, as Price contended, any right in the people at large to choose or change their governors. As for equality, it was a dangerous myth. In any society some are always at the top, some at the bottom; and those who try to level do not equalize but merely turn the social order topsy-turvy. To give power to the unpropertied masses would turn them against the propertied few in a scramble for spoils, and in the end would give each of them an infinitesimal share in the plunder of the wealthy.

A government subservient to the popular will, as expressed through universal suffrage, would be heading for disaster, Burke argued, because wise public policy cannot be determined by the simple arithmetic of counting votes. "Absolute monarchy is tyranny," Bolingbroke had said a generation earlier, "but absolute democracy is tyranny and anarchy both." Burke would have agreed, for he had no faith in the democratic dogma that the people best know their own interests. They frequently do not, he claimed, and when their will conflicts with their good they must, for their own sake, be restrained by an authority that is independent of them.[1] Otherwise they will use their freedom to destroy themselves. "The restraints on men, as well as their liberties, are to be reckoned among their rights. . . . Men have no right to what is not reasonable, and to what is not for their benefit."

Burke, in other words, attacked the first principle of the Revolution, that sovereignty resides in the entire body of citizens and is expressed in the law that their representatives make. The people may arrogate to themselves the *power* of governing; but, he said, that does not give them the *right* to govern. "Government is a contrivance of human wisdom to provide for human *wants*," and such wisdom comes only from long ages of experience. No man or group of men has a right to flout experience and destroy a constitution that has been centuries in the building, for no one has the sagacity to create a better one from whole cloth. The rationalists argue that they have such sagacity, but their "new conquering empire of light and reason" is an illusion; they misconceive the nature of society and government, and try to apply a logic of human rights that is "the offspring of cold hearts and muddy understandings."

Burke revered history as the medium of divine creation. In his own way he had as deep a religious conviction as Whitefield or the Wesleys; he saw

---

[1] The same question of popular sovereignty posed by the French Revolution had also been to the fore during the Puritan Revolution, and Burke's stand had been foreshadowed by that reluctant revolutionary, Oliver Cromwell. The people were bent on doing as they pleased even if it meant their destruction, Cromwell decided; and his answer was to force upon them "what's for their good, not what pleases them."

in the social order, fashioned through countless generations, the handiwork of God, and regarded those who would jettison it as infidels. The value of man's historical heritage needed to be stressed in a time of revolution. The *Reflections*, it is true, had dangerous seeds, which sprouted in later Toryism into an idolatry of the past, a belief that whatever had stood the test of time was good and that innovation was *ipso facto* bad. But seeds of the future did not concern the conservatives of the 1790s. What mattered to them was that Burke provided an articulate credo with which to defend their threatened world.

By the time this credo appeared in 1790, the upheaval in France was dividing British public opinion. Men were having to examine what they believed and to take a stand on the issue of reform. Many stood with Burke. Others, such as Charles James Fox, insisted that true Whiggism was dedicated to the cause of liberty and that the Revolution, whatever its mistakes and even its crimes, was furthering that cause. These factions were relatively moderate, but on each side of them were extremists. To the right of Burke were the arch conservatives, who identified liberalism with treason. To the left of Fox were radicals, even republicans, who sent addresses and delegations to the National Assembly in Paris and worked to promote French principles at home. The views of one of these Francophiles were thus parodied by a contemporary:

> Whatever is in France is right;
> Terror and blood are my delight;
> Parties with us do not excite
>   Enough rage;
> Our boasted laws I hate and curse,
> Bad from the first, by age grown worse;
> I pant and sigh for univers-
>   Al suffrage.

The most famous of the republicans was Tom Paine. He had already made a name for himself in 1776 by his fiery pamphlet, *Common Sense,* supporting the American Revolution; and he now threw his heart into supporting the French. He answered Burke in 1791 by publishing *The Rights of Man,* a violent and uncompromising attack, in the name of democracy, upon the whole nature of British oligarchical society. The pamphlet was inexpensive as well as provocative and had an enormous circulation — partly subsidized by democratic clubs — among the working classes. The government replied by indicting Paine for seditious libel. He fled to France, where he was elected to the legislature and barely escaped being guillotined, and then ended his days in the United States.

The fear of a popular rising in Britain, which underlay the government's prosecution of Paine, proved to be unfounded. The common people were as much divided as their betters. Agitators wandered the country, preaching that a republic was at hand and that all property would be divided equally; and in some areas mobs responded by rioting against the established order. But in other areas the riots were against reformers, of whom Joseph Priestley was the most prominent victim. His house in Birmingham, with his manuscripts and scientific instruments, was sacked and destroyed; and he too, like Paine, was eventually forced to find refuge in the United States. The old days of embattled factions, of political trials and forced exile, seemed to be returning.

The War in Europe (1793–1797)

For almost four years after the outbreak of the Revolution, Pitt tried to keep peace at home and abroad. He hoped to contain the agitation of domestic radicals without resorting to stringent repression, and to avoid a conflict with France that would undo all the progress he had made in financial retrenchment. But by November 1792 the second hope was fading: French armies had turned back the Austro-Prussian invasion in the previous summer, had overrun the Austrian Netherlands, and were menacing Holland. In Paris the monarchy had given place to a republic and the National Assembly to a new legislature, the Convention, that was increasingly dominated by its most radical element, the Jacobins. The Convention had proclaimed that "France will grant her help to all peoples who desire to recover their liberty." The Jacobins, as the only judges of who these desirous peoples were, could use the proclamation as ground for conquering any part of Europe that they pleased.

Britain was faced by the kind of threat that had aroused her for a century past. Since the days of Marlborough she had fought French expansion into the Low Countries, into Germany, across the Alps; and French armies were no less of a threat under the new tricolor of the Republic than under the Bourbon lilies. Pitt had no desire to fight the Revolution while it remained within the frontiers of France, as Austria and Prussia had done; but no responsible British prime minister could sit by while the French established their hegemony in western Europe. The Convention was launching an idealistic conflict, spiced with the hope of aggrandizement. Whitehall, which cared little about the ideals and a great deal about the aggrandizement, was being drawn into a struggle to defend the old balance of power.

In February 1793 France declared war on Britain, Holland, and Spain, and so added them to a coalition that already included Sardinia, Prussia, and Austria — a ring of enemies that would have done credit to Louis XIV. Their aim, in which even Pitt now acquiesced, was to despoil France of border provinces and overseas colonies, and to reimpose upon her people the regime that they had shaken off. To the Revolution the allies opposed a stark negative, with no hope for the future. They intended to crush French power along with French ideas; if they had succeeded, as Fox said, they would have given "all the kings of Europe a perpetual guarantee against all peoples who might be oppressed by them in any part of the world."

The allies seemed to have every chance of succeeding. The War of the First Coalition, on the face of it, should have crushed the Revolution in its infancy. The bureaucratic and military system of the Bourbons was in ruins; factions in the Convention struggled for power and for their own lives, under the periodic threat of the Paris mob; the royalists of northwestern France were in arms in a counterrevolution. Yet a nation that seemed to be disintegrating won the war with ease. In 1795, when the Jacobin Republic gave place to the bourgeois regime of the Directory, Holland was conquered and Prussia and Spain forced out of the war; only Sardinia, Austria, and Britain continued to fight. In 1796–1797 a young French general from Corsica, Napoleon Bonaparte, eliminated Sardinia and Austria by a whirlwind campaign in the Po Valley. Britain was left alone. France annexed Belgium, turned Holland into a satellite republic, extended her eastern frontier to the Rhine, and dominated northern Italy. What the Bourbons had dreamed of the Directory achieved.

The military force that the Revolution generated in France deserves explanation, or it remains as mysterious as it was to its victims in the war. French armies, first under the Republic and then under the Directory, defied all the rules and went from triumph to triumph; they produced such a military overturn as had never been seen before, and it was only a foretaste of what was to come. Small wonder that contemporaries were bewildered. They could not grasp the fact that a military revolution, growing out of the social revolution within France, was producing a new kind of warfare. Change of such magnitude is seldom fully understood even by those who initiate and profit from it, let alone by those who are beaten and demoralized by it.

The War of the First Coalition was a conflict between two kinds of society, and the contrast between them was mirrored in their armies. Those of the *anciens régimes* were products of a world sharply divided between the privileged and unprivileged: officers were gentleman; common soldiers were mere canaille, creatures to be insulated from contact with civilians, supplied with their needs by the commissariat, and controlled by rigorous discipline.[2] An army in consequence moved and fought under a tight rein, and the premise that its individual soldiers could not be trusted to act on their own affected both tactics and strategy.

This premise disappeared in France as a result of the Revolution. When the Jacobins had to improvise a military system in 1792, they called the country to arms in a *levée en masse,* which was in itself a major act of revolution. It created a new kind of army, which had to fight in a new way if it was to fight at all. The army was huge and was largely composed of recruits who had little training and great enthusiasm. Because these citizen soldiers were numerous and ill trained, they were expendable, for the government could draw on the manpower of the nation to replace them in short order. Because they were enthusiastic, they did not need to be tightly controlled. They

---

[2] For a discussion of eighteenth-century warfare see above, pp. 68–70.

could live off the countryside, through which they foraged on their own; the army therefore did not have to carry many supplies, and moved at a speed that its opponents could not match. Even more important, it had the capacity, which the enemy had not, to exploit a victory to the full. These raw troops were formidable.

The nature of battle changed to match the changed nature of the fighting man. The French opposed mass to specialized training, fervor to discipline, and could afford much heavier losses than the enemy. French soldiers soon learned how to utilize their advantages on the battlefield, flowing around the static lines of regulars, and how to turn their opponents' retreat into a rout. Battle thereupon began to yield them rich dividends. It ceased to be "the remedy of the desperate," and became the means of winning a campaign, a province, an empire. The old days of limited war for limited ends were over; the Jacobin military revolution had opened almost unlimited possibilities of conquest.

These conquests, which began the disintegration of the old order on the continent, staggered the ruling classes in Britain. The oligarchs became so deeply alarmed for their own society that they saw in every critic of the status quo a Francophile conspirator, and their alarm infected the government and the judiciary. Any attempt at change came to be regarded with suspicion; a motion to reform parliament, for example, which had won 174 votes in the House of Commons in 1785, mustered only 41 when it was reintroduced in 1793. Pitt's ministry, reflecting this changed mood in the ruling class, began to adopt repressive measures. Aliens were put under severe restrictions in 1793, and the government was authorized to expel them at its discretion. From 1794 to 1801 habeas corpus was suspended, so that suspects could be — and were — held in prison for years without trial. In 1795 the Treasonable Practices Act broadened the law of treason to cover any writing or utterance that incited to contempt of the sovereign, the authorities, or the constitution. In the same year the Seditious Meetings Act required the license of a magistrate for any gathering of more than fifty persons; this drastic interference with freedom of assembly broke up most of the radical clubs that had been flourishing since 1789. Freedom of the press was as drastically curtailed: cheap newspapers were forced out of business by stamp duties, and printers were held strictly accountable for publishing anything that displeased the government. The rights of the citizen, in short, no longer included the right even to grumble at the established order.

The judges enforced the new legislation with a rigor of their own. They were trained in conservatism, like all the legal fraternity. They also shared the general belief that a conspiracy was afoot to subvert the constitution, of which they considered themselves the guardians, and they rallied to its defense. Whoever preached the necessity of reform, one of them said, was guilty of sedition. Whether or not this was good law was beside the point; what mattered was not how the law read but how it was interpreted from the bench. The government needed only to bring him prisoners, declared a Scottish judge, and he would find the law to hang them. In Scotland this was no idle boast, for the bench selected the members of the jury and instructed them in their findings; against such a system the accused had little protection, and treason was likely to be whatever the court said it was. English jurymen could on occasion be more independent, as they showed in 1794 by acquitting twelve reformers who were being tried together for treason. But this was a rare exception; for the most part the judges stretched the law to serve their purposes, and no one gainsaid them. An extreme example was the trial of some journalists in 1799 for criticizing Russian tariff regulations as detrimental to British trade, at a moment when a Russo-British alliance had just been formed. The astounding charge against the accused was that they had libeled the Russian Czar; if the libel went unpunished, the judge solemnly informed the jury, the Czar might call Britain to account for insulting him. Judge-made law, working in such preposterous ways as this, became a gag for every form of opinion that the government disapproved. "God help the people," said Charles Fox, "who have such judges."

But the people at large feared and hated French Jacobinism so much that they gave little thought to what was happening to their liberties. The panic that gripped the upper classes spread to the rest of the nation and grew, as such hysteria often does, by feeding on its own fancies. Magistrates all over the country were unearthing what they considered proofs of sedition; spies and informers were turning up the lurid titbits that they were paid to find; and a voluntary association of snoopers was gathering "evidence" from the gossiping servant, the disgruntled peasant, the drunken innkeeper, and other similarly reliable sources. Fear of the traitor and the foreign agent was in the air men breathed.

But fear was only one of the factors that united the country behind its government; another was the growing hostility to the Revolution on religious grounds. The Jacobins in Paris were moving not only toward greater radicalism but also toward more and more open atheism, and they were thereby alienating all British Christians; the Methodists in particular, with their vast lower-class membership, were discovering in Jacobinism the figure of Antichrist. The common people had a traditional antipathy to the French, which was now heightened by apprehension and religious antagonism. In the grip of these emotions the masses, restive as they were under the hardships that beset them, followed the lead of their rulers and accepted the idea that only a traitor would want to change the established order. The reform movement, which had been so active before the war, was forced underground for a generation to come.

One man stood out almost alone against official repression. Charles James Fox continued to insist, in the teeth of misrepresentation and obloquy, that the true strength of the nation lay in the citizen's freedom to think and speak and criticize; and he himself showed the way. Year after year he proclaimed in parliament the virtues of the French Revolution and the iniquity of fighting it, and flayed the government with all the power of his oratory. He paid for his courage by political ostracism, but he served his country well. At a time when Pitt was allowing conservatism to become identified with curtailing popular rights, a policy based on fear, Fox kept alive a liberalism based on confidence in the people. The legacy of Pitt's regime was the narrow, ossified Toryism of 1815–1830; the legacy of Fox was the reforming spirit of Whiggism that triumphed in the years after 1830.

Pitt and his colleagues had much reason to be fearful. The ills of industrialization were aggravated by the archaic system of poor relief, and by bad harvests and agrarian unrest. Ireland was in ferment. From Paris and from domestic crackpots came talk of invasion supported by insurrection. The war, above all, was going from bad to worse. The government concluded that drastic measures were needed to save the nation, and the error behind the conclusion is apparent only by hindsight. The British people, for all their grievances, were far from insurrection. Their provincialism insulated them from the ideas of the Revolution, as geography insulated them from its power. They were therefore largely immune to the moral and physical forces that were reshaping the continent, and deserved more trust than their rulers put in them.

The Naval War (1793–1797)

The triumphs of France on land in the War of the First Coalition had no counterpart at sea. The revolution that put new power into the hands of her generals did not help her admirals, for their problem was different in kind. Although they too had numerous and enthusiastic recruits, they could not recreate the old Bourbon navy on revolutionary lines. The reason was simple. The square-rigged ship of the line, which was the mainstay of the fleet, was so complex that her crew needed years of training in discipline and seamanship before she was an effective fighting instrument, let alone a smoothly functioning part of a squadron. A general could soon fashion an army out of inexperienced men and officers promoted from the ranks; an admiral who put to sea with ships so manned was inviting disaster. The factors that made military innovation possible and successful did not apply to war under sail.

From the beginning of hostilities, in consequence, Britain had the wherewithal for naval predominance. The expeditionary forces that she sent to the continent suffered as humiliating defeats as the armies of her allies, and she squandered some 80,000 troops on useless expeditions to the West Indies; but her power at sea was beyond challenge throughout the War of the First Coalition. In 1793 she had half again as many serviceable ships of the line as the enemy, with far better crews; and her naval administration, by comparison with the French, was a model of efficiency. If she had immediately capitalized on her strength to establish a tight blockade, she could probably have brought France to starvation.

Instead she frittered away her chance, and the principal blame lay with the naval command. The senior admirals were an undistinguished lot, most of whom had helped to lose the American war; they were still governed by the notion that a battle should be fought between two parallel lines firing at each other, and such tactics were bound to be inconclusive.[3] The Admiralty had no more idea of how to plan a blockade than it had had in 1778; in winter it recalled its fleets to port to protect them from storms, and permitted the enemy to come and go as they pleased. British naval predominance was consequently used to little purpose while it lasted; and it did not last long.

In 1797, when the collapse of the First Coalition left Britain to fight alone, she faced the same ring of enemies at sea that had nearly ruined her in the War of Independence. France had gained the Dutch navy by conquering Holland and had bullied Spain into alliance; the British, faced by these combined fleets, were forced onto the defensive. They withdrew entirely from the Mediterranean, and even their hold on the Channel was endangered. To add to their troubles came mutiny in their navy and rebellion in Ireland. Their worst crisis in the whole quarter-century of war was in the years 1797-1798, when they were in greater peril than ever again until the dark days of 1940-1941.

They might not have weathered the crisis if the new generation of admirals rising to high command had not contained, at long last, some men of genius. One of the best of the new school was Sir John Jervis, the commander in chief of the fleet that had withdrawn from the Mediterranean. He was a cold, awesome disciplinarian, but he had a fighting spirit. In February 1797 he encountered off Cape St. Vincent, the southwestern tip of Portugal, a large Spanish fleet sailing to join the French and cover an invasion of the British Isles. Jervis, outnumbered by almost two to one, attacked with a confidence that was justified in the event. At the decisive moment of the battle one of his officers, who commanded the smallest ship in the line, left his post without orders and interposed his vessel between the divided segments of the enemy to keep them from uniting; he then boarded and captured two of the huge Spaniards. Jervis acknowledged this bold initiative in his subordinate, who had flouted the time-honored principle of holding the line and had thereby converted an indecisive action into a triumph. London was soon buzzing with the officer's name, Horatio Nelson.

The Battle of Cape St. Vincent shattered the Franco-Spanish plan of invasion, and in the autumn of 1797 a defeat of the Dutch ended the threat from that quarter. But between these two victories the Royal Navy had to meet and surmount a greater danger, which came from within itself. In April mutiny broke out in the Channel Fleet at Portsmouth and soon spread to

---

[3] For a discussion of traditional naval tactics see above, p. 69. The classic study of the British navy during the period covered in this and the following chapter is Alfred T. Mahan, *The Influence of Sea Power upon the French Revolution and Empire* (10th ed., 2 vols., 1898). For more modern accounts, briefer and eminently readable, see William O. Stevens and Allan Westcott, *A History of Sea Power* (1944), chaps. 10-12; and E. B. Potter and Chester W. Nimitz, eds., *Sea Power: A Naval History* (1960), chaps. 6-9.

the squadrons guarding the Thames against the invasion that was then momentarily expected from Holland. For weeks the nation was stripped of its defenses. The spirit of disaffection seemed suddenly to be everywhere, and even the army was suspect.

The mutiny had nothing to do with French revolutionary ideas, but was the spontaneous outburst of men tried beyond endurance. The sailors were the roughest and toughest members of the King's service. Some had been forced into it by the press gangs that roamed port towns in search of likely victims, some by parochial authorities who wanted to be rid of them; some were foreigners, some Irish jailbirds. The great majority were loyal and grumblingly accepted their cramped quarters, abominable food, and ferocious discipline; what they would not accept, and what finally touched off the explosion, was their rate of pay. Wages in the merchant marine had risen, under pressure of demand and of wartime inflation, to four times the naval rate. Although soldiers had recently received a slight raise, sailors were paid what they had been for more than a century, and rarely got even that when it was due. They had families to feed. When wages were in arrears and prices were soaring, the families starved.

The Admiralty had ignored petitions from the Channel Fleet, which on Easter Sunday, 1797, took matters into its own hands. The men pushed their officers politely aside and seized the ships, then waited for the government to redress their grievances. The Admiralty for once acted with speed and good sense: the First Lord hurried to Portsmouth and conceded the substance of the men's demands, subject to parliamentary approval; the crisis seemed to be resolved. But the mutineers' taste of power was intoxicating. Parliament acted too slowly for them, and they again took over the ships; the contagion spread to the fleets at Plymouth, Yarmouth, and the Nore, off the mouth of the Thames. The navy was paralyzed.

When Admiral Duncan sailed from Yarmouth to watch the Dutch coast, all but two of his ships deserted him. With those two the indomitable old man took up his blockading station, and to keep the enemy from attacking him he signaled over the horizon to his nonexistent fleet. For some days his bluff succeeded, until one by one his mutinous ships rejoined him. For the Admiralty had managed to pacify all the malcontents except those at the Nore, where trouble continued for weeks. When supplies to the fleet were cut off, the mutinous sailors retaliated by seizing every ship that tried to enter or leave the Thames. But before long they began to realize the futility of their defiance, which the public regarded as treason, and by the middle of June the last resistance at the Nore fizzled out.

Twenty-nine ringleaders were executed and others variously punished, but the men in general profited from what they had done. They had taught their superiors a salutary lesson, that obedience could not be taken for granted. Sailors were men, and if driven too far they would, like the Frenchmen they despised, assert their rights. The most pressing of their grievances were redressed and the worst abuses remedied. Slowly but surely conditions in the fleet began to improve, and with them morale, until within a few years the Royal Navy was the finest fighting instrument that Britain had ever known.

The Egyptian Expedition (1798)

In the spring of 1798 all signs pointed to an imminent French invasion of England, the one unconquered enemy. General Bonaparte, fresh from his triumphs in Italy, commanded an army massed on the Channel coast of France, where the ports were bustling with preparation. Pitt called the people to arms, and thousands of volunteers responded; plans were made for laying waste the countryside and fortifying every tenable point. "The nation had not yet learnt to know its own strength or its resources," wrote a foreign observer. "The government has taught it the secret and inspired it with an unbounded confidence almost amounting to presumption." [4] Presumption indeed it was, for yeomanry armed with fowling pieces would have been no match for Bonaparte's veterans.

But the Corsican had no idea of attempting invasion, which he knew would be suicidal as long as the Royal Navy held the Channel. His preparations were disguise for a quite different plan, to attack Egypt. He intended to open the Mediterranean and Near East to French influence, cut the British route to India by way of Suez, and perhaps eventually move against India itself. The Directory supported him with an enthusiasm born of self-interest: his success would bring wealth and glory to a shaky regime, and his failure would rid it of a general who was too popular for comfort. In May, Bonaparte sailed from Toulon for Alexandria.

His Egyptian expedition was the first sign that his genius, dazzling as it was, had a serious limitation. No leader in history had greater gifts for commanding an army or organizing and administering a state; but he was inferior to many of his pedestrian contemporaries in his understanding of sea power. He understood it well enough to foresee, in the spring of 1798, that landing in Britain would be disastrous, and not well enough to foresee that landing in Egypt would be equally so. He expected to establish on the Nile a base of operations against the Near East or India. The base itself did not offer resources for such operations, which therefore would depend on water-borne communications with Europe; if those communications were cut, his army would sooner or later be imprisoned between sea and desert. He was acting on the assumption that Britain would not or could not regain control of the Mediterranean, and the assumption was fallacious.

[4] Quoted by Arthur Bryant, *The Years of Endurance, 1793–1802* (1942), p. 228. This is a vivid and lively account of the first phase of the war. See also W. T. Laprade, *England and the French Revolution* (1904). One of the best recent histories of the whole period is the sequel to Dorothy Marshall's *Eighteenth Century England* in the ten-volume *History of England* edited by W. N. Medlicott: Asa Briggs, *The Age of Improvement* (1959), which covers the years 1783–1867.

Pitt had begun to demonstrate the fallacy before he knew of the French design. He realized that Britain could not make headway alone and that her best chance of creating a new coalition lay in reasserting her naval power in the Mediterranean. He had consequently weakened the fleet at home, despite the threat of invasion, in order to reinforce the squadron at Gibraltar under Admiral Jervis — now Lord St. Vincent in honor of his victory — and permit him to reenter the inland sea. St. Vincent thereupon sent most of his battle line to join Nelson, who was cruising off Toulon to observe the French preparations. The Royal Navy was resuming a blockade in force.

On May 19 Bonaparte sailed from Toulon, convoyed by thirteen ships of the line. On June 6 Nelson, joined by his reinforcement, set off in pursuit with thirteen of the line and one heavy frigate, but without light frigates for scouting. On June 22 he learned that the French had captured Malta from the Knights of St. John, who had long possessed it, and had then sailed eastward; he guessed that their destination was Egypt, and in a fever of impatience set sail to overtake them. The future of the war hinged on whether he succeeded. The supreme naval figure of the age was hunting the supreme military figure, and an encounter at sea could have had only one outcome: Bonaparte's career would have ended then and there.

On the night of the 22nd Nelson passed the French fleet in the darkness. The enemy heard his signal guns and made off, and by sunrise were safe over the horizon. He soon outdistanced them and, on reaching Alexandria, found to his chagrin no sign or rumor of them. Immediately he left to hunt along the Syrian coast. As Egyptian observers watched his sails disappear over the eastern horizon, they saw other sails rise from the sea to the west. Bonaparte was arriving; sheer luck had saved him for his future.

He landed his army, crushed native resistance, and was soon secure in the mastery of Egypt; but his fleet was far from secure. The coast offered it no refuge, no fortified harbor like that of Toulon; and Nelson was hunting blindly but indefatigably. He had no more idea of the enemy's whereabouts after a month of cruising than he had had at the start; "the Devil's children," he said, "have the Devil's luck!" He beat back westward to Sicily, turned east again, and on July 28 learned that the French had gone to Egypt after all. Once more he pressed for Alexandria. His captains knew what was expected of them, because he had used the long days at sea to talk with them until they shared his way of thinking. He was a master of teamwork, and he had trained his team — what he called his band of brothers — to cooperate by instinct.

On the afternoon of August 1 the fleet sighted the enemy ships moored in Aboukir Bay, near one of the mouths of the Nile to the east of Alexandria. The French Admiral had anchored in line ahead, facing the mouth of the bay; shoal water to port seemed to preclude attack from that side, and only the starboard batteries were cleared for action. The wind blew from the sea, and the British ran before it as they bore down on the enemy van. Their tension was at fever pitch. They knew that their chief was determined on victory at any cost. "If we succeed," asked one of his captains, "what will the world say?" "There is no *if* in the case," Nelson answered. "That we shall succeed is certain; who will live to tell the story is a very different question."

The only way to complete success, when the enemy had almost as many ships as the British and larger ones, was to concentrate in full force on one part of the French line after another. Nelson gambled on there being enough room to pass between the line and the shoals without running aground; his five leading ships got through, by superb seamanship, and anchored on the west side of the van while the rest of the fleet assaulted the other side. Darkness fell, and the battle raged on. Nelson himself was dazed and disabled by a flying splinter, but his captains knew their job. The French were caught between two fires and could reply to only one because their port batteries were useless. Their ships in the van surrendered one by one; the attack moved on to the center, where their huge flagship caught fire and blew up, with a glare that lighted the bay and a shock felt for ten miles. All night the cannonading waxed and waned, until both sides were too exhausted to man the guns. At dawn two enemy ships at the rear of the line slipped their anchors and escaped to sea, the lone survivors of thirteen. No conflict between fleets of comparable strength had ever before produced such an overwhelming victory.

It was epochal because it revealed a new approach to naval war. Even Jervis had broken off action at Cape St. Vincent while the enemy still had a substantial fleet intact. This Nelson would not do. His aim was to destroy every ship that he could reach, and he pursued this aim with whole-souled concentration, undeterred by fear of damage to his ships, of casualties in his crews, of wounds or death for himself; the kind of victory that he sought justified all losses. His goal, like Bonaparte's, was a battle of annihilation; and at the Nile he achieved it.

The results were far-reaching. The Corsican and his army were cooped up in Egypt, the prisoners of his miscalculation. In the spring of 1799 he tried to break out by moving into Syria to attack the Turks, who had declared war on him; he dreamed of emulating Alexander the Great by conquering the Near East and advancing from there against India, or of moving on Constantinople and taking Europe in the rear. These grandiose fancies evaporated before the city of Acre, when a small British squadron captured his siege artillery and landed it to strengthen the Turkish garrison. The French were repulsed, the invasion collapsed, and Bonaparte fell back on Egypt. For the first time in his career he had, thanks to sea power, met defeat.

In August 1799 he and his staff sailed for home in two frigates. He evaded British cruisers and in early October landed in France, where he was received as a savior. His skillful propaganda had magnified his triumphs and concealed his underlying failure, whereas the failure of the Directory at home was all too apparent. In November he overthrew it and established the Consulate, with himself as first consul; and where he was first no one else was

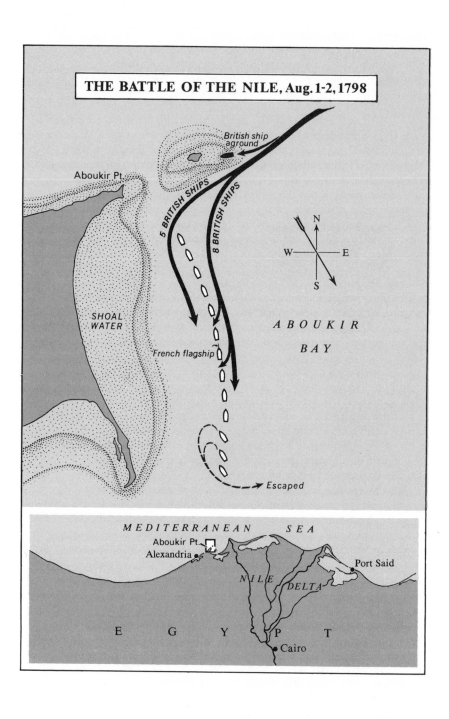

THE BATTLE OF THE NILE, Aug. 1-2, 1798

British ship aground

Aboukir Pt.

5 BRITISH SHIPS

8 BRITISH SHIPS

N

W E

S

SHOAL WATER

ABOUKIR BAY

French flagship

Escaped

MEDITERRANEAN SEA

Aboukir Pt.
Alexandria

Port Said

NILE DELTA

E G Y P T

Cairo

second. The Revolution had come full circle. It had destroyed a decrepit absolutism only to create in its stead an efficient one, a military dictatorship.

The War of the Second Coalition (1799–1801)

The Egyptian expedition impressed the French people, thanks to Bonaparte's publicity, but did not impress Europe. The powers saw in it the long-awaited sign that France had overreached herself. Her ambitions were clearly insatiable: she had occupied Switzerland and the Papal States before Bonaparte's departure for Alexandria, and had mulcted them to pay for his expedition; she had seized Malta from the Knights of St. John, whom Czar Paul, the half-insane Russian autocrat, regarded as his particular protégés; she was infiltrating the German states and the Kingdom of the Two Sicilies, the feeble Bourbon power in southern Italy. She was undermining the political structure of the continent, and only proof of her weakness was needed to rekindle armed opposition.

The Battle of the Nile was staggering proof. In its aftermath the French position in the Mediterranean began to collapse. The British seized Minorca, which they had lost in 1783, and so regained their base for blockading Toulon; their troops strengthened the fragile Bourbon hold on Sicily; their fleet encouraged a revolt on Malta and blockaded its French conquerors. This reversal of fortune persuaded Austria and Russia that the time had finally come to overthrow the Revolution, and by the spring of 1799 they were allied with Britain in the Second Coalition.

At first the allies swept everything before them. A Cossack general, Suvorov, stormed through Italy; the Austrians defeated the armies of the Directory in Switzerland and Germany; a French fleet that had ventured into the Mediterranean retreated ignominiously; rebellion again broke out in western France; an Anglo-Russian expeditionary force invaded Holland. In that summer of 1799, when Bonaparte was still in Egypt, the French empire was tottering. A concerted push might well have brought it down, but the allies lost their opportunity by bickering among themselves. The novel participation of Russia in the war was an incalculable factor, made all the more so by the Czar's eccentricity. The eruption of Suvorov into Italy disturbed the Austrians, who had no desire to see the peninsula pass from French to Russian dominance; they were glad when he was transferred to Switzerland, and they failed to support him there. Anglo-Russian cooperation in Holland was little better, and the expedition failed dismally. By autumn the French had suppressed rebellion at home and regained control of Holland, Switzerland, and western Germany. The Austrians held Italy, but at the price of infuriating Czar Paul. In the autumn he withdrew from the war, just as Bonaparte was seizing the reins in Paris.

The next two years were disastrous for Britain. The First Consul justified his coup d'état to the French people by dealing promptly with Austria, in a campaign that broke her grip on Italy and forced her, in February 1801, to make peace. Meanwhile Bonaparte had courted and won the favor of the mercurial Czar, who was persuaded to turn against Britain and put an embargo on her ships; Russia also joined Sweden, Denmark, and Prussia in a new League of Armed Neutrality, like that of 1780, to enforce its members' right to trade as they pleased. This defiance of Britain's blockade revealed how low her stock had fallen. Her allies had deserted her; her navy had done nothing of moment since the Battle of the Nile except force the surrender of Malta; her troops had been ferried around the coasts of Europe on a series of pointless and fruitless expeditions. The strategy of Whitehall was as its nadir.

But the main instrument of strategy, the fleet, was stronger than ever before. Between 1795 and 1800 it made ready for its central task of blockade by conquering what had hitherto been its most lethal enemy. This was not the French but scurvy. The disease is caused by a deficiency of vitamin C, found in fresh fruits and vegetables, both of which were lacking in the sailor's diet; prolonged cruising without some source of vitamins had always meant that scurvy would decimate the crew. Although nothing was known about vitamins, since the early seventeenth century lemon juice had been recognized as an anti-scorbutic, or corrective of scurvy; and during the War of the Austrian Succession a way had been found to concentrate and preserve the juice. Not until 1795, however, did the Admiralty order a regular issue of this remedy throughout the fleet. The effect within the next five years was virtually to eliminate the disease in the navy. Crews might remain healthy at sea for indefinite periods; the ships of a blockading squadron no longer needed to be replaced in alternation by ships fresh from home, but could hold their station month after month. The result was an enormous increment in naval power.

The navy had also learned the techniques of effective blockade. They were extremely arduous, but Lord St. Vincent, now in command of the Channel Fleet, enforced them with a ruthless disregard for wear and tear on ships or men. He cruised in all weather and seasons off the western approaches to the Channel, where he was in touch by frigate with smaller squadrons masking the exits from Brest; if the enemy dared to come out, one of these detachments would summon help from the main fleet. The enemy did not dare. Their ships of the line were penned into the roadstead of Brest like helpless sheep, and the First Consul's repeated orders to put to sea were not obeyed. He was having his second lesson in the uses of sea power.

By the spring of 1801 he had a plan for circumventing that power through the League of Armed Neutrality. If the Baltic states combined their navies against Britain, they would be enough of a threat so that the Channel Fleet, to meet it, would have to relax its stranglehold on Brest. But Whitehall had no intention of waiting passively for this plan to mature. The keystone of the neutral coalition was Denmark, and Pitt resolved to demonstrate to the Danes, and so to their would-be allies, the futility of their designs. He prepared in great secrecy to deliver an ultimatum to Copenhagen, backed by what Nelson called "the best negotiators in Europe," twenty ships of the line.

The Admiralty, with the obtuseness it often showed in choosing men, entrusted the mission to an incompetent old admiral, Sir Hyde Parker, but had the good sense to name Baron Nelson of the Nile as his second in command. Nelson had done almost nothing since his victory except acquire a glamorous mistress. He had returned home with her and her complaisant husband, and had broken with his own wife and been snubbed by the King; his career seemed to be over. But in a crisis the Admiralty wanted his talents, whatever the shortcomings of his private life, and gave him a second chance.

The Danes rejected the ultimatum. The only way to coerce them was to destroy their fleet, moored in Copenhagen harbor under strong shore defenses; and Parker was most reluctant to do so. To conquer the enemy Nelson had first to conquer his superior; this he did, and received permission to attack as he pleased. But in the middle of the battle Parker, watching from a distance, lost his nerve and signaled the ships to retire. They could not have done so if they would, and Nelson would not. He put his telescope to his blind eye and said that he saw no signal. His coy disobedience might have earned him a court-martial; instead, after he had battered and bluffed the Danes into submission, he superseded Parker and sailed to negotiate with the Russians. Czar Paul had been assassinated. His successor, Alexander I, agreed to reopen his ports to British trade and admit the Royal Navy's right of search.

The League of Armed Neutrality had dissolved at the touch of force, and Britain had made clear that she could at will control the Baltic. Meanwhile she had reemphasized her control of the Mediterranean by landing an army in Egypt to begin the reduction of the French garrison there. The long arm of her sea power now reached around Europe from the Gulf of Finland to the mouth of the Nile. Although she was once more alone and France was stronger than ever before, the effective limit of French ambitions was the water's edge.

The Irish Crisis (1797–1801)

Pitt was no longer in power by the time the operations that he had planned in the Baltic and Egypt came to fruition. He had been unseated, after having been in office almost eighteen years, by a complex of developments growing out of the Irish problem. He had tried and failed to deal with that problem in time of peace, and almost inevitably it returned to plague him in time of war. The pattern has been repeated over and over in British history, from the days of Elizabeth I to the days of Lloyd George: Irish grievances have gone unredressed until Britain has entered into a conflict at home or abroad, when the Irish have seized their opportunity for making trouble. They revolted against Elizabeth during her war with Spain. They revolted against Charles I on the eve of civil war in England, and went on fighting until Cromwell crushed them. They rose in the cause of James II as King William was beginning his struggle with France, and again were crushed. They threatened revolt when Britain had her back to the wall in the War of Independence, and this time succeeded in winning both economic and political concessions. But they were far from satisfied, and in the 1790s the story was once more repeated.

The legislative "independence" they had acquired in 1782 was proving illusory. Even by British standards the Irish parliament was corrupt, and it represented only the small Anglican minority; neither the Presbyterians of Ulster nor the Roman Catholics of the south were allowed to vote. The executive, drawn from the core of the Anglican group and ruling from Dublin Castle, was appointed by and dependent on the British government, and was adept at manipulating a legislature to which it had no constitutional responsibility. That legislature was no more than an empty symbol of nationhood. Real power remained where it had always been, in the hands of a small Anglo-Irish clique that bitterly opposed any concessions to the majority.

The French Revolution brought discontent to a head. Presbyterians and Catholics alike were soon agitating for reform, and the fact that they could agree on anything was ominous; their hatred of each other had long been one of the chief factors in maintaining British ascendancy. Now that they were drawing together, Pitt decided to conciliate one of them. In 1793 he secured Roman Catholics the right to vote for members of the Dublin parliament. But he failed to secure them the right to be members themselves, for the bogey of a legislature dominated by Catholics terrified all shades of Protestant opinion. And he did nothing to conciliate the radicals of Ulster, who were soon arming themselves and drilling against the day of deliverance.

The source of deliverance was obvious. For some time past, Irish emissaries had been assuring the government in Paris that Ireland, if given a stiffening of French troops, would chase the British into the sea. At the end of 1796 a strong French expedition sailed from Brest, eluded the fumbling British blockade, and appeared off the Irish coast. A storm prevented the troops from landing, but their coming at all stirred wild excitement in Ulster, which by the spring of 1797 was ripe for revolt. The Dublin government acted with the brutality of panic. Troops, largely Protestant militia, were sent to disarm the province; and what little discipline the soldiers had soon vanished in an orgy of looting and burning and killing. The principal victims were Catholics, who were intermingled with the Presbyterians; refugees, with their tales of rapine, fled in thousands to the south. The harrying of Ulster had crushed disaffection there, and ended the dream of a united Ireland; but it rekindled the religious furies of a hundred years before. The Orange and the Green, Protestant and Catholic, were at each other's throats as they had been on the Boyne. By the spring of 1798 Catholic Ireland was seething and, like Ulster the year before, looking to France for deliverance.

Again deliverance did not come. Pitt had weakened the fleet guarding the coast in order to send reinforcements to the Mediterranean; when he heard of Bonaparte's departure from Toulon he assumed that the enemy were bound for Ireland, where at the moment the southeastern counties were at the mercy of 30,000 peasants, bent on loot and massacre. But the French sailed instead for Egypt, while the British poured troops into Ireland and savagely suppressed the rising; a few French soldiers did land during the summer and autumn, but they were promptly rounded up. Whether the Directory could have exploited the crisis is an open question, like all historical might-have-beens. The stakes were high: landing an army in Ireland would have been hazardous in the face of the Royal Navy, but would also have been a knife in Britain's back, whereas landing in Egypt turned out to be a blow in the air. France first encouraged the Irish and then left them to their fate.

By the late summer of 1798 Ireland was again a conquered nation. The Dublin clique had destroyed the fragile union of Protestants and Catholics, had then provoked the latter to revolt, and had crushed them with almost the brutality of Cromwell's Ironsides. Dublin had only one policy, to repress, and considered voices of moderation as treasonable. But this narrow, frightened executive had at last overreached itself. Pitt was no Cromwell; he would not govern through an army of occupation, and in any case he could not afford one during a European war. He was determined upon a more lasting solution, which meant one that would be acceptable to Catholic Ireland — and therefore unacceptable to Dublin Castle. His worst troubles were beginning.

He had a solution in two parts, which were integrally connected. One was a political union of Ireland and Great Britain, akin to the union of England and Scotland in 1707, with a single parliament in which the Irish would have proportional representation. The other was Catholic emancipation, in other words the admission of Roman Catholics to the newly enlarged Westminster parliament. They could not feasibly be admitted to the existing Dublin parliament, as he had discovered, because the Protestant interest feared their domination. At Westminster they would be a small and unthreatening minority in a legislature overwhelmingly Protestant, but they would have a voice in government. The scheme had great advantages for both sides. The Irish would for the first time have members of parliament of their own choosing, commercial barriers between the two countries would disappear, and the British would be rid of a governmental system that was artificial, antiquated, and unworkable. But the scheme could succeed only as a whole. Neither half by itself was viable: Protestant Ireland would never accept emancipation without union, and Catholic Ireland would never accept union without emancipation.

Pitt, with his orderly mind, decided to tackle the two halves of his problem separately, and achieve first legislative union and then Catholic emancipation. Union met little resistance in Britain but much in Ireland, where the Dublin parliament was understandably reluctant to pass an act that would end its own existence. Pitt's Irish agents resorted to a campaign of corruption such as the eighteenth century had never witnessed, buying votes with peerages, honors, and simple bribes. Meanwhile the cabinet agreed informally to emancipation, and the Prime Minister's assurances of it won Irish Catholic support for union. In the summer of 1800 both parliaments passed the Act of Union, which went into effect at the beginning of 1801. Twenty-eight Irish peers, elected for life, and four Irish bishops took their places in the British House of Lords, and a hundred Irish members in the House of Commons.[5] Virtual free trade was established between the two countries, along the lines that Pitt had tried and abandoned in 1785. The cross of St. Patrick was superimposed upon those of St. George and St. Andrew to form a new flag, the Union Jack, symbolizing the United Kingdom of Great Britain and Ireland.

The symbolism was hollow. The kingdom had not been united by the voluntary agreement of two nations acting through their representatives, as England and Scotland had been, but by the British government's imposing its will on a parliament that did not represent either Protestant or Catholic Ireland. Pitt had achieved a settlement with the only means at hand, unsavory as they were; and nothing but success could make men forget the corruption out of which union had been born. Success, furthermore, was problematical. The Prime Minister had won only half a victory, and that by itself was not enough. Because Ireland could not be saved without union, one of his lieutenants remarked, "you must not take it for granted that it will be saved by it."

Pitt had not laid the groundwork for completing his victory. He had no binding pledge from his colleagues to support Catholic emancipation, and on this crucial point he had failed to convince the King. The blunder proved to be irretrievable. Supporters of the old order in Dublin and London were adamant against any concession to Catholics, and they could always appeal to the bigotry latent in the British electorate. But it turned out that they had no need to; they appealed instead to the bigot on the throne. George III, at his coronation, had taken an archaic oath to uphold the supremacy of the established Anglican Church; and he believed, as he had long since made clear to Pitt, that permitting Catholics in parliament would violate that oath. "I shall reckon any man my personal enemy," he said, "who proposes any such measure." He was in an excitable frame of mind, which threatened to lapse into the insanity that had already attacked him twice during his reign. But, if his mental balance was unreliable, his conscience was not.

For the last time the King's stubbornness produced a major crisis. The tradition of ministerial loyalty to the sovereign was still strong, and

[5] The act allowed an Irish peer, if not elected by his fellow peers to the House of Lords, to stand for election to the House of Commons from a British constituency. This provision accounts for the continuance of titled Irish members in the lower house, some of whom, such as Lord Palmerston, played prominent roles in nineteenth-century politics.

George had reigned so long that by now he himself was a tradition; in the face of his stand the cabinet refused to press for emancipation. Pitt was in a dilemma that had no good solution. Fulfilling the assurances that he had given the Irish Catholics was impossible; repudiating them was dishonorable. He chose the only course that preserved a shred of honor, and offered his resignation. The King, who hated to part with the man who had so long been his mainstay, reluctantly accepted the resignation; but before it could take effect George went out of his mind and was near death. He recovered, and when he informed Pitt of his return to health he added a reproach typical of his egoism: "what has he not to answer for who is the cause of my having been ill at all?" In response Pitt promised that never again while his sovereign lived would he reopen the Catholic question. Then he left office.

He had staked his ministry on an equitable solution to the Irish problem, and he had lost. The Act of Union could not satisfy the Irish. They had surrendered the symbol of their own parliament in order to be governed from London, on the understanding that they would be represented in that government; and what they were left with was a travesty of representation. The men who ostensibly guarded their interests in Westminster, the Irish members of the new House of Commons, were part of the same Protestant clique that had misgoverned Ireland into rebellion in 1798. To the old grievances that had produced rebellion was now added a sense of betrayal, of having been hoodwinked into union on false pretenses.

The Irish detested their new status, and went on detesting it for almost thirty years until, with the threat of a new rebellion, they forced emancipation. By then the harm had been done, for they had come to look on union as a British contrivance. What Pitt intended as part of a larger reconciliation became a mere political bond, which galled the Irish more and more as time wore on. Under a different king the problem might have been settled at the beginning of the nineteenth century; instead it grew for more than a hundred years, and in the end brought the United Kingdom to the verge of civil war. This was the price paid for George III's conscience.

The Peace of Amiens (1802)

Pitt's resignation came at a time when the country's will to fight was at low ebb. Twice Britain had joined in coalitions to stop French aggrandizement, and twice had seen them destroyed; now she was on her own and could no more hope for victory on land than France could at sea. After eight years of war the burden of her national debt was staggering; it had more than doubled since 1793, and stood at over £530 million. Prices were rising far faster than wages, so that by 1800 farm laborers, for example, were receiving in real wages less than half of what they had at the start of the war; in some villages mobs threatened to hang farmers who would not cut the price of their grain. Trade and industry, it is true, were booming; between 1796 and

1800 the value of British exports and imports increased by £12 million. But the spread of machinery in the manufacturing areas was throwing manual laborers out of work and creating bitter discontent, which was further heightened by a succession of calamitously bad harvests. Continuing the war seemed pointless, when rich and poor alike were longing to be free from the burden of what promised to be an interminable conflict. Their views were summed up by an admiral in the blockading squadron off Brest, who wrote that "nothing good can ever happen to us short of peace."

If Pitt had remained in office he might have opened peace negotiations, but he would not have conducted them as his successor did. The new Prime Minister, Henry Addington, was an amiable nonentity unversed in foreign affairs; and he had the gentleman's illusion that Bonaparte would behave like a gentleman. All began smoothly. The First Consul was ready to negotiate; he needed a breathing space to consolidate his position at home, to organize France's conquests and satellite states, and to create an effective navy. But his need did not make him easy to deal with. First he bullied Whitehall into an armistice that removed the pressure of blockade; then he haggled over terms for months, using bluff, threat, and deception, and ended by driving a hard bargain. In March 1802 the treaty of peace was signed at Amiens.

The British people went wild with rejoicing, but they had little to rejoice about. The government had returned virtually everything conquered overseas to France and her satellites, Holland and Spain; it had agreed to restore Malta to the Knights of St. John under a flimsy international guarantee, and to evacuate both British and French troops from Egypt; and it had done nothing to secure British trade with Europe. Most humiliating of all, Whitehall had accepted the First Consul's haughty insistence that the affairs of Germany, Switzerland, and Italy were not subject to negotiation; in those areas he considered his will to be sovereign. For him the peace was a substantial triumph, short-lived as it proved to be. He ceded nothing of moment, marked out western Europe as his preserve, and regained access to the world overseas. The French people hailed this success by making him First Consul for life, and he now began to call himself Napoleon.

The Peace of Amiens marked the end of an era during which Britain had been groping for security. She had entered the war in 1793 with little idea of how her armed forces should be used, with public opinion deeply divided, and with no overriding purpose to steel her will. Pitt had hoped that, after a quick victory, she would rearrange the affairs of the continent to her liking. When the hope had faded, he had made abortive efforts to negotiate peace with the Directory; and he favored renewing the negotiations with Bonaparte. The war was for Pitt not ideological but essentially defensive, to curb the expansion of France rather than destroy her as a power or undo the Revolution; and the British public, by and large, took a similar view.

But over the years Pitt had come to see, more clearly than many of his contemporaries, the scale of the threat inherent in French aggression.

Shortly before his resignation he was asked in parliament to define his war aims without the qualification of any *but*'s or *if*'s. "In one word," he answered, "security, security against a danger the greatest that ever threatened the world. . . . Peace is most desirable to this country. *But* negotiation may be attended with greater evils than could be counterbalanced by any benefits which would result from it. And *if* it afford no prospect of security, *if* it threaten all the evils which we have been struggling to avert, *if* the prosecution of the war afford the prospect of attaining complete security, then I say that it is prudent for us not to negotiate. These are my *but*'s and my *if*'s. This is my plea, and on no other do I wish to be tried by God and my country." [6]

The Peace of Amiens did not make Britain secure, for Napoleon had no intention that she should be; instead it ended her hope of finding security as long as he ruled western Europe. For her the uncertain phase of the war, with its periodic gropings for a settlement, was drawing to a close. During that phase she had slowly and painfully learned how to use her strength, particularly her sea power, but had not recognized the need to fight through to final victory. In the second phase, which opened in 1803 and lasted with one brief intermission until 1815, there was an early, abortive attempt to negotiate peace; but thereafter the nation settled down to the job of destroying the French empire, whatever the effort might cost and however long it might take.

This later phase, like the previous one, was replete with military stupidity, bright chances lost, allies defeated; but in it the British harnessed their power as never before and exerted it with more and more effect. When Napoleon rejected his opportunity to make a lasting peace with them, he evoked a force that contributed, perhaps more than any other, to driving him step by step down a long road. The road led from Paris to Moscow to Leipzig to Elba, and from Elba to Waterloo and St. Helena.

[6] Winston Churchill, just after he became prime minister in May 1940 at the start of Britain's great crisis in the Second World War, dealt with the same question of war aim; and his words bore a striking resemblance to Pitt's. "You ask, what is our policy? I will say: it is to wage war . . . against a monstrous tyranny, never surpassed in the dark, lamentable catalogue of human crime. That is our policy. You ask, what is our aim? I can answer in one word: it is victory — victory at all costs, victory in spite of all terror, victory however long and hard the road may be; for without victory there is no survival." Walter L. Arnstein, *Britain Yesterday and Today: 1830 to the Present.*

8 The Napoleonic Wars

The Renewal of Hostilities (1802–1803)

The Peace of Amiens had much in common with the Munich settlement that the British reached with Hitler in 1938. In both cases the dictator, whether French or German, had no intention of keeping faith or desire for a lasting accord, but was playing for time to prepare further agression. The British public, by accepting the offer of peace at face value, exerted pressure on the government to come to terms; and the government acted in the hope, though not in the conviction, that real peace could be bought at the price of concessions. The year that followed the settlement put an end to hope, roused anger instead, and so kindled in the nation a will to fight that had been lacking.

Napoleon, like Hitler after Munich, soon showed his hand. He drastically restricted British trade with his dominions, tightened his control of Holland and Italy, made Switzerland into a satellite, sent French agents to stir up trouble in India and Ireland and even to survey British ports, renewed his active concern with Egypt, and brushed aside all protests as impertinent. Addington's government, by the standards of traditional diplomacy, might claim compensation for the increase of French power in Europe; and the First Consul's continuing interest in Egypt meant that a British naval base in the Mediterranean was vital. Addington decided that Britain would compensate herself, despite the terms of the Treaty of Amiens, by holding onto Malta. Napoleon was furious. "Woe to those who do not respect treaties," he burst out at the British Ambassador. "They shall answer for it to all Europe." For his own actions, presumably, he saw no need to answer.

He spurned several last-minute efforts to compromise the quarrel, and in May 1803 the British government renewed the war. The First Consul's high-handedness had defeated his own ends. He wanted peace in order to prepare for more effective war, particularly at sea, and had ordered a fifty percent increase in ships of the line. With the shipyards of the Low Countries, France, and northern Italy at his command, he might have had this great increment within another year or two. Instead he provoked the British before he was ready, and they promptly reestablished a blockade that he was powerless to break. His naval plans evaporated, and with them his dreams of

reconquering Egypt and moving against India, and even his hope of
retaining a colonial empire.

The renewal of the war had an immediate impact upon the United
States. In 1800 France had regained, by a treaty with Spain, the territory of
Louisiana that she had ceded in 1763; this vast tract had indeterminate
frontiers, but it stretched from the Mississippi to the Rockies and from the
Gulf of Mexico to Canada. The prospect of its passing from the frail hands of
Spain into the grip of the First Consul roused angry excitement in America.
Napoleon realized that he could not reassert French control without war
against the United States, and that he could not fight such a war if the
British closed the Atlantic to him; their navy insulated the young republic
from his power. As soon as he understood that Whitehall was about to
renew the struggle, he concluded that Louisiana was as worthless to him as
it was valuable to the Americans, and offered to sell it to them for $15 million;
in May 1803, just when London declared war, the transaction was completed.
Thus the United States, with the quite inadvertent help of the British government and navy, almost doubled its territory.

The War at Sea (1803–1805)

Napoleon was as thoroughly resolved to destroy Britain as the
British were to destroy his empire, and he had only one sure way to do so — to
invade. The prerequisite was the same for him as it had been for the
Spaniards in 1588, to secure control of the Channel. Unless he had control,
invasion was out of the question. A few regiments might get across under
cover of night or fog, or by rowboats in a calm that immobilized sailing
ships; but his troops when landed could not be supplied. To supply them he
had to concentrate in the Channel a fleet strong enought to beat back whatever
the British brought against it and to keep position until the invaders had
crushed resistance ashore. Here the Spanish Armada had failed, but Napoleon
was not accustomed to failing. He was approaching the zenith of his career, for
in 1804 he had himself made Emperor of the French; and his one sure way to
secure his empire was by breaking the islanders' will to fight.

While awaiting his chance for a naval concentration, he prepared
small craft and drilled the soldiers that they were to carry. The shipyards of
western Europe were mobilized, and turned out a flotilla of some two
thousand flat-bottomed boats, propelled by sail and oar, to ferry the elite of the
French army across thirty-odd miles of water from Boulogne to the beaches of
Kent. As the boats were completed they moved, under protection of shore
batteries, to the points of concentration near Boulogne. There Napoleon had
massed 100,000 men, and he trained them month after month until they
became as superb a fighting force as any general ever commanded; this was the
Grande Armée with which the Emperor subsequently overawed the continent.

But that army, fine as it was, could not march on the water, or be carried in boats until the French navy mastered the Channel.

Mastery for six hours, Napoleon said, would make him master of the world. But he presumably knew that this was grandiloquent nonsense, for by the spring of 1804 he faced formidable British defenses on land as well as at sea. Addington was no man for the crisis, which swept Pitt back into office; and he quickly saw to it that the country was prepared. Light vessels and fortifications protected the coast; Regulars and militia numbered 180,000, and in reserve were 400,000 volunteers armed with a variety of crude weapons. The southeastern counties were denuded of any supplies that invaders might use, and plans were made for defending the Midlands if London fell. The island was a tough nut to crack, and Napoleon could not have cracked it without weeks of undisputed naval control. British admirals knew that such control was impossible. They had finally learned the business of blockade, after years of fumbling; and they held the enemy in a grip that could not be broken for long.

But the newly crowned Emperor was determined to try. He had naval forces for his purpose that were superficially imposing: Spain had recently joined France in the war; and the Dutch, Spanish, and French fleets, if they could combine, were roughly equal to the British in numbers though in nothing else. Combining them all was out of the question, for they were scattered in ports from the North Sea to the Mediterranean. Concentrating even a substantial part of them in the Channel would be difficult — and pointless as well unless the British fleet could somehow be removed from the scene.

In the spring of 1805, when the final campaign opened, the disposition of forces was that shown on the map. The main French fleet, twenty-one ships of the line, was cooped up in Brest by Admiral Cornwallis, cruising in the western approaches to the Channel with twenty-five of the line; Admiral Keith, with eleven, guarded the Channel itself. A minor French squadron at Rochefort and Franco-Spanish contingents at Ferrol and Cadiz were contained by small British forces. The French Mediterranean fleet at Toulon, eleven of the line under Admiral Villeneuve, was watched by Nelson with thirteen. Although the geographical focus of the impending campaign was the Straits of Dover, the naval elements involved were dispersed along the whole coast of western Europe.

Napoleon planned to disperse them more widely. He hoped that his fleets, if they escaped from port and eluded British pursuit, could then converge on the Channel while the enemy was still hunting them blindly across the ocean. He misunderstood his problem. He could not depend on decoying the British, whatever the bait, away from the Straits of Dover for the time he needed; the only way to secure his army's communications was to defeat the Royal Navy and drive it from the seas. But he believed that its *absence,* not its destruction, would be enough for his purpose.[1] He consequently elaborated

---

[1] His strategy is in marked contrast to that of the Germans in the First World War. They then faced the same problem of overcoming the superiority of the

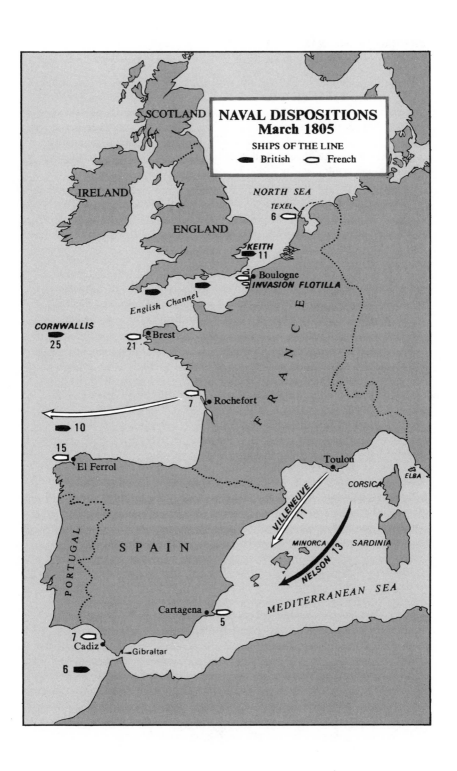

**NAVAL DISPOSITIONS
March 1805**

SHIPS OF THE LINE

British ◗ French ◖

SCOTLAND

IRELAND

ENGLAND

NORTH SEA

TEXEL
6

KEITH 11

Boulogne
INVASION FLOTILLA

English Channel

CORNWALLIS
25

Brest
21

Rochefort
7

10

15
El Ferrol

Toulon

ELBA

CORSICA

VILLENEUVE 11

MINORCA

SARDINIA

NELSON 13

F R A N C E

P O R T U G A L

S P A I N

Cartagena
5

Cadiz
7

Gibraltar

6

MEDITERRANEAN SEA

a series of schemes for luring it away, only the last of which was tried, in the spring of 1805. The best that can be said of the final plan is that it showed, like most concoctions of that fertile brain, daring and imagination.

On paper the design looked feasible. Villeneuve would slip out of Toulon past Nelson's guard, pick up the Franco-Spanish squadron at Cadiz, and make for the Caribbean; the fleet at Brest and the Rochefort contingent would escape simultaneously and sail for the same destination. The British would have to pursue, to save the West Indian islands on which the "nation of shopkeepers" set such store; the French would join forces in the Caribbean before their enemy arrived, and then double back to the Straits of Dover to convoy the invading force. Britain would be conquered while her fleet was half a world away.

This design rested on two premises, and both were ridiculous. One was that the Royal Navy would behave as Napoleon expected; the other was that the French navy would. The Emperor assumed that the British would relax their guard on Toulon, Brest, and Rochefort simultaneously, to allow his squadrons to escape, and would then follow them to the West Indies and stay there, bemused, while the French returned to Europe. The British blockade, it is true, was not completely effective. With sailing ships it could not be; a storm might blow a covering squadron off station and allow the enemy to come out and disappear in the waste of ocean, or a frigate with a crucial dispatch might miss the admiral to whom it was addressed. Yet, for all the accidents of wind and weather, the noose of sea power that the British had drawn around the continent was far stronger than Napoleon supposed, and the Admiralty far more resourceful. He was predicting a weakness and incompetence that were not there.

He was also predicting a competence in his own navy that it did not have. For years its strength had been declining, sapped by every month that passed with nothing to do. Morale that could not feed on action deteriorated, and so did gunnery; crews became slack when their ships rode idly at anchor, and captains and admirals lost the sixth sense that they needed for maneuvering in battle. The Emperor assumed that his orders would suddenly galvanize these men into breaking out of their long confinement, and that they would then cross the Atlantic for a precisely timed rendezvous in the Caribbean

---

Royal Navy; but they realized, as Napoleon did not, that control of British home waters was inseparable from control of the seas. The Germans planned accordingly: they would lure a part of the British fleet into a battle in which it was outnumbered, then repeat the performance as often as necessary until the enemy's strength was whittled down to the point where the entire Royal Navy could reasonably be challenged to a climactic engagement. The German plan went awry at the Battle of Jutland in May 1916. But the plan itself was intrinsically sound, whereas Napoleon's plan was chimerical.

For works dealing with Britain's role in the Napoleonic Wars see, in addition to those cited in the previous chapter, Sir Charles Oman, *Britain against Napoleon* (1942), and Arthur Bryant, *The Years of Victory, 1802–1812,* the sequel to the same author's *The Years of Endurance.*

and return in a victorious armada sweeping up the Channel to Boulogne. It
was a glittering dream.

The wonder is that any part of it materialized. In January 1805
the Rochefort squadron escaped to the West Indies, waited for support that
did not arrive, and then returned in May with nothing accomplished. The
main fleet at Brest stayed prudently in harbor. But in March, after an
unsuccessful attempt two months earlier, Villeneuve got out of Toulon,
evaded Nelson, and set off in turn for the Caribbean. None of the other
contingents that he expected was there to meet him, and when he learned
that Nelson was hot in pursuit he doubled back to Spain. So did Nelson.
Napoleon's chief purpose in the campaign, to combine his three fleets, had
failed; but Villeneuve's was now of formidable size, thanks to French and
Spanish ships that had joined him, and after refitting in Spain and gathering
in additional ships the Admiral put to sea in a forlorn effort to reach the
Channel. His morale was gone. He complained of bad masts, bad sails, bad
officers and seamen, bad tactics; "we know only one maneuver, to form line,
and that is just what the enemy wants us to do." In August he gave up,
turned southward, and took refuge in Cadiz. His force had risen to more
than thirty sail of the line, French and Spanish; and this armada allowed itself
to be blockaded initially by three British ships.

Villeneuve had brought the bulk of the Franco-Spanish navy under
his command, by liberating squadrons that had hitherto been immured in
various ports; but he had done nothing to further the invasion. His great
fleet was wasted at Cadiz, and he was badgered by the Emperor to justify its
existence. When the Admiral continued to do nothing, he was superseded.
News of this disgrace was the last straw for Villeneuve; he felt impelled to
make a sortie, if only as a gesture, before he was replaced. In his heart he may
have known it for a gesture of despair, because Nelson had now taken
command of a blockading force that numbered twenty-seven ships of the line.
On October 19, 1805, the Franco-Spanish fleet, thirty-three of the line, put
to sea and headed southward from Cadiz.

At dawn on the 21st it sighted the British. In the darkness far to the
west lay Cape St. Vincent, where Nelson had first made his name; to the
eastward the surf rolled against the cliffs of Cape Trafalgar. The British
approached from the west with a light wind behind them; Villeneuve, as
they drew near, reversed course and headed back for Cadiz. "We know only
one maneuver, to form line, and that is just what the enemy wants us to do."
Indeed it was; Nelson intended to tear the line apart. He divided his force
into two divisions, one to break through the allied rear and his own to break
through the center. As he led his column he flew the famous signal, "England
expects that every man will do his duty." A sailor supposedly responded, in
words that ring true even if they were never spoken, "Does the old bitch
think we shan't?"

Battle was joined at noon and raged for the next four hours; but the
issue was never in doubt. Early in the action Nelson was mortally wounded,

H.M.S. Victory, Nelson's flagship, being towed into port after Trafalgar.
Engraving by J. Sousen after a painting by Clarkson Stanfield.

(*National Maritime Museum*)

and he died at the moment of victory. Partly in consequence, the British did not achieve a battle of annihilation as they had at the Nile; but they did break the back of French sea power. They captured or destroyed roughly half of Villeneuve's fleet; thereafter Napoleon had no force of any consequence except the squadron at Brest, which dared not venture out. For the rest of the war — in fact for the next hundred years — Britain was free not only from threat of invasion but from any serious challenge at sea. Her power extended as far as the tides ran. After Trafalgar she used her naval preponderance to contain and destroy Napoleon, and after Waterloo she used it to maintain the Pax Britannica throughout the maritime world.

The War of the Third Coalition (1805–1807)

Napoleon's attempt to invade Britain did not end at Trafalgar; it had ended months before. Since the spring of 1805 he had realized that he faced a renewal of the continental war: his expansion in Germany and Italy was alienating Sweden, Russia, and Austria; and Pitt's diplomacy was bringing them into alliance against him. The Emperor had waited until late August to see whether Villeneuve's fleet might yet open the Channel to him, and then, deciding that it would not, he had turned to a campaign on the Danube. Two months before Trafalgar, in other words, he had tacitly admitted the bankruptcy of his naval plans, and the battle itself was a mere postscript to their failure.

Napoleon's genius and army were at their peak, and he launched the greatest offensive of his career. He marched from the Channel to the Danube, like Marlborough a century before, with a speed that his enemies thought impossible; and on the day before Trafalgar he captured an Austrian force of 60,000 men. He pressed on to Vienna, occupied it, and in December moved north to annihilate an Austro-Russian army at Austerlitz. Austria for the third time made a humiliating peace, and the Russians fell back toward their frontiers.

In London, during these catastrophes, Pitt was dying; the strain of the war years had worn out his frail body. When the news of Austerlitz reached him, he recognized what it meant: the old map of Europe, he said, would not be needed for another ten years, a prophecy that was fulfilled almost to the letter. He died in January 1806, murmuring, "my country, how I leave my country!" He certainly did not leave it triumphant, but he did leave it indomitable. It was sufficiently united, thanks in great part to his leadership, so that it carried on the struggle for the next nine years without any single leader of his stature.

The next administration had an optimistic name, the Ministry of All the Talents, which included at last those of Charles James Fox. But the talents were largely wasted. Fox promptly put to the test his long-standing sympathy for the French Revolution, and for Napoleon as its heir, by opening peace negotiations. The Emperor encouraged them with one hand, and with the other tightened his grip on Europe. Even Fox became disillusioned. The French, he concluded, did not want peace and were not to be trusted; they "fly from their word." In September 1806 he also died, only nine months after the death of his life-long rival, Pitt; the negotiations virtually died with him.

In his brief tenure of office Fox did achieve one aim that had been as dear to him over the years as the cause of peace. Just before his death he secured the consent of parliament to abolish the slave trade throughout the empire, and the measure was formally passed into law in the spring of 1807. Although slavery itself remained legal in the colonies for another quarter-century, and only the importation of slaves was forbidden, this prohibition was recognized at the time for what it was, the crucial step in abolishing the whole institution of slaveholding. The statute was not the work of Fox alone. For nearly twenty years William Wilberforce had been waging the parliamentary campaign for abolition, and in the country at large the cause had won the support of many prominent men, among them John Wesley, Samuel Johnson, and Adam Smith. But Fox led the final phase of the battle, and the victory that he assured before he died is a fitting tribute to his indomitable spirit.

The Ministry of All the Talents, which did not long survive the loss of Fox, resigned in the spring of 1807. It failed in its central task, for it neither made peace nor showed any talent for making war. Britain apparently knew no more about how to cooperate with allies than she had in 1793. Pitt's successors continued his long-established policy of subsidizing any power that would fight France on the continent, so that Britain maintained her role as "the paymaster of Europe." But the millions of pounds that she poured out were largely wasted, because she had no real plan for integrating her efforts, by land or sea, with those of Napoleon's faltering opponents. Her strategic influence on the War of the Third Coalition was consequently negligible, and by 1807 that conflict was drawing to a close in a way that was peculiarly threatening to her. In the previous autumn Prussia had joined Russia against the French Emperor, who was more than a match for them both; in June 1807 he defeated them with finality. Prussia was conquered, Russia ready to come to terms; and the terms he offered her were directed against Britain.

Napoleon met the young Czar Alexander, who was dazzled by him; and a series of interviews between them produced the Treaty of Tilsit. This settlement, signed in July 1807, was a landmark in the Napoleonic Wars. It was an alliance between the two Emperors, by which the whole continent was divided into French and Russian spheres of influence. Prussia was temporarily reduced to impotence, and Austria was in eclipse. The Emperor of the French had become Emperor of the West, dominating Germany and Italy; and in the east the Czar ruled the only other great power that was left.

"What is Europe, where is it," Alexander exclaimed to Napoleon, "if it is not you and I?" He was melodramatic, but for the moment he was right.

The two sovereigns bound themselves at Tilsit to cooperate in any war that either one might undertake in Europe. As a result, when Britain refused to come to terms, Alexander changed sides and turned against her. By now he detested her, and she had given him cause: in the recent war she had done nothing effective to aid him, either by arms or subsidies, and had even seized some of his merchant marine. To his proud and mercurial temperament the only answer was to join Napoleon and bring her to her knees.

Once more the islanders stood alone, with no hope of creating another coalition like those of the past. They seemed to have only enemies left in a Europe more solidly united against them than ever before. The climactic phase of the struggle was beginning, and it brought into sharp relief both the strengths and the shortcomings of British society. One source of strength was industrialization, which was advancing at a forced pace under the impetus of war; Britain supplied the continent with much of its manufactured goods, and even her enemies were compelled to buy from her. War also stimulated the enclosure movement, as did the rising population that had to be fed; even bad harvests did not halt the increasing productivity of the land, but domestic foodstuffs still had to be supplemented by foreign imports. The British merchant marine, despite the best efforts of French privateers, retained the lion's share of the European carrying trade. Mines, factories, farms, and ships created the wealth that the government converted, by taxation and borrowing, into the sinews of war.

"A nation that by her activity and the genius of her citizens," wrote an admiring German observer, "manufactures its numberless articles of merchandise infinitely finer, in much superior workmanship, in far more exquisite goodness than all other nations without exception, and that is able to sell them infinitely cheaper, owing to her admirable engines, her machines, and her native coal; a nation whose credit and whose capital is so immense as that of England; surely such a nation must render all foreigners tributary; and her very enemies must help to bear the immense burden of her debt and the enormous accumulation of her taxes." [2]

But the shortcomings were also apparent. Both industrialization and enclosure dislocated the economic order, and consequently bred unrest. Artisans who could no longer compete with the products of machinery, such as the hand-loom weavers, were not ready to be docilely unemployed; they much preferred to smash the machines. Villagers who lost their rights in the common, or found that their small holdings had been filched from them in

---

[2] Quoted in William Cunningham, *The Growth of English Industry and Commerce in Modern Times* (1892), pp. 516–17; I have modernized spelling and punctuation. Cunningham's work, although long out of date, contains much useful detail.

the process of enclosing, were as angry as the weavers, and discontent among
the lower classes was potentially explosive. Moneyed men were also unhappy.
The number of poor who were on relief was mounting fast; and the Speenhamland system for dealing with them, by supplementing wages from local
rates, was putting a greater and greater strain on the rate-payer.[3] At the same
time, the financial demands of the war and the interest charges on the
swelling national debt put a similar strain on the taxpayer. In 1798 Pitt had
instituted a graduated income tax on incomes between £60 and £200, and a
flat ten percent rate on those of £200 or more; this innovation was retained
through the war years. The propertied classes, who had to pay both local
rates and national taxes, were groaning under the burden that the war imposed
on them.

Yet many members of those classes, to judge by literary evidence,
lived as if there were no war. The great novelist of the period was Jane
Austen; her books deal with middle-class county society, which she saw
with an amused and keen eye and described in lucid detail. Her characters
are entirely absorbed with their own affairs and those of the neighborhood.
They move through their daily rounds, flirting, drinking tea, making de-
lightful conversation, with never a hint that the country is in the grip of
economic revolution and is standing at bay against Napoleon. Though Miss
Austen's two brothers were in the navy throughout the war, her world is
untouched by anything outside itself; it is tranquil and timeless. This
tranquillity is not the aberration of a single author, but the reflection of a
significant truth. War, even on the Napoleonic scale, was still limited in its
impact; and so was economic change. Every inhabitant of the British Isles
was in some way and to some degree affected by what was happening, but the
effect was often too subtle to be perceived. Men continued in the traditional
frame of their society, almost unaware that they were living through upheavals that would fascinate historians.

If Jane Austen reflected the myopia of many of her contemporaries,
William Wordsworth spoke for others who were passionately involved in the
struggle against France. The poet had changed his tune. The young man who
had regarded the French as heroes was now a middle-aged patriot who regarded them as "slaves, vile as ever were befooled by words," and who
gloried in Britain's isolated stand against the enemy.

> Another year!—another deadly blow!
> Another mighty Empire overthrown!
> And We are left, or shall be left, alone;
> The last that dare to struggle with the Foe.
> 'Tis well! from this day forward we shall know
> That in ourselves our safety must be sought;
> That by our own right hands it must be wrought;

[3] For the origins of the Speenhamland system see above, p. 113.

That we must stand unpropped, or be laid low.
O dastard whom such foretaste doth not cheer!

Rational calculations gave little cause for cheer. Although the Czar's
volte-face meant almost nothing to Britain in military terms, because his fleets
were insignificant and his armies no more amphibious than the French, it
meant a great deal in commercial terms. He closed the ports of Russia to
British goods, and agreed to bully the other Baltic states into doing likewise.
He thereby enabled Napoleon to implement on a large scale a project with
which the Emperor had already been experimenting — to cut off Britain's
entire trade with Europe. Out of the Tilsit settlement came the far-reaching
design for economic warfare known as the Continental System.

Economic weapons were the only ones left that could be effective.
The French naval offensive had failed, and with it all chance of invading
Britain. The French military offensive, on the other hand, had given
Napoleon direct or indirect control of a large part of the European coastline,
and the adhesion of Russia accounted for much of the rest; the few holes
that remained did not seem difficult to plug. The Emperor intended to
answer the British naval blockade by a blockade on land, enforced in every
port of the continent and extending like a gigantic dike from the Baltic to
the Black Sea. This dike, he reasoned, would accomplish two purposes
simultaneously. On the one hand, by eliminating France's greatest competitor
it would give French products a virtual monopoly of the European market.
On the other hand, by damming the flow of British manufactures it would
turn the islanders' greatest strength into a fatal weakness. Britain was already
so far industrialized, the Emperor believed, that she was highly vulnerable.
She could not exist unless the factory system continued to function, because
she must either export or starve. Once her markets were cut off, the machinery
of mass production would break down. As it did so, factory owners would
rage, hungry workers would riot, and the pressure on Whitehall would
mount until the government was forced to capitulate. This was the design,
and it determined the whole future of the war.

The Continental System could succeed only on two conditions. One
was the continuance of the accord with Alexander, for only his collaboration
made the dike complete and kept central Europe docile. The other was that
Napoleon could make his power effective along the vast stretch of European
coast that lay outside the Russian orbit. Either his system was truly continental,
or it was nothing. In order to develop its full force he had to make sure that
it operated in every saltwater harbor that had good communications with the
interior. Balkan and Scandinavian ports were relatively unimportant because
of the poor communications between these peninsulas and the land mass of
Europe; but all the rest of the coastline, from northern Germany to Naples,
was Napoleon's concern.

The implications for him were enormous. He soon discovered that
he could almost never enforce a strict embargo through satellite governments

because they were too weak, even if they were willing, to suppress the smuggling of British goods. He was compelled to bring in his own bureaucracy of customs officers, backed by troops, which meant extending his dominions; and this he did over the next four years. The attempt to make his economic system work involved him in more and more expansion of his political system, until in the end even he overreached himself.

Results of the Continental System (1807–1809)

The ink was scarcely dry on the Tilsit agreement before Napoleon was planning further moves. They were directed at two corners of Europe that were far apart but vital to his schemes. One was Scandinavia, where he intended to revive the old idea of a naval coalition, with Denmark for its focus, to seal off the Baltic from British penetration. The other was the Iberian peninsula, where Portugal was in his bad graces because of her traditional friendship with Britain, and Spain seemed ripe for absorption into his system. If British goods were excluded from the Baltic and from Portugal and Spain, as they already were from the Low Countries, France, and Italy, the blockade would be complete, at least in theory; and the islanders would face a choice of ruin or surrender.

London recognized the danger in the Baltic, and responded at once. In September 1807 a powerful British expedition attacked Copenhagen for the second time, bombarded the city into surrender, and sailed away with the entire Danish fleet. This act, whatever its justification as self-defense, was almost Napoleonic in its brutality; but it did accomplish its purpose, for the Baltic remained open. In November, when Napoleon's troops were at the gates of Lisbon, another British squadron convoyed the Portuguese fleet and royal family to refuge in Brazil. The Royal Navy was becoming adept at filching fleets from under the emperor's nose.

Almost simultaneously London counterattacked on another front by tightening the operation of its blockade. A series of orders in council redefined to Britain's benefit, and therefore narrowly curtailed, the right of neutrals to freedom of the seas. The complex provisions of the orders were not designed to ruin neutral commerce, which was vital to the British themselves, but to control and profit by it while diverting it from the enemy. Neutral ships were encouraged to trade with Britain and prohibited, unless they had first called at a British port and received a license, from trading with any continental state that excluded British ships and goods. The principal impact of these restrictions was upon the United States, the only remaining neutral that had a large carrying trade. American merchant captains were in a dilemma. If they disobeyed the restrictions they risked capture by British men-of-war; if they obeyed them they were fair game for French privateers at sea and customs officials on land. American opinion was incensed against both sides, and the only question was which was the greater enemy.

To the peoples incorporated into the Continental System the answer to that question became clearer with every month that passed. For them Napoleon was the enemy. Britain had what they wanted, the products of the Industrial Revolution and the produce of the overseas world — silk and sugar and coffee and spices and a thousand others; these imports were in such demand that the black market flourished even as prices soared. Britain offered European consumers the satisfaction of their material wants. Napoleon offered them, in return for tightening their belts and foregoing their wants, the benefits of the French Revolution enforced by French arms; and the benefits he conferred at bayonet point were not popular. "We come to give you liberty and equality," announced one of his marshals to a newly subjugated people, "but don't lose your heads about it. The first person who stirs without my permission will be shot." Before this kind of pronouncement the sins of the Royal Navy paled into insignificance.

A year after Tilsit, Napoleon was challenged for the first time by a people in arms. His troops crossing Spain, ostensibly to subjugate Portugal, were actually intended to win him the entire peninsula. In the spring of 1808 he kidnapped the Spanish royal family and elevated his brother Joseph to the vacant throne. This kind of procedure was almost routine with him, but he did not reckon on the nature of the Spaniards. They had no taste for the reforms that King Joseph dangled before them; they wanted their own despicable monarchy, obscurantist church, and moth-eaten aristocracy, and were ready to fight for them. Revolt germinated almost overnight. In June a French army of 20,000 men surrendered, and the shock was felt through Europe. King Joseph was discovering what the British had learned a century earlier from their attempt to install Archduke Charles in Madrid, that foisting a regime on the Spaniards against their will was a dangerous game.

Napoleon was incensed at Spanish resistance. But, having no idea of the hornets' nest he had roused, he supposed that suppression would be easy; for he knew that the Spanish irregulars, or guerrillas, could not stand up to his troops in the field. He did not know the difficulties that faced those troops, which proved in the end insuperable. Communications with France, thanks to the British navy, were almost entirely by land; and the roads south from the Pyrenees ran over a series of mountain ranges where guerrillas could take a heavy toll of men and supplies. Left to themselves, the French would have been hard put to hold down a people ferociously determined to oust them; and they were not left to themselves. The Spaniards appealed to the British, who responded at once. So began the Peninsular War, which lasted for the next five years.[4]

[4] The classic history of the Peninsular War, written by a historian who was also a participant, is Sir William F. P. Napier, *History of the War in the Peninsula and in the South of France, from the Year 1807 to the Year 1814* (5 vols., 1828–36). For an equally full modern account see Sir Charles Oman, *A History of the Peninsular War* (7 vols., 1902–30). The standard work on British military operations as a whole is Sir John W. Fortescue, *History of the British Army* (13 vols.

The war gave Britain two new opportunities to use her resources. One was commerical. The collapse of the Bourbon regime at Madrid loosened the hold that Spain had had on her American empire, which began to disintegrate. Spanish colonists, hungry for manufactured goods, opened their ports to Britain and so gave her, at the moment when Napoleon's blockade was beginning to produce serious economic repercussions at home, the market that her merchants had coveted for a century. It was too limited a market to end her difficulties, but it did help to tide her over the most critical phase.

Her other opportunity was strategic. After years of landing expeditionary forces on the continent and having them chased back into the sea, she had the chance to use her army effectively. Control of the Spanish coast enabled her to strike where she pleased, supply her troops, and evacuate them if need be; the Spaniards' hatred of the French gave her a base of popular support. Her redcoats alone, or the Spanish irregulars alone, might have been crushed, but not the two in conjunction. The French could not concentrate against the former without opening their communications to the latter, or disperse over the countryside to hunt down guerrillas without exposing their detachments to the British army. For the first time since 1793 that army was able to prove itself.

It was a different kind of army from the French. Britain, untouched by social revolution, had maintained her eighteenth-century military structure; but since the beginning of the war she had taken great pains to overhaul it. The pay, drill, and equipment of the troops had been improved, and their administration reorganized; riflemen and rangers had been introduced, to operate on their own as scouts and skirmishers; the artillery had adopted Major Shrapnel's new explosive shell; the infantry had become so skilled in marksmanship that the volley of a British line was devastating. The result of all these changes was still an eighteenth-century army, small, professional, and highly trained; but it was a more effective instrument than that century had ever developed.

A reformed army with unreformed leaders would have been useless. "In war *men* are nothing," wrote Napoleon in the summer of 1808; "it is *a man* who is everything." The British hitherto had not produced a man worth mentioning; their generals, in contrast to Nelson and his "band of brothers," had been almost uniformly incompetent. But by the beginning of the Peninsular War a commander was on the scene, though not yet in command, whose talents were comparable with Marlborough's a century before. Just as the navy had had the luck of finding genius at the climax of its struggle against France, so now the army in its struggle had the same luck.

Arthur Wellesley, the younger son of a minor Irish nobleman, had

in 20, 1899–1930). Fortescue handles his subject in almost overwhelming detail, as the number of volumes suggests; but his judgments on men and campaigns are often open to question.

his way to make in the world like most younger sons. He elected the army, and in 1796 was sent with his regiment to India; there fortune smiled on him, for in 1797 Pitt appointed his older brother, by then Lord Wellesley, to be governor general. In the next eight years the two Wellesleys made names for themselves. The French were everywhere, stirring up trouble among the native princes; and the Governor General, despite the lamentations of the East India Company's directors, promptly took the offensive. He waged a series of wars which shattered the princely coalitions and affirmed the supremacy of the British Raj, and in them his younger brother performed brilliantly and rose to high command. By the time the two men returned home in 1805 Britain's position as the paramount power, which Hastings had established, was expanding into the Empire of India. Lord Wellesley's work was done, but his brother's was only beginning.

In August 1808 Arthur Wellesley landed in Portugal with a small army. He defeated a French force guarding Lisbon, and might have annihilated it if he had not been superseded by a blunderer who threw away most of the fruits of victory. Wellesley and his inept superior were recalled; the command in Portugal devolved upon Sir John Moore, who advanced into Spain to aid the insurgents. But Napoleon by now had crossed the Pyrenees with a quarter of a million men; he destroyed the Spanish levies and reached Madrid, where he heard that a British army of only 27,000 was on his flank. The prospect of capturing it turned him away from his plan for reducing the rest of Spain, and he set out on one of his lightning pursuits. But Moore, racing to the sea and the waiting transports, moved even faster, until the disgusted Emperor turned over the chase to a subordinate and returned to France. Moore reached his destination, Corunna, early in January 1809; there he turned on his pursuers and repulsed them in an action that cost him his life. But he had saved his army and distracted Napoleon from the best opportunity the French ever had to conquer Spain.

The Emperor's reason for returning to France had been news that Austria was again preparing for hostilities. He had defeated her three times, but she was not yet crushed; now that he was embroiled in Spain and the exactions of his Continental System were making him more and more unpopular in Germany, she hoped that the time had come for revenge. She fought alone, however, and he brought her to heel in a single campaign. Yet it was not easy; he met tougher resistance than ever before, because he was now fighting a people as well as a government. When the two together defied him, they gave pause even to the *Grande Armée*.

As Napoleon's involvement in Spain had encouraged Austria to turn on him, so his consequent involvement on the Danube gave new life to the Spanish rising. It also gave an opportunity to Britain, which the government botched with an ineptitude reminiscent of the 1790s. Instead of assisting either the Austrians or the Spaniards in the summer of 1809, it sent 40,000 men to capture Antwerp; the question of how the city could be held, once captured, did not arise because the expedition was an ignominious failure.

The troops would have been invaluable to Wellesley, who had returned to Portugal in the spring as commander in chief. Without them he had only 25,000 regulars and could make no lasting impression. He advanced on Madrid, and won victories that earned him a peerage as Lord Wellington; but his Spanish allies proved unreliable, and he barely managed to extricate himself and retreat to Portugal. There he waited to be attacked, for in the autumn Napoleon, having crushed Austria, began to pour troops back across the Pyrenees. It was the dismal end to a dismal year.

The British Counterattack (1810–1811)

Fortunately for Lord Wellington, the French elected to conquer Spain before moving against him, so that he had many months in which to prepare his defense. He put the time to good use, for he knew that the crisis of the war was approaching. His plans were based primarily upon food: he set out to prove the Napoleonic dictum that an army marches on its belly. The French lived off the countryside, he reasoned, and could not long remain stationary; they had to move like locusts from region to region, stripping each one of everything edible. The British, in contrast, lived off the sea; if they held Lisbon for access to water-borne supplies and maintained their communications with the city, they could exist anywhere. Their two necessities were an impregnable base and the means of supplying the army from it; Wellington attended to both by fortifying the approaches to Lisbon and by creating an effective transport service. He also built up an excellent staff and medical corps, drilled his troops until they were the equal of any in Europe, and trained an army of more than 10,000 Portuguese that gave a good account of itself. His gift for military organization was what Thomas Carlyle defined as genius, "the transcendent capacity for taking trouble." Nothing that concerned the smooth functioning of an army escaped his eye. He was never popular with his men, or cared to be; but he was as meticulous in watching over their needs as he was remorseless in his demands on them.

The test of his preparations came in September 1810, when Marshal Masséna began his long-heralded invasion of Portugal with more than 60,000 French veterans. Wellington fell back on Lisbon, fighting as he went, while the Portuguese peasants laid waste their farms in the invaders' path. In October Masséna's advance halted abruptly. Before him were the lines of Torres Vedras, fortifications that ran across the neck of the Lisbon peninsula for almost thirty miles, from the Atlantic to the Tagus River. The Marshal was helpless. The lines were too strong to be carried by assault, and the defenders could not be starved out while their navy commanded the sea. The French, on the other hand, could starve and did. The land offered them no subsistence, and only a trickle of supplies from Spain got through the swarms of Portuguese irregulars operating in their rear. Masséna held out until the spring of 1811, while his army dwindled; then he retreated by a route already picked bare of food during his advance. Wellington harassed his rear, and guerrillas hung on his flanks. He lost 25,000 men and returned to Spain with an army of scarecrows.

His retreat had large repercussions. Napoleon had ordained, with his usual public fanfare, that the British should be swept into the sea; instead the Emperor had suffered a disaster to his arms and prestige. French morale in Spain sank, and Spanish morale was toughened; the tide of war in the peninsula had turned. The subject peoples of Europe began to hope again, and the Russian Czar took a more independent tone than he had since the Treaty of Tilsit. What Napoleon later called the Spanish ulcer was draining the health of his empire.

Not the least important effect of Wellington's success was at home, where good news was sorely needed. By the beginning of 1811 Britain was in a parlous state. The King had lost for good both his sight and his sanity; his eldest son, the Prince Regent, was popular only with the sycophants around him; the Prince's younger brother the Duke of York, Commander in Chief of the army, had been driven from office by a noisome scandal; and the country was governed by a ministry with no discernible talents. After the death of Pitt and Fox only two men of real ability were left, Lord Castlereagh at the War Office and George Canning as foreign secretary. The public distrusted them both, they loathed each other, and in 1809 their quarreling forced them simultaneously from office. For the next three years the government, run by mediocrities and riven by factions, had no clear-cut policy at home or abroad.

The immediate danger by 1811 was at home, for Britain was at last feeling the full effects of the Continental System. Her commerce was little impaired, but her industrial population was suffering almost the hardships that Napoleon had anticipated. Raw materials were in desperately short supply, and prices soared accordingly; the market value of silk almost quadrupled, and wool, timber, and hemp were not far behind. Food was becoming as dear as these products; in 1812 the price of wheat in some areas rose from 10 to 25 shillings a bushel, and famine stared the country in the face. Bankruptcies were coming thick and fast, unemployment was rife, and riots were a commonplace. The workingman's job was a life-and-death matter for him; his smoldering resentment of machines, which he blamed for curtailing employment and depressing wages, finally broke into violence.

At the end of 1811 organized bands of men, masked and working at night, began to destroy textile machinery throughout the Midlands. Local opinion supported the rioters, and their activities spread. Their leader was said to be a mysterious "General Ludd," who may or may not have existed; and from him they took the name of Luddites. At first they abstained from bloodshed, but before long, when some of their men were shot by the soldiery, they retaliated with murder. The government took severe repressive measures, and in a mass trial at York in 1813 many leaders were sentenced to hang and many more to be shipped to Australia; the movement then disintegrated, although it revived briefly after the war. The Luddites were not revolutionaries, because they had no motive except the blind fury of the dispossessed, no aim except to return to a bygone era before machines had complicated life; they were the old England protesting against the new. The protest was hopeless, but for the moment they terrorized employers and scared the government. How long, men wondered, would the common people endure their miseries?

Most politicians took a gloomy view. They knew that the popular hardships were real and dangerous, and that radical agitation was making the most of the danger. The nerve of the ruling class began to falter, and defeatism was in the air. The nation seemed to be too close to ruin to dare continue the war. And why continue it? Many men believed in their heart of hearts that Napoleon was invincible on land, and that the British army would go on repeating in Spain the failures that had dogged it since 1793; the struggle, they argued, was hopeless. This mood was so strong in Westminster that Wellington, during his campaign against Masséna, expected at any moment to have his army called home. But the government blundered on doggedly, and he justified its doggedness. By the close of 1811 the British public was realizing that its cold and taciturn general had a gift for victory.

While the army was redeeming itself in Spain, the navy was gathering in new conquests. Guadeloupe and Martinique in the West Indies, Java in the East Indies, Mauritius and the Cape of Good Hope — all over the world the colonies of France and her satellites fell into British hands. Around the European coast bases were established, on Heligoland in the North Sea, on Malta, Sicily, and the Ionian Islands in the Mediterranean, for blockading squadrons and for the smuggling of British goods into the continent. Napoleon had no answer but wider and more stringent control. He annexed to France a strip of territory on the northeast, running through the Low Countries and the North Sea coast of Germany to Lübeck on the Baltic, and on the southeast he incorporated Piedmont, the Papal States, and the eastern coast of the Adriatic; he and his brother-in-law Murat, King of Naples, ruled such of Italy as was not annexed. The French grip on the coastline seemed to be secure.

But by the end of 1811 it was less secure than ever, because each time the Emperor tightened his grip he added to his enemies. Annexing the Papal States roused against him a power that he could not understand — that of a gentle and unbending old man, who excommunicated him and became his prisoner; the sight of the Pope at the imperial chariot wheels was an insult to Catholic Europe. Napoleon's intrusion into Germany, and his increasingly overt domination of his satellites there, waked in opposition to him a new sense of German nationalism, particularly in the young; in Italy, integrated for the first time since the days of Rome, nationalistic dreams were also stirring. The Emperor had forcibly disseminated the ideas of the Revolution through Europe, and now they were working against him.

The American and Russian Wars (1812)

While the Napoleonic system was stretching French power toward the breaking point, Britain was also paying a price for her method of making war. She was embroiled in a second Anglo-American conflict, which from her viewpoint was merely a regrettable and minor by-product of the great struggle in Europe; but from the American viewpoint it was momentous. The War of 1812, the first on which the new republic embarked, confirmed the emotions in which the United States had been born; hatred of Britain became part of orthodox American patriotism. That hatred, and the reciprocating British resentment, obscured the fact that the two countries had common interests and poisoned their relationship for generations to come.

The war grew directly out of the struggle in Europe, even though for many years that struggle was a chief source of American prosperity. As European neutrals disappeared into the maw of the French empire, Britain swept their flags from the seas; and the United States inherited the bulk of the continent's carrying trade. But the Americans inevitably fell foul of the navy that was bringing them their business. They needed more and more ships, hence more and more seamen; and they offered high wages. Soon they were attracting deserters from the Royal Navy, which was also expanding and was desperate for sailors. British press gangs gathered in Americans who could not prove their citizenship; British men-of-war stopped and searched American vessels and appropriated any of the crew who were thought to be deserters. The United States protested, but Whitehall would not mend its ways because, for the British, manning the fleet was a matter of self-preservation.

Both the great European belligerents imposed more and more restrictions upon neutral trade, which roused a resentment in the United States that brought it to the verge of war in the 1790s, first against Britain and then against France. But the crises passed, partly because American commerce was thriving despite all trammels, and primarily because the European struggle was not yet focused upon economic warfare. After 1806 it was. Neither Britain nor France would permit a neutral to give comfort to her enemy; each aimed at manipulating American trade to her own advantage and exerted increasing pressure to that end. Here Britain was at a disadvantage. Sea power, usually far less conspicuous than land power, was more so for once: while Napoleon was confiscating American merchantmen in the distant ports of France, British warships were invading American territorial waters and outraging national pride.

The United States, caught between the upper and nether millstone, at first attempted to escape by putting an embargo on all foreign trade; but the effect at home was ruinous. The next move was to inform France and Britain that American trade would be open to whichever one abandoned its restrictive policy, and closed to the other. Napoleon pretended to rescind his decrees in compliance; he duped President Madison, who believed that the French were acting in good faith and that the British would not act at all. Whitehall did act, by repealing the orders in council. But a few days earlier the United States, antagonized beyond endurance, had declared war against Britain.

It was a needless conflict, provoked by prickly emotions on the American side and haughty ineptitude on the British; neither contestant had an intelligible war aim. The Americans had the will to conquer Canada, but not the power. Neither did they have the power to achieve their ostensible goal, the right to trade as they pleased. For Britain, fighting for existence, would not compromise the effectiveness of her blockade unless compelled to do so; and the United States Navy of that day could not compel any one. As for the British, they had no goal; they lacked both the will and the power to conquer the United States, and could ill afford a contest that further strained their resources, already spread thin, and that offered them nothing in return.

The conduct of operations was as faulty as the logic that had caused them. An American attempt to invade Canada was a fiasco. A British raid on the Chesapeake had no results except to burn public buildings in the new capital at Washington, thereby further embittering the Americans, and to inspire *The Star-Spangled Banner*. The infant United States Navy won a number of minor actions, on inland lakes and at sea, that jolted British complacency and exalted the American public, but had little effect on the outcome of the war. A British attack on the mouth of the Mississippi had no effect at all; veterans of Wellington's Peninsular army were defeated in the Battle of New Orleans, which started Andrew Jackson on his road to the White House but which was fought after the war was over. Peace was concluded in December 1814 in the Treaty of Ghent. As if to emphasize the pointlessness of the conflict, the treaty kept discreetly silent on all the issues out of which hostilities had grown.

For the United States the war had great significance, but in Britain it was little regarded at the time and has long since been forgotten.[5] It was a sideshow, played out just when the great drama on the Continent reached its climax. In the years 1812–1814 Napoleon made his supreme gamble for the mastery of Europe, and by the time the Treaty of Ghent was signed his empire had shrunk to a Mediterranean island. Small wonder, then, that events in America received scant attention overseas.

The declaration of war by the United States in June 1812 coincided almost to the day with the opening of Napoleon's gamble, which was his invasion of Russia. It was forced upon him, he believed, by a change in Russian policy. Soon after the Tilsit agreement Czar Alexander's enthusiasm for his new ally had begun to cool, as conflicts of interest between the two had become more and more apparent. Napoleon's activities in Germany disturbed the Czar, because they were undermining the influence of Russia

---

[5] The present place of the War of 1812 in British history is suggested by the anecdote — whether true or not makes no difference — of a modern Englishman's reaction when told that his countrymen had once burned Washington. "Really? I knew of course that we burned Joan of Arc, but George Washington — ?"

in an area with which she had been concerned for half a century. Still more disturbing, because closer to home, was Napoleon's encouragement of Polish nationalism; for in the eighteenth-century partitions of Poland Russia had absorbed vast territories, which she stood to lose if the Poles reasserted themselves. Last but not least, the Czar's embargo on trade with Britain was losing him popularity at home and straining the Russian economy. For political and economic reasons he was ready to break the Tilsit accord, and in 1811 he issued a series of decrees that reopened his ports to British goods.

This defiance jeopardized the whole structure of the Continental System. Napoleon could not understand what was happening. Russia, he had thought, was a planet revolving about himself; but now it was moving into a new course. Either he could let it go and abandon his method of war against Britain just when it seemed to be succeeding, or he could force Russia back into orbit. For him this was no choice. Both his nature and his position precluded retreat; he had to go on.

He did not delude himself that coercing Russia would be easy, and for the task he gathered the greatest army that Europe had ever seen. Its core was 250,000 French veterans, but large contingents of Germans, Italians, Poles, and other nationalities brought the total to 600,000; Prussia and Austria, bullied into alliance, provided another 50,000 to guard the flanks of the invasion. In the whole of continental Europe only one small power stood out: the Napoleonic Marshal Bernadotte, whom his master had recently installed as Crown Prince of Sweden, defied him and allied with the Czar. But Sweden was in no position to give effective help, and neither was Britain; Russia stood alone against a continent in arms.

In June 1812 Napoleon's vast horde crossed the Russian frontier and rolled eastward. It failed by a narrow margin to encircle the defending army, which fell back before it and, like the Portuguese, laid waste the countryside. In mid-September the French entered Moscow, and there they stayed for a month. They were in much the same position that Masséna had been in before Lisbon: the enemy hung on their flanks, their lines of communication were stretched to the limit, and they faced starvation. Napoleon's overtures for peace were met by silence. He had to retreat. As soon as he did so his whole supply system disintegrated, and his nightmare began. In December he reappeared in the west, and only then did Europe learn what was behind the rumors that had been circulating for weeks. Out of the host that had entered Russia some 20,000 men returned, and they were more dead than alive. Half a million had disappeared, and with them had gone the foundation of the Napoleonic Empire.

The Fall of Napoleon (1813–1815)

Even the catastrophe in Russia did not break Napoleon's hold on his people. He hurried back to Paris, and by the spring of 1813 had succeeded in raising a new army of 200,000 to meet the onslaught that he knew was coming. Alexander had not halted on his frontiers but continued westward, and his advance roused the Germans to a national war of liberation from their oppressor. Prussia joined the Czar, Crown Prince Bernadotte crossed from Sweden, and in the summer of 1813 Austria, thanks in part to British pressure and loans, threw in her lot with the allies. Napoleon won several battles, but with his raw troops he could not win the campaign; never had he so sorely missed the 200,000 veterans who were fighting in Spain. In October Swedish, Russian, Austrian, and Prussian armies converged upon him at Leipzig, and in the three-day Battle of the Nations broke his hold on central Europe. With the remnants of his forces he fell back behind the Rhine; his empire was gone, and only France remained.

Meanwhile Wellington, after two years of fluctuating success and failure against greatly superior numbers, had finally expelled the enemy from Spain. At the close of 1813 he crossed the Pyrenees, in the first invasion of French soil since 1792. His adversary, Marshal Soult, put up a skillful and dogged defense, but with fewer and fewer troops as Napoleon called for reinforcements to hold the eastern frontier. By April 1814 the British were in Toulouse. There they learned that the war was over. During the spring Napoleon, in eastern France, had fought one of the most brilliant campaigns of his career, but against odds that even genius could not overcome. On March 30 his capital surrendered, and on April 11 he abdicated; in return for giving up the crowns of France and Italy he was made sovereign of the minuscule island of Elba. Bourbon rule was reestablished in France under the late King's brother, who was proclaimed as Louis XVIII; and in the autumn the powers convened at Vienna to make peace.

It was a staggering task. The reactionaries who had "learned nothing and forgotten nothing" imagined that the world of 1789 would reemerge with all its trappings of monarchy and privilege, and that the map of 1789 would be recreated; but that world and that map were gone. New concepts of nationalism, of representative government and individual rights, had been carried through the length and breadth of the continent; they could be contained, perhaps kept from growing rapidly, but not rooted out. The crazy-quilt pattern of little states in Germany and Italy had been destroyed, the partition of Poland undone; neither Russia, Austria, nor Prussia wanted to restore the old map in its entirety, for each hoped to aggrandize herself.

The peacemakers were confronted with two problems, each of which was a challenge to their statesmanship. The first was how to protect the new order that they were establishing, of which France would necessarily be a part, from the subversion of French revolutionary ideas. The second was how to adjust the spoils of victory among the continental powers without

precipitating another war. Prussia, Austria, Russia, and Britain had bound
themselves together in the Quadruple Alliance, to arrange the settlement
and then to cooperate in maintaining the peace; but soon after the sovereigns
and plenipotentiaries met at Vienna peace was hanging by a thread. Russia and
Prussia wanted to make annexations in central Europe that Britain, Austria,
and France threatened to oppose by force. War was averted through
compromise, thanks largely to the skillful diplomacy of Metternich, the
minister who had directed Austrian policy since 1809. But the shrewd observer
on Elba had taken note of the crisis.

Napoleon concluded that his enemies were about to fly at each
other's throats, and that France would welcome his return. From all over
Europe his veterans, released from captivity, had come home to find themselves
cold-shouldered by the Bourbon government; many of them longed to have
him back, and with them he could build such an army as he had not had
since 1812. The reduction of France to her prerevolutionary frontiers,
furthermore, outraged French patriots and endangered the regime of Louis
XVIII, who had only the humdrum virtues of peace and retrenchment to
offer a nation that had so long lived on glory. The King was unknown to his
countrymen, after his years of exile, and looked to them like a pigmy replacing
a giant. Some were eager to have the giant again; few would lift a finger
to oppose his return.

In March 1815 Napoleon landed in the south of France; three weeks
later he was installed in the Tuileries, while the Bourbons fled again into exile.
But the Emperor knew that he was not yet master of the country: the people,
he said, "have let me come just as they let the others go." To win support he
had to prove himself, again by the sword. His return had united the quarreling
allies, who had outlawed him as an enemy to the peace of the world; and their
forces began to converge on France. He had the material for rebuilding the
Grande Armée, but he did not have the time. For 170,000 Russians and 250,000
Austrians were lumbering slowly but inexorably toward the eastern frontier,
while close at hand in Belgium were 120,000 Prussians under Marshal Blücher
and to the west of them, barring the road to Brussels, a polyglot force of
100,000 men in British pay. These allied armies determined in outline
Napoleon's plan of campaign. He had to strike into Belgium, divide and
destroy the enemy there, and then deal with the Austrians and Russians.

Wellington, now a duke, had been Britain's representative at the
Congress of Vienna; he was hastily recalled and put in command of the
improvised forces guarding Brussels. They were a far cry from his Peninsular
veterans, most of whom had been shipped to America and had not yet returned.
Every soldier available in the British Isles was sent to him, but he had only
30,000 of them. The remaining 70,000 were a scratch collection of Dutch,
Belgians, and Germans, some raw recruits, some veterans of Napoleon's
armies; their fighting spirit and even loyalty were doubtful. The Iron Duke
needed all his imperturbability.

Napoleon moved at top speed. He had to, because each of the two

(*Wellington Museum*)

The Duke of Wellington. Portrait by Sir Thomas Lawrence, ca. 1814.

armies before him was roughly equal to his in size; his only hope was to outmarch them, get between them and drive them apart, and then crush each in turn. His first target was Blücher. On June 16, while a French detachment under Marshal Ney held off the British at Quatre Bras, the Emperor with his main force fell on the Prussians at Ligny and cut their army in two. Napoleon assumed that it was shattered and would retreat eastward; he sent a corps under Marshal Grouchy in pursuit and then turned to destroy Wellington. The Duke barely managed to extricate his army and retire hastily northward from Quatre Bras, hunting a position strong enough to defend. On the 17th a torrential rain slowed his pursuers, and that evening the British commander found what he wanted, a low ridge south of the village of Waterloo; there he turned at bay.

Wellington knew, as Napoleon did not, that the entire Prussian army was nearby and coming to his aid. It had not been demoralized by the Battle of Ligny, and it had retreated not eastward but northward to Wavre, on a route roughly parallel to the British; Grouchy had lost touch with his quarry and was miles away. But the Prussians moved slowly — far more slowly, in the event, than Wellington had supposed they would — and everything depended on whether the Duke could hold until they arrived. His position was strong and gave scope for the kind of defense at which he was adept: in front he had little protection, for the slope was gentle; but behind, where the ground fell away to the northward, he could maneuver his reserves under cover and out of sight of the enemy. In artillery and cavalry he was much weaker than they, and his chief reliance was on the fire power of the British infantry.

Napoleon, after delaying until almost noon of the 18th, put that power to the test by ordering a frontal attack. Marshal Soult had learned from his Spanish experience how costly such an attack could be, and he cautioned his chief. The Emperor's reply was both brutal and unrealistic. "Because you have been beaten by Wellington you think him a great general. And I tell you that Wellington is a bad general, that the English are bad troops, and that this will be a picnic for us." He soon learned better, and he did not forget the lesson. "The Duke of Wellington," he confessed a few weeks after the battle, "is fully equal to myself in the management of an army, with the advantage of possessing more prudence."

During the battle Napoleon showed no prudence at all, and little finesse; his one aim was to overwhelm resistance by sheer mass. In the early afternoon his columns broke through Wellington's center, scattering a force of Dutch and Belgians in wild rout, but were counterattacked and driven back by British reserves. Then the Emperor threw in his cavalry, some 15,000 under Marshal Ney, in three waves of assault which, though torn by artillery fire, flowed up the slope and poured through gaps in the enemy line. The defenders formed squares, within which the artillerymen took refuge. French round shot ripped the squares, but they held. The attack broke against them twice, reformed and broke again, until by six in the evening it was spent. Wellington had committed his last reserves. Napoleon had not; although his right was by then heavily engaged against the Prussians, who at long last had arrived from Wavre, he made one more effort in the center with the Guards, the elite of his army. They too failed, and the last tide of the Empire ebbed down the hill.

Wellington ordered his whole line forward. As it swept into the valley, and the Prussians broke through on the flank, the French army dissolved in rout. All night the panic-stricken mob fled down the roads toward France. The British were too exhausted to follow, but the Prussian cavalry took up a relentless pursuit. The Emperor, his face streaked with tears, tried time and again to make a stand. But his authority was gone, and at last he gave up and led the race to Paris.

Although he had no thought of surrender, his countrymen had; his own legislature forced him to abdicate. The French provisional government threatened to arrest him if he did not leave the country at once, and the Prussians were hunting him in order to shoot him. He fled to the port of Rochefort, hoping to escape to the United States; but the wind was against him, and the British were waiting for him. Their blockade, which had done so much to bring him to the end of the road, now claimed his person. He surrendered to the captain of H.M.S. *Bellerophon,* and with supreme effrontery wrote to the Prince Regent, as "the most powerful, the most constant, and the most generous of my enemies," to claim asylum in England. Instead he was brought to Plymouth but not permitted ashore, then exiled to the small British island of St. Helena, in the south Atlantic more than a thousand miles off Africa. There he lived for six years, and died of cancer in 1821.

His second defeat and abdication were essentially a postscript to his first defeat in 1814, as the Battle of Trafalgar was a postscript to the preceding naval campaign. But the Hundred Days of 1815 also determined, as Trafalgar did, much of what came after. Europe was brought together in a new unanimity born of the final, unexpected French aggression. Bonapartism was discredited in France for a generation to come; the fallen Emperor of 1814 was a hero to many, but the man who fled from Waterloo to Paris, then from his own countrymen to the *Bellerophon,* was not. Lastly the prestige of Britain was raised to a higher point than ever before.

When Napoleon called the British, as personified in the Prince Regent, "the most powerful, the most constant, and the most generous of my enemies," he was wrong only on the last point. They were not generous to him, beyond frustrating the Prussian hope of putting him before a firing squad, and they had no cause to be; he represented to them the same force of ruthless imperialism that they had fought in the French Revolution. In struggling against that force they had not always been constant or powerful. But they had been more constant than any other people, if only because less vulnerable, and had fought on alone when the future seemed without promise. Their naval power had slowly but surely increased until it held the continent in a vice; and their military power, for fifteen years the laughingstock of Europe, had redeemed itself in the Peninsular War and the Waterloo campaign. The Spaniards had helped in one, the Prussians in the other; but the hero of both was Wellington. He was at the zenith of his fame, and his country was at the start of its greatest influence in the world. The years had amply borne out the prophecy in Pitt's last public speech: "England has saved herself by her own exertions, and will, as I trust, save Europe by her example."

9 The Twilight of Aristocracy

The Settlement of 1815

While Napoleon was marching toward Waterloo, far away on the Danube the diplomats and sovereigns were winding up their business at the Congress of Vienna, so that after Waterloo all that remained was to make peace with France. This was done in the autumn, as part of the general settlement. French frontiers were reduced to those of 1790, before any of the Revolutionary conquests; the nation was obliged to return to their former owners the art treasures that Napoleon had filched from all over Europe, to pay a large indemnity, and to turn over a number of its border fortresses to allied troops until payment was complete. These provisions were anything but punitive, and with good reason; the victors had no other choice. If they destroyed France, they would once more revolutionize the continental power structure, an unthinkable prospect. If they punished France severely without destroying her, they would arouse such resentment that Louis XVIII could never be secure on his throne; and instability in Paris meant instability in Europe. The only peace that could endure was one that was tolerable to France.

But the allies did all they could to prevent a recurrence of French aggression. In their territorial arrangements at Vienna they erected barriers across the two principal routes by which France, since the seventeenth century, had invaded central Europe. The first route, and the one with which Britain was deeply concerned, was through the Low Countries. Here the Belgian provinces, which had been under Austria until 1792, were joined with the Dutch provinces, which had been independent before the wars, to form the Kingdom of the Netherlands. The peacemakers hoped that this new state would be large and strong enough to repel French attack; and to make assurance doubly sure they gave to Prussia the Rhenish territory immediately to the eastward, so that if need be Prussian armies could again march into Belgium as Blücher had done. The second invasion route from France was into northwestern Italy. Here, in the upper Po valley, the Kingdom of Sardinia was enlarged to be an Italian equivalent of the Kingdom of the Netherlands; and Austria took on the same supporting role as Prussia in the north by acquiring the provinces of Lombardy and Venetia that occupied the lower valley of the Po. In the rest of the peninsula the old non-Italian dynasties were restored. North of the Alps the German states, considerably reduced in number, were joined together in the German Confederation; one of its members was Hanover, enlarged and converted from an electorate into a kingdom, of which the aged and insane George III was king.[1] In the east, Russia gained the lion's share of Poland, largely at the expense of Prussia; and the latter was compensated with part of Saxony and the Rhineland.

These arrangements, relatively minor as they seemed on the map, affected the future of Europe. Sardinia became the only Italian state that was both ruled by a native Italian dynasty and was strong enough to be a factor in the affairs of the peninsula. Austria was the dominant power there, and by shifting from the Netherlands to the Po she relinquished her old role of protecting the German states against France. Prussia assumed that role by acquiring the Rhineland, where she also gained, quite inadvertently, the area that was to be crucial for the future industrialization of Germany. Russia advanced westward into the heart of the continent, and thereafter played a more important part in its power politics than ever before.

Britain had little direct concern with most of these territorial adjustments, and so could afford to be detached. Her principal aims in the peacemaking were less controversial than those of the land powers: she wanted security for the Low Countries, with which her own security was involved; she wanted a lasting, and therefore an equitable, settlement with France; and she wanted to safeguard her communications with India. At the end of the war she occupied the colonies of almost all the maritime states, and therefore had strong means of persuasion during the peacemaking; only if her wishes were met could the former owners be sure of regaining their possessions. She had her way on almost every point, and gave up the bulk of her conquests. In the West Indies she retained a few small islands won from France, in the North Sea Heligoland, and in the Mediterranean Malta and a protectorate over the Ionian Islands. To guard the route to India she kept the former French island of Mauritius, off the east coast of

---

[1] The Hanoverian crown, unlike the British, descended only in the male line. At the accession of Queen Victoria in 1837, consequently, the Hanoverian throne went to her uncle, the younger brother of King William IV; and the long dynastic connection between the two countries was broken.

Good general works dealing with the period covered by this chapter are the first two volumes of Elie Halévy, *A History of the English People in the Nineteenth Century,* entitled respectively *England in 1815* and *The Liberal Awakening, 1815–1830* (2nd ed., 6 vols., 1949); Asa Briggs, *The Age of Improvement, 1783–1867* (1960); J. A. R. Marriott, *England since Waterloo* (3rd ed., 1919), the sequel to Robertson's *England under the Hanoverians* in the eight-volume *History of England* edited by Sir Charles Oman; George M. Trevelyan, *British History in the Nineteenth Century and After* (1937); and E. L. Woodward, *The Age of Reform, 1815–1870* (1938) in the *Oxford History of England* series.

Africa, and two erstwhile Dutch possessions, Cape Colony and Ceylon, for which she paid compensation to the Kingdom of the Netherlands.

That compensation was nothing to what Cape Colony would cost her in the long run, for there she was buying trouble. The Cape of Good Hope was a valuable possession, largely because it grew the fruit and vegetables that were the standard preventive of scurvy; ships on the long voyage to or from India made Capetown a port of call in order to preserve the health of their crews. But the colony was populated by Boers — Dutch who had been settling there since the seventeenth century and had preserved their old ways; and they soon proved to be among the most intractable inhabitants of the British Empire. Cromwell or William III might have known how to handle them; Victorian administrators did not, and the South African problem developed until it produced, in the 1890s, the greatest imperial crisis since the American War of Independence.

If the Vienna settlement had in it seeds of trouble for the British Empire, it also had seeds of European trouble. The latter sprouted fast; and in the postwar years the problems of the continent influenced British history almost as much as they had during the war. Those problems arose primarily from the conflict of two forces, the revolutionary idea of nationalism that the French had sown, particularly in Germany and Italy, and the determination of the continental powers to maintain peace by suppressing any revolution anywhere. Britain at first cooperated with her allies and then defied them, and her policy is comprehensible only in terms of the conflicting forces in Europe.

The arrangements made at the Congress of Vienna betrayed the dreams of patriots in many countries. Napoleon's armies had destroyed the *anciens régimes* all over Europe, much as the Japanese armies in the Second World War destroyed the European colonial regimes all over southeast Asia; and in both cases, after the conquerors had gone, the attempt to reconstruct the Humpty Dumpty of the past touched off a series of revolts by peoples who wanted to determine their own affairs. To German nationalists, who had dreamed that the War of 1813 would lead on to unification, the loosely structured German Confederation was a poor sop; and to Italian nationalists the change from French to Austrian hegemony was no sop at all. This was not accidental; one powerful man at Vienna had designed it that way. Prince Metternich, the Austrian chancellor, was a Rhinelander by birth but a Viennese by policy; and the policy of Vienna was necessarily opposed to unification in Germany or Italy. The Austrian Empire, composed of Germans, Hungarians, Poles, Czechs, and a host of smaller minorities, was the living denial of nationalism. A united Germany would deprive the Habsburgs of the influence that they had exerted there since the fifteenth century, and a united Italy would deprive them of Lombardy-Venetia. Those losses would only be the beginning; the end would be the breakup of the empire itself into its constituent national parts. The French virus menaced the existence of the state over which Metternich presided; and for more than thirty years after the Congress of Vienna he tried to guard against the danger, until it materialized in the great explosion of 1848.

His attempts to stop national risings, like Napoleon's attempts to stop British imports, involved him in every corner of Europe. A rising anywhere might be contagious and spread to Italy or Germany and thence to Vienna and Prague and Budapest; the only protection was to intervene at the start. This Austria could not do alone, but she was not alone. All the great powers, in varying degree, feared a resurgence of French Revolutionary ideas; and the fear brought them together. They were aware as they never had been before that they were parts of a single community, which they described as the Concert of Europe. Whenever a threat to the peace arose, they agreed to assemble in a congress like that at Vienna, and there to concert action against the danger.

This so-called congress system scarcely deserves the name of system. It had no formal organization, no agreement upon methods of coercion or even of procedure; it committed its members to nothing except to meet. In international relations, nevertheless, it was an advance from the anarchic world of the eighteenth century because it recognized the principle that all the powers had a common stake in maintaining peace. "The immediate object," said Lord Castlereagh, the British Foreign Secretary, "is to inspire the states of Europe with a sense that the existing concert is their only perfect security, . . . and that their true wisdom is to keep down the petty contentions of ordinary times and to stand together in the support of the established principles of social order."

Czar Alexander attempted to Christianize this new spirit of unanimity. In the autumn of 1815 he announced that he had formed with the Emperor of Austria and the King of Prussia a Holy Alliance, the members of which bound themselves in indissoluble fraternity to act according to the precepts of Christ, and that they invited the adhesion of other sovereigns. "Sublime mysticism and nonsense" was Castlereagh's comment, and the Prince Regent politely declined to join; so did the Pope. The other European heads of state, with tongue often in cheek, accepted the Czar's invitation. But only Russia, Austria, and Prussia ever took the alliance seriously; and for them it soon became more reactionary than holy. Britain was still tied to them, however, in the Quadruple Alliance formed against Napoleon in 1814; and in 1818 France, after a probationary period, was admitted as a fifth partner. These were the powers at the center of the congress system.

Britian's Breach with the Concert (1815–1823)

A concert is as a concert does, and the fundamental question was how the new order would operate. This question of what means to employ in keeping peace is inherent in any such international collaboration, and has since arisen in the League of Nations and the United Nations. It has no easy answer. A threat to peace is most difficult to assess correctly at just the moment when it is easiest to deal with — its early stages. At that moment the collaborating powers are in danger of doing either too little or too much. Too little, if they allow a real threat to grow until it gets out of hand. Too much, if they regard every alteration of the status quo in any country as a threat that justifies intervention to reestablish "principles of social order," for their policing to maintain peace then becomes a tyrannical suppression of change.

Castlereagh and his colleagues were aware of the difficulty. They regarded the Concert of Europe in its early years much as President Wilson regarded the League of Nations, as an international framework within which change could take place. The Concert could not be more than that. It was unable, they argued, to "secure and enforce upon all kings and nations an internal system of peace and justice," and until it could ensure equitable government within a country it had no right to intervene in that country's affairs; to do so would be to buttress whatever power was established there, "without any consideration of the extent to which it was abused." Keeping the peace was one thing, supporting misrule quite another; and Britain's collaboration with her allies depended on whether they preserved the distinction between the two.

At first all went smoothly. But after 1818, when the Congress of Aix-la-Chapelle withdrew allied troops from France and admitted her to full standing in the Concert, the mood of the continental powers began to change. Liberals, restive under their static regimes, were resorting to sporadic violence; Czar Alexander had posed for three years as their champion, but he was wavering erratically; Metternich was turning to repression as the only security. In 1819 the Spanish army, with which the King of Spain had hoped to regain his American colonies, revolted against him and touched off a revolution that spread from Spain to Portugal, the Kingdom of the Two Sicilies, and Sardinia. Metternich responded by convoking the Congress of Troppau, where in November 1820 the Holy Alliance got down to work. Prussia, Austria, and Russia bound themselves to intervene in any state where a revolution endangered its neighbors, and a few months later Austrian troops moved against the two Italian culprits. This action was based on sound logic, for revolution had in fact proved itself highly contagious; and the spread of contagion had demonstrated the force of Metternich's argument that the peace of Europe was indivisible and that the only way to preserve it, and with it the social order, was to intervene before trouble got out of hand.

But Castlereagh strongly dissented. He took much the same stand that his master, Pitt, had taken toward France before 1793, and carried it further: he denied that the Holy Alliance had the right to interfere in the domestic affairs of independent states. In taking this position, it may be argued, he could not help himself. The Spanish and Italian revolutionaries were moderates, who demanded the kind of constitutional, parliamentary regime of which Britain had long been the chief exemplar; and no minister responsible to the Mother of Parliaments could well have agreed that such a regime menaced the social order. In the 1820s, nevertheless, revolution of any sort was disturbing. Castlereagh and his colleagues, who sometimes feared it at home, needed the courage of their convictions to defend it abroad and to take a stand that tacitly admitted a people's right of revolution. But for the moment their stand was merely verbal; and, while they protested, the continental powers acted. Austrian arms made Italy safe for reaction; the Congress of Verona, in 1822, authorized France to do likewise in Spain, whereupon a French army crossed the Pyrenees, restored the despicable King, and kept guard while he wreaked his vengeance on his subjects.

Meanwhile Castlereagh had died and been succeeded at the Foreign Office by his old rival, George Canning. The change affected the direction of British policy much less than its style. Canning had a gift for drama, in words and actions, that his predecessor had lacked; and, where Castlereagh had regretted Britain's alienation from her allies, Canning welcomed it. He did not believe in the Concert of Europe; "it will necessarily involve us deeply," he had said, "in all the politics of the continent, whereas our true policy has always been not to interfere except in great emergencies, and then with a commanding force." By the beginning of 1823 he was encouraged to think that the Concert was breaking apart and that international relations were reverting to a wholesome state — "every nation for itself, and God for us all."

France was certainly acting for herself by invading Spain, and seemed to Whitehall to be behaving uncomfortably like the France of Louis XIV. Her ascendancy in Madrid was bad enough; worse still was the possibility that she would go on to regain for her new protégé the Spanish American empire, in which Britain had so long been interested. The Holy Alliance considered the Spanish colonists as revolutionaries, whose virus had once infected the mother country and might again; the sooner they were brought to heel the better. The British government, in contrast, considered them as independent *de facto*, and held that Spain had lost her claim to them and France had none.

The crisis revealed a strong community of interest between Britain and the United States, for Washington was as much opposed as London to European intervention. The Americans wanted to loosen the ties between the New World and the Old; they had recently recognized the colonies as independent, as Britain had not, and were determined to do all in their power to keep them so. The physical power of the United States, with no army or navy worth the name, was negligible; but Britain had at last the "commanding force" of which Canning had spoken. While repression had been confined to Europe he had been limited to protests; now that it threatened to reach across the Atlantic he could act. In October 1823 he brusquely informed the French government that intervention in America would not be tolerated. This ultimatum was decisive because it was backed by the force of the Royal Navy.

Meanwhile in Washington, as the trend of British policy became unmistakable, President Monroe recognized and rose to a great opportunity. On December 2, before he knew of Canning's ultimatum to Paris, he delivered to Congress the message known ever since as the Monroe Doctrine. It proclaimed that the United States would not interfere in the internal affairs of any European state or of an existing colony in America, and would oppose both European interference in any independent American state and future European colonization on either American continent. The doctrine was a bold gesture. The United States seemed to be throwing the mantle of its protection, by fiat, over the entire hemisphere; but in fact the President had no mantle to throw. Instead he appropriated, by dexterous timing, the mantle of British sea power. For the rest of the century, with one brief interlude, the Royal Navy rather than the American gave teeth to the Monroe Doctrine.

The British were delighted with the President's message. They had little wish to gain more colonies themselves in the Americas, and less wish to see European powers do so; and they were glad to share with the United States the onus of defying the Holy Alliance. The crisis evaporated, for the French did not dream of challenging Monroe's words when backed by Canning's threat. Reaction was stopped, as the Napoleonic system had been, at the water's edge.

British withdrawal from the Concert of Europe resembled the defection of the United States from the League of Nations a century later, in that it destroyed the unanimity upon which the experiment depended; but the *kind* of unanimity that Britain repudiated in the 1820s was more dangerous than hopeful. The great powers were high-handed as well as repressive. They were ignoring the wishes of the smaller powers, one of whose kings accused them of exercising "the influence arrogated by Napoleon"; and, if they had held together, their control might have become as tyrannical as the Emperor's and even more stifling. By defying them, it may be argued, Britain served the best interest of Europe.

Her action was dictated, of course, not by such considerations but by her own interests and tradition. She had been accustomed, as Canning said, to interfere on the continent only in great emergencies, growing out of overt naval or military threats. Her interests were worldwide, as those of Prussia or Austria were not; and she was deeply involved only when European developments touched the security of her home islands, her empire, or the routes of empire. She accepted for a time the idea of collective security, but it was essentially alien to her. When her reactionary allies used the idea to further their own ends, she had no reason to cooperate with them and every reason not to. Her past history and present concerns worked to draw her away from the Concert and, as Thomas Jefferson said in 1823, to "bring her mighty weight into the scale of free government."

The Tory Reaction (1815–1823)

The ministry that carried out this momentous shift in British foreign policy was, ironically enough, notorious for its opposition to freedom at home. Since Fox's death in 1806 liberalism had been in eclipse. Under the pressure of war, economic dislocation, and popular unrest, the mood of the ruling classes had become increasingly apprehensive and averse to new ideas. The Whigs who remained faithful to the tradition of Fox had dwindled to a small minority, doomed to what seemed to be permanent opposition; they were divided among themselves, and offered a wide range of criticism but no coherent program. The shifting groups of politicians who held office during the war years had set their faces against reform and come to stand for a rigid, repressive conservatism. By 1812, when Lord Liverpool formed an administration that lasted until 1827, these conservatives were assuming the name of Tories. A two-party system was more clearly perceptible than it had been at any time since the Hanoverian accession a century before; party labels again had meaning, although the meaning had changed since the days of Queen Anne. The Whigs, little as they could agree on specific measures, insisted on the need for change. The Tories denied the need; they clung to the status quo as the only safeguard against revolution, and they were firmly in power.

The heyday of this static conservatism was the first decade of the Liverpool ministry, from 1812 to 1822. The Prime Minister himself was colorless and undistinguished, and he acted more as umpire than as leader. Three men in his cabinet were chiefly responsible for governmental policy: Lord Eldon, a diehard conservative who was Lord Chancellor; Henry Addington, now Lord Sidmouth, who was Home Secretary; and Lord Castlereagh at the Foreign Office. Under the leadership of this triumvirate the cabinet, particularly between 1816 and 1819, followed a repressive policy almost worthy of Metternich. The liberties of British citizens were more drastically curtailed than in any other peacetime period of modern history. The government acted from fright, as it had in the 1790s; and this time the fright infected the Whigs and paralyzed their opposition. Charles Fox must have turned over in his grave.

The postwar problems that beset the country, it is true, might have frightened any government. Public finances were in disorder, and the business community suffered accordingly. Since 1793 the net annual revenue — from customs and excise, various forms of taxation, the income from crown lands, and so on — had increased more than fourfold, thanks in part to the institution of the income tax in 1798; and by 1815 this revenue was just under £83 million. But in 1816 the income tax, which had been an emergency war measure, was abolished; and the annual revenue soon fell off to a mere £58 million. The struggle with France had cost Britain, in subsidies to her allies and the expenses of her own operations, more than £830 million, a sum that was almost four times the total outlay for all the nation's wars between 1739 and 1783. The money had been raised for the most part by loans, with the result that the national debt had more than tripled during the twenty-two years of fighting. By the time of Waterloo the debt had climbed above £860 million. The carrying charges on this sum remained virtually constant when the revenue declined; before long, therefore, more than half the annual budget was absorbed in servicing the debt. The government's financial position was little better in peacetime than it had been during the war.

The Bank of England had long since suspended payment in gold and was issuing only paper currency. Bank notes were also put out by a host of country banks that had recently sprung up, some with shaky assets. The effect was twofold: to debase the value of the currency, and hence bring on inflation, and to produce great financial instability. The worth of the paper notes, even those of the Bank of England, fluctuated from month to month; and prices rose and fell accordingly. Business was a gamble for all concerned; and the working classes, solely dependent on their wages, could never tell when they would receive enough to keep body and soul together. They were cursed by paper money, according to the young poet Shelley, because it forced them

> to let the Ghost of Gold
> Take from Toil a thousandfold
> More than e'er its substance could
> In the tyrannies of old.

The private sector of the economy was as badly strained as the public. During the war the problem of the food supply, with European imports greatly reduced, had become acute. The only way to feed the nation had been by more efficient farming, and in consequence British landlords had enclosed some three million acres. For these men peace was a disaster because imported grain, or corn in British parlance, sent domestic grain prices tumbling. The landed interest had long used the Corn Laws, which imposed duty on grain from abroad, as its weapon against foreign competition; and a parliament dominated by landlords did not hesitate to use the weapon again. In 1815 the Corn Laws were revised to prevent the importation of foreign wheat until the price on the domestic market rose to 10 shillings a bushel.

The result was tumult. Mobs ranged London, insulting members of parliament and threatening cabinet ministers; the young Lord Palmerston, Secretary for War, defended his town house by arming the servants with shotguns. More significant if less dramatic opposition to the government came from the manufacturers. They protested that the high price of grain, and hence of bread, would inflate wages and thereby raise the cost of production and the price of the finished goods, which had to be marketed abroad in competition with foreign products; British industry, therefore, would be penalized for the sake of the British landlord. Parliament held to its course. The landed interest was deaf to argument, and had as yet no inkling of the future. The great struggle over the Corn Laws was still thirty years away, but already the lines were being drawn. On one side were the industrialists and the workingmen in town and country who were the chief consumers of bread, in other words the bulk of the nation. On the other side were the landlords.

Laborers had enough grievances without an increase in the price of bread. During the war Britain, despite Napoleon's best efforts, had come to supply the needs of much of the outside world for manufactures; her exports in the year before Waterloo were more than three times as great as in 1792. In the same period, furthermore, her population had risen by some thirty-five percent. Peace brought a rapid decline in the European demand for goods, the termination of governmental war contracts, and the return to civilian life of half a million soldiers and sailors. The result, inevitably, was massive unemployment and destitution.

British society was ill prepared to cope with a sudden increase of paupers. The machinery of the Poor Law, inefficient before the war, had become even more so during it, largely because of the Speenhamland system for supplementing inadequate wages out of public funds.[2] The system was not nationwide. But, where it operated, the results were pernicious: because the wage-earner received an extra dole for each child, the poor were invited to be fruitful and multiply; the employer, not having to pay a living wage, was free to forget whatever social conscience he might have; the laborer had no incentive to work when the lazy and the diligent were treated alike. Last, and most important in a world dominated by the propertied classes, the rate-payer was saddled with a burden that was fast becoming intolerable, and that was not serving the end for which it was designed. Between 1803 and 1818 the cost of poor relief rose by more than 400 percent, from £4.25 million to £18 million; yet the agricultural laborer, in the regions where the Speenhamland system operated, became almost synonymous with the pauper.

The eighteenth-century working classes had not been supine, but had aired their grievances in riots and other forms of direct action. Industrial laborers, particularly in the wool trade, had combined in associations to hinder the introduction of machinery and keep up the wages of hand labor. These associations, the remote ancestors of the modern trade unions, had petitioned parliament, conducted strikes, bargained with employers, and in general made such a nuisance of themselves that they had precipitated a series of repressive statutes. The most important was the Combination Act of 1799, which gave capitalists a powerful weapon: any group of laborers who collectively refused to work for a reduced wage, or any unemployed individual who refused an offer of work in his trade, could be prosecuted

---

[2] For the origin and operation of the Speenhamland system see above, pp. 113, 168.

and imprisoned.[3] Workingmen's associations continued despite the law, and during the war years had some notable successes. But in the postwar depresssion, with wages falling and jobs scarce, the employer had the whip hand. The laborer could not look for redress to his trade or to the magistrates; he either accepted his lot or turned to violence.

The government had no way of knowing which he would do. It is difficult, in today's era of mass communications, to realize how little communication existed a century and a half ago between the rulers and the ruled. The masses had few ways to communicate. The popular press was still in its infancy; petitions to parliament, even if they were read, seldom revealed a consensus among the petitioners; riots were not a tactful way of making a point to authority, but they remained almost the only way. The government, in turn, had no reliable method for feeling the pulse of the masses. Spies and informers, widely used as they were, tended to produce what they thought their employers were looking for; investigations by parliamentary committees and commissions were at best a ponderous and limited procedure; reports from local magistrates were distorted by the reporters' upper-class prejudices and fears. The amateurs who still governed Britain had far better means of gathering information than their grandfathers had had.[4] But, when they tried to gauge the will of the unrepresented and mute majority, they had to rely on their instinct.

That instinct, though experienced, was fallible, all the more so when dulled by apprehension. The men of Whitehall and Westminster had to read such signs as came their way, and then guess what was going on in the hearts and minds of the workingmen. When the signs were ominous, as they were in the postwar years, the danger was easily exaggerated: a plot concocted by a few hotheads, a riot with a few fatalities, or a mass meeting with a few wild speeches became a portent of revolution. And *if* revolution were brewing, the authorities had to nip it in the bud or not at all; for they lacked the force to put down a full-blown insurrection. They had as yet no police in the modern sense, even in London; the regular army at their disposal was extremely small, and they could not rely on the ill-trained volunteers of the militia. Because they did not have the knowledge to evaluate a threatening situation, or the strength to wait and see whether the threat materialized, they could be frightened into precipitate action.

[3] Combinations of employers, either to reduce wages or to blacklist troublesome workers, were also forbidden; but these practices continued without hindrance from the magistrates. See Graham Wallas, *The Life of Francis Place, 1771–1854* (4th ed., 1925), pp. 198–99. Place was one of the leading radicals of the period, and was chiefly responsible for the repeal of the Combination Acts in 1824, for which see below, p. 204.

[4] A major example is the census of population, which was first taken in Britain in 1801. Another is the reports of parliamentary commissions, which in this period became more detailed and circumstantial than ever before; the commissioners took voluminous testimony, from witnesses called from all over the country, on the subject under investigation.

Britain after the war, with her load of debt and a disordered currency, her markets slumping, her unemployment rising to add to the burden of poor relief, was certainly going through difficult times. The misery of the people was obvious, and misery bred violence. The government interpreted the first acts of violence to mean that insurrection was starting; and it reacted, much as the Irish executive had reacted in 1797, with a ruthlessness born of anxiety. The year 1816 saw an outbreak of political agitation. Some of it was lurid: the Luddites again took to smashing machinery in the Midlands; mobs rioted in London, displaying the tricolor, and on one occasion pillaged firearms and invaded the heart of the city. Some of the agitation was respectable: the sober Corporation of London petitioned the Prince Regent for financial retrenchment and parliamentary reform. In the following winter secret committees of both houses of parliament made alarming reports, whereupon the government suspended habeas corpus, banned seditious meetings, and ordered local magistrates to prosecute authors of dangerous pamphlets. For a time agitation died down, less because of these measures than because of economic improvement; but soon the depression returned, and with it political unrest.

In August 1819 a meeting of some 60,000 people was held in St. Peter's Fields in Manchester. The crowd was unarmed and contained many women and children, but carried banners demanding annual parliaments, universal suffrage, "representation or death"; and a well-known rabblerouser mounted the platform to harangue the concourse. At that point the magistrates panicked and ordered mounted militia — local businessmen in uniform — to arrest the speaker. The men charged in with drawn sabers and were reinforced by regulars; the result was pandemonium. Several people were killed and hundreds wounded — sabered or trampled in the fleeing crowd.

The shock of the "Manchester Massacre," which was also derisively nicknamed from St. Peter's Fields "the Battle of Peterloo," was felt through the country and beyond. From the safe distance of Italy the young republican, Shelley, sent a call to revolution.

> Rise like Lions after slumber
> In unvanquishable number —
> Shake your chains to earth like dew
> Which in sleep had fallen on you —
> Ye are many — they are few.

At home even moderate opinion was outraged. But the government was profuse in its thanks to the soldiers, and inflexible in the line of action that had produced their handiwork. In the autumn of 1819 parliament passed the notorious Six Acts, which were the highwater mark of repression. They were substantially a return to Pitt's policy in the late 1790s, but this time without the excuse of war. The acts provided for the seizure of firearms, muzzled the cheap press by imposing a stamp duty, and limited freedom of assembly to such meetings as were held under official auspices. This legislation, most of which was soon repealed, served its purpose of silencing the radicals. Whether the purpose was worth the price is another matter.

The events of 1816–1819 revealed as never before the distance between the propertied classes and the masses. The former, smelling revolution in the air, closed ranks in self-defense, as they did again a generation later during the Chartist agitation. In parliament the Whigs, with few exceptions, were acquiescent; party labels meant nothing when oligarchy itself was threatened. Outside parliament the businessmen and magistrates, if Peterloo is a fair sample, eagerly supported the government. A Lancashire merchant boasted to a radical leader about how the people had been kept in their place: "the sons of bitches had eaten up all the stinging nettles for ten miles round Manchester, and now they had no greens for their broth. . . . Damn their eyes, what need you care about them? How could I sell you goods so cheap if I cared anything about them?" Economic forces alone scarcely account for such bitter brutality.

In January 1820, a few months after the passage of the Six Acts, George III died. The event seemed unimportant, because for ten years the "old, mad, blind, despised, and dying King," as Shelley called him, had lived in seclusion while his son was king in fact. But when the Prince Regent came to the throne as George IV he precipitated a crisis that shook the monarchy, revivified the Whigs, and gave the mass of the people a chance to show that their anger was still a force to be reckoned with.

In 1795 George IV, then Prince of Wales, had married Caroline of Brunswick and had promptly separated from her. He possessed all his father's qualities, said Lord Byron,

> Except that household virtue, most uncommon,
> Of constancy to a bad, ugly woman.

Caroline subsequently left England to live on the continent, where her flighty conduct gave rise to much gossip; but as soon as she heard of her husband's accession she hurried home to be queen. Instead the government, at the King's insistence, started proceedings for a divorce. Immediately the Whigs took up the Queen's cause for its political value, and the populace rallied to her with wild enthusiasm. She was, if not bad, vulgar and foolish and of questionable morals. But her husband's morals were beyond question. In his private life George IV followed the example of Charles II, rather than any of his own ancestors; and he made no attempt to conceal his profligacy. No matter what his wife had done, he had done worse; in the eyes of the nation she was the injured party.

When the bill for divorce was introduced into parliament in the summer of 1820, the King was in fact on trial; and as the weeks went by it became clearer and clearer what the verdict would be. The most brilliant of Whig lawyers defended the Queen, the idol of the populace; and excitement

mounted into a threat of revolution. In November the divorce bill was
dropped, amid tumultuous rejoicing. For the last time a king had persuaded
his ministers to introduce a measure at his personal behest, and he had been
defeated by the minority party because it had the people behind it. The
lesson was not lost on the Whigs. One of their younger members, Lord John
Russell, remarked that "the Queen's business had done a great deal of good
in renewing the old and natural alliance of the Whigs and the people, and
of weakening the influence of the Radicals with the latter." The Whigs of
the 1820s had strayed a long way from that old alliance, personified in
Charles Fox; and they were beginning to realize that renewing it might be
politically profitable.

But the profit was delayed, because by 1823 the Tories were showing
a new vitality. In their domestic policy they had hitherto followed the
injunction attributed to Metternich, "govern, and change nothing." Any
change had seemed to them like a hole in a dike, which threatened to let
in the flood; and they had forgotten the warning of their patron saint,
Edmund Burke, that "a state without the means of change is without the
means of its conservation." But now new faces were appearing, and with
them new ideas. Of the triumvirate only Lord Eldon remained, a monument
to the past. In 1822 Castlereagh's mind had failed, and he had committed
suicide; Canning, his successor as Foreign Secretary and leader of the House
of Commons, was far more open-minded on the need for reforms. Lord
Sidmouth, who had taken the odium of enforcing the Six Acts, had resigned
as Home Secretary and been replaced by the son of a Lancashire cotton
manufacturer, Robert Peel, who was developing a strong distrust of any
Toryism that did not move with the times. William Huskisson, one of the
ablest financiers of his day, was the new President of the Board of Trade.
The static, repressive period was over, and the state was recovering the means
of change.

The Near East Crisis (1821–1830)

After 1822 change appeared in both foreign and domestic policy.
Canning's interference with the Holy Alliance in 1823 over the issue of the
rebellious Spanish American colonies was only the beginning of Britain's
concern with rebels. In 1821 the Greeks had revolted against their rulers,
the Ottoman Turks; and from this revolt came a crisis that tormented Europe
for a decade. Until 1825 the decrepit Ottoman Empire tried without success
to regain control of Greece, in a war that was one of grisly atrocities on both
sides. But a wave of sympathy for the Greeks swept over Europe. The ruling
class of Britain and the continent had been nurtured on the classics and,
knowing little or nothing of modern Greece, saw in rough peasants the ancient
Spartans and Athenians. The cause not only aroused the sympathy of the
classicists; it also appealed, in its exotic wildness, to devotees of the romanticism

that was then in full flower. Philhellenes, or supporters of the Greeks, were soon found everywhere from Russia to the American frontier.

Lord Byron, one of the best known literary figures of Europe and the idol of romantics, set his seal upon the revolt. He wrote about it in a tone that blended nostalgia for the Greeks' past with anxiety about their future, a combination that was calculated to rouse Philhellenes to frenzy.

> The isles of Greece! the isles of Greece
>   Where burning Sappho loved and sung,
> Where grew the arts of war and peace,
>   Where Delos rose, and Phoebus sprung!
> Eternal summer gilds them yet,
> But all, except their sun, is set. . . .
>
> Fill high the bowl with Samian wine!
>   Our virgins dance beneath the shade —
> I see their glorious black eyes shine;
>   But gazing at each glowing maid,
> My own the burning tear-drop laves,
> To think such breasts must suckle slaves.
>
> Place me on Sunium's marbled steep,
>   Where nothing, save the waves and I,
> May hear our mutual murmurs sweep;
>   There, swan-like, let me sing and die:
> A land of slaves shall ne'er be mine —
> Dash down yon cup of Samian wine!

Byron not only wrote; he took action. In 1823 he went to Greece to help the revolt, which he did most efficiently; and in 1824 he gave his life for it. He died, not singing on the promontory of Sunium but at Missolonghi from fever; and he proved to be worth even more to the cause dead than alive. He became the hero-martyr of the Philhellenes. They sent money, supplies, and volunteers to the Greeks until the war, like the Spanish Civil War of the 1930s, took on the aspect of an international crusade.

Although the idealism that stirred such excitement put pressure on the great powers to intervene in Greece, they were not accustomed to act on idealism. Their policies rested on calculations of interest, and in this case the interaction of their interests was enormously complex. But the underlying forces at work are clear in retrospect, and they are worth examining. They operated, like forces pressing on a fault in the earth's crust, to produce a series of European upheavals, from the first tremor in the Greek crisis to the Balkan disturbances that began the earthquake of 1914.

The geographical focus of these forces was the Ottoman Empire. For almost two hundred years its dominions had been shrinking, and the Sultan's government, the Sublime Porte at Constantinople, had been growing more feeble. By the 1820s Russia had conquered the north coast of the Black Sea and was pressing toward the mouth of the Danube; the Serbs had revolted in the Balkans before the Greek rising and had gained substantial autonomy; and the Sultan's ambitious vassal in Egypt, Mohammed Ali, had an effective army and navy with which to build an empire for himself. The Ottoman state appeared to be on the verge of disintegration.

But the great powers could not allow it to disintegrate before they had agreed on dividing the spoils, and agreement proved impossible. Russia longed for Constantinople and the Sultan's Balkan provinces, in order to open the Straits and get access through the Aegean to the Mediterranean. Statesmen in Vienna had good reason to fear such Russian expansion in the Balkans, and statesmen in London had equally good reason to fear the Russians in the Mediterranean; the Ottoman Empire, shaky as it was, served a vital function for both Austria and Britain as a barrier against the Czar. The affairs of the Porte also concerned France, whose government, if only for domestic reasons, needed to reassert its influence abroad; and Napoleon himself had pointed the way to the Near East. Every great power except Prussia, in short, had a stake in the Sultan's empire and therefore in the revolt of the Greeks against him.

In the years 1824–1827 the crisis deepened. First the Sultan called in the army and fleet of his vassal, Mohammed Ali; the Egyptians set to work, with efficient ferocity, to end the Greek rebellion by exterminating the rebels, whose only hope soon lay in intervention by the powers. At the end of 1825 Czar Alexander died, and his successor, Nicholas I, made clear that he would intervene alone if need be. In that case Russia would probably make Greece into a satellite, and be a long step nearer to realizing her expansionist dreams. Metternich, who disliked this prospect slightly less than he disliked the principle of intervening to *aid* rebellion, refused to join in concerted action; and Prussia followed his lead. Neither France nor Britain wanted to apply force for fear of bringing down the whole Ottoman edifice; but they dared not let Russia proceed alone. They decided, in order to keep some influence on events, to cooperate with the Czar in whatever measures might be necessary. The Holy Alliance of the three eastern powers gave place for the moment to a new triangular grouping of Russia, France, and Britain.

In August 1827 Canning died; and power in Whitehall passed to a group of mediocrities whose one idea was to retreat into what looked like the safety of inaction. But events were out of their control. In October a combined squadron of Russian, French, and British men-of-war, which had been sent to the Greek coast, was observing the Turko-Egyptian fleet in the Bay of Navarino. The allied admirals were uncertain what they had been sent to do, but the question became academic when they were fired upon. They returned the fire and wiped out the enemy fleet.

The Battle of Navarino saved the Greeks, but it roused consternation in London. At the beginning of 1828 the Duke of Wellington became prime minister; he was strongly opposed to any action that would impair Ottoman power, particularly if Russia reaped the benefit, and had the King express to parliament his hope that the battle, "this untoward event," would not interrupt Britain's friendly relations with her "ancient ally," the Porte. This diplomatic nonsense made no impression in Constantinople, where the Sultan called for a holy war against the powers that had destroyed his fleet. Russia responded by doing what Canning had worked so hard to prevent, going to war on her own. British diplomacy was bankrupt. From the beginning it had had two conflicting objectives: to protect the Greeks from being slaughtered by the Turks or dominated by the Russians, and to preserve the integrity of the Ottoman Empire. Canning, when the chips were down, had been willing to compromise the second objective for the sake of the first; Wellington had relinquished the first for the sake of the second; and at the outbreak of war Britain seemed to have failed in both.

She was saved from utter diplomatic defeat by an unforeseen factor, the fighting power of the tatterdemalion Turkish army. After the Russian troops had sustained a number of reverses, Nicholas became more amenable. Metternich urged an independent Greece, and Wellington, much against his will, was persuaded to agree. The negotiations between the powers dragged on until the spring of 1832, when at long last Greece was formally established as a sovereign kingdom under the guarantee of Britain, France, and Russia. Meanwhile, in 1829, the Russo-Turkish war had ended in the Treaty of Adrianople, which considerably strengthened Russian influence in the Balkans outside Greece, and proportionately weakened Ottoman control. There for the moment the eastern question rested.

It was far from closed. For almost a hundred years it reopened periodically, bringing with it wars and the threat of wars. The settlement of the Greek phase left an uneasy three-cornered balance of power in the eastern Mediterranean between Russia, Britain, and France, which operated for a time to British advantage. When France became disturbingly ambitious in the Near East in the late 1830s, Britain and Russia drew together to restrain her. When Russia attempted to dominate the Porte in 1853, France and Britain opposed her, diplomacy fumbled, and the result was the Crimean War. After the eclipse of France in 1870 Austria took her place, and in 1876–1878 Austro-British pressure prevented the Ottoman Empire from becoming a Russian preserve. Not until Russia and Britain came to terms in 1907 could that empire, so long "the sick man of Europe," be allowed to die. Until then the powers kept it alive, not because they relished its existence but because they could not agree on how to divide the inheritance.

The Disruption of Toryism (1823–1830)

The period 1822–1827, when Canning was the leading figure in the ministry, was one of legislative change that foreshadowed the upheaval of the 1830s. The Tories were belatedly realizing that conservatism was doomed if it did nothing. They were not always agreed among themselves on what to do, and they were determined not to budge on the central issue, the constitution of parliament. But the House of Commons sanctioned so many reforms in so many other areas that by 1827, when Canning died, the question was not whether but when the house would consider reforming itself.

The first change, initiated by Robert Peel, was in the criminal code. As early as 1819 Peel had made a name for himself as a rising financier by regularizing the currency and providing for the resumption of specie payments; now, as home secretary, he carried through a massive program to amend the substantive law and the system of law enforcement. The death penalty was abolished for all but the most serious offenses; the medieval anachronism, benefit of clergy, by which any cleric accused of a crime might claim trial in a church court, was at long last ended; criminal procedure and the functioning of juries were improved; and in 1829 a London metropolitan police force was created, the members of which are still popularly known by Peel's first name or nickname—Roberts or Bobbies.

The Combination Act of 1799, like the old criminal code, had proved impossible to enforce. In 1824 it was repealed, and masters and men alike were freed to organize as they pleased. The result was an epidemic of strikes and lockouts, which precipitated a new statute in 1825 that narrowly limited the right of combination. The law was weighted against labor: penalties were provided for using force or intimidation against employers, or against workingmen who did not wish to join what was then called an association and soon came to be known as a trade union. For years to come the union remained in a limbo; it was neither illegal, provided that it was voluntary and uncoercive, nor recognized by the law. Parliament had established one of the principles sacred to Victorians, freedom of contract, whereby an employee might contract with his employer on any terms that were mutually acceptable, without interference from any organization of employees or, in theory, of employers. This was laissez-faire with a vengeance, for it permitted the capitalist to exploit the laboring man as much as the market would bear.

Victorian economic doctrine was also foreshadowed in the reforms instituted by William Huskisson, the President of the Board of Trade. In principle he was for his day an advanced free-trader; and, although in practice he proceeded cautiously, the sum of his achievements was impressive. He relaxed the Navigation Acts, primarily to stimulate the trade of the British colonies and thereby cement their loyalty to the mother country; he changed the Corn Laws to reduce the tariff on imported colonial grain; he also lowered tariffs on foreign manufactured goods and, even more drastically, on foreign raw materials, and in the process dealt a lethal blow to smuggling. British trade boomed.

The prosperity that followed, however, brought a wave of speculation almost as wild as the South Sea Bubble, and a crash in 1826 that was almost as shattering as that when the Bubble burst. The resultant unemployment was aggravated by bad harvests, and hunger stalked the countryside. Much foreign grain was in storage, waiting for the domestic price to rise to that stipulated in the Corn Laws. Parliament hastily authorized the sale of this grain, and thereby tacitly admitted that the Corn Laws worked hardship on the nation. Two years later a sliding scale of duties was introduced, decreasing as grain prices rose on the domestic market; and this principle remained operative until 1846. Parliament was willing to compromise in an emergency; but, once the crisis passed, the legislature put the welfare of the landed interest ahead of the general welfare.

For the moment the question of the Corn Laws was overshadowed by political developments. Early in 1827 a stroke incapacitated Lord Liverpool, the titular head of the government since 1812; and a bitter battle ensued for the succession. Canning won, at the cost of disrupting his party. Rank-and-file Tories distrusted his liberal views, especially on Catholic emancipation, and also distrusted him. He was too brilliant for more pedestrian men, and he could not blunt the shafts of his wit; every time he delivered a major speech, it was said, he made an enemy for life. When he was named prime minister six of his colleagues resigned, including Peel and Lord Eldon; and Tories harassed him more than Whigs during his term of office. It was brief. In August 1827 he died; and without him his few followers could not carry on. After a short interlude the Duke of Wellington formed a government, in January 1828, which appeared to be a return to the Toryism of an earlier day. But in fact that Toryism was dying, torn by factions and haunted by the ghost of Canning; and the Duke was forced to surrender its principles one by one.

The first surrender seemed to be insignificant. The new cabinet unwillingly accepted a Whig bill, introduced by Lord John Russell in 1828, to restore dissenters to full citizenship by repealing the Test and Corporation Acts that barred them from local and national office. This legislation of the Cavalier Parliament had lost most of its teeth after 1727, thanks to annual suspending acts, but had remained on the books as a nostalgic Tory symbol of the day when Anglicans had monopolized political power.[5] The chief effect of repeal was psychological rather than legal: it gave new force to the movement for Catholic emancipation. If Protestants outside the established church deserved full recognition, why not Roman Catholics?

The man who posed this question dramatically was Daniel O'Connell. Ever since 1801 Irish Catholics had been agitating for repeal of the union and for emancipation, and O'Connell had recently come to the fore as the leader and organizer of their discontent. He was a big man in every way, in body and intellect and humor; and he was as patient as he was astute. He had no faith in persuading the British by logic or coercing them by violence; his aim was to generate irresistible political pressure, and in this he succeeded. In 1828 he stood for parliament from the Irish county of Clare, and experts were startled to discover that a Catholic might legally be nominated and even elected, though he might not sit. The Anglo-Irish gentry were solidly opposed

[5] See above, p. 26.

to the candidate, and they were used to controlling county elections. But the peasants in their thousands marched to the poles, regimented by their priests, to vote for O'Connell. He was triumphantly returned.

The Clare election put Wellington's government in a serious dilemma. The Duke and Peel, his leader in the House of Commons, were against Catholic emancipation on principle; so were the King and the great majority of the House of Lords. But to refuse to seat O'Connell would clearly mean rebellion in Ireland, which would have widespread support in Britain. The followers of Canning, true to his memory, championed the Irish cause, as did many Whigs. If emancipation were to be carried at all, Wellington would have to carry it; only he could overcome the opposition of the upper house. The bill was introduced, to the scandal of the diehard Tories. For a moment it seemed as if Wellington would be stopped as Pitt had been: the King balked. George shared all his father's bigotry, which he mistook for principles; but, after haranguing his ministers for six hours while he helped himself to brandy, he gave way before their threat to resign. In April 1829 the bill became law.

The effect was profound. Emancipation created a third party, of Irish Catholics in the House of Commons, which was not committed to Whig or Tory principles but solely to the interests of Ireland; and for more than a century that party played a role in British politics out of all proportion to its numbers. The way in which O'Connell had achieved his ends showed that efficient organization, backed by the threat of violence but operating within legal channels, could force the hand of a reluctant British government; and the lesson was not lost on the Irish. In domestic politics the emancipation crisis was a further step in the disruption of the Tory party that had begun at Liverpool's retirement. Wellington and Peel were discredited with their own rank and file, and the Canningites were driven into coalition with the Whigs. While the impetus to change was accelerated, the barriers to it were revealed as feeble when the King and the House of Lords, those champions of the status quo, gave way before the ministry. The path was open for changing the structure of parliament itself, and the drive for reform began that culminated in 1832.

The Tory defenses crumbled rapidly. In June 1830 George IV performed his one good deed for his country: he died. He was an opinionated, meddlesome, stupid rake, who brought the popularity of the crown to its nadir in modern times; and he was adamant against reform. His younger brother, who succeeded him as William IV, was a far less ponderous obstacle. He was a bluff and genial man, with some pretensions to liberalism but little political common sense, and as conscientious and well-meaning as he was irresolute.

His accession necessitated a new parliamentary election, which coincided with a revolution in France. It was a moderate revolution, like that in England in 1688, because it was carefully managed by the upper classes; out of it came, not a Jacobin Reign of Terror, but a staid bourgeois regime with a bourgeois king, Louis Philippe. Developments in Paris made a deep impression across the Channel. If even the volatile French could change their government without opening the floodgates of democracy and chaos, surely the British could.

In the new parliament the Tories had a shaky majority, which melted away as soon as Wellington made clear that he would not consider any measure of reform. He stood for a Toryism that had starved to death for want of ideas, and his speech in the House of Lords in November 1830 was its funeral oration. Parliament as it then existed, he said, "possesses the full and entire confidence of the people. I will go further. If at the present moment I had imposed upon me the duty of forming a legislature . . . for a country like this, in possession of great property of various descriptions, I do not mean to assert that I could form such a legislature as we possess now, for the nature of man is incapable of reaching such excellence at once, but my great endeavor would be to form some description of legislature which would produce the same results." At a time when the people were clamoring for change and were backed by holders of "great property of various descriptions," the Duke could only extol the surpassing excellence of the status quo. A few weeks later he was forced to resign, and the battle for reform began.

The Reform Program

The Industrial Revolution, by creating a new wealth that demanded power, began the process that culminated in the Reform Bill. Preindustrial Britain had seen agitation for making the House of Commons more representative of the people, as witness the mobs that had rioted for John Wilkes; this left-wing radicalism, which continued under the surface and sometimes broke through it, as in the Battle of Peterloo, was essentially popular and carried a threat of social revolution that alarmed the propertied classes. Against that kind of reform the factory owner was united with the landowner; both, as employers, could foresee that extending the suffrage to the laboring man would eventually mean, if only because of his overwhelming numbers, government that was more in his interests than in theirs. By the 1820s, however, the progress of industrialization was creating pressure for reform of quite another sort. A large propertied group, the magnates of foundry and mine and mill, now stood outside the narrow world of parliament and demanded entrance to it. These new plutocrats dreaded radicalism as much as the bluest-blooded Tory did. What they wanted was a share of political power for themselves, not for the people; and they backed their demand with a logic that was hard to refute.

Until the accession of George III the composition of the House of Commons, despite all the anomalies of rotten boroughs, had borne some rough relationship to the distribution of wealth and population. The country had still been chiefly engaged in trade and agriculture, and a case could be made for a legislature in which the commercial and landed interests predominated.[6] But by the time George III died a vast new interest had come into being, and it had no representation worth the name. The great industrial centers were in parts of the British Isles that had hitherto been sparsely populated, and in which parliamentary boroughs were few and far between. Most of the mushrooming cities sent no members to parliament, and the barons of industry who dominated those cities had almost no voice in national politics. These men accepted wholeheartedly the oligarchical principle that no one deserved such a voice unless his property gave him a stake in the social order; what they repudiated, just as wholeheartedly, was the Tory identification of property with land. Why, they asked, should industrial wealth be discriminated against in favor of landed wealth? The question was hard to answer, and they pressed it more and more insistently with every year that passed.

The Tories refused to budge. Although they had in their ranks a few scions of industrialists, such as Robert Peel, the party was in essence that of the landed interest. The heads of the great territorial houses still made up the bulk of the peerage, and their relatives and dependents the bulk of the House of Commons. That house could not be enlarged to take in the clamorous outsiders without becoming hopelessly unwieldy; the only way to accommodate them was to wipe out most of the rotten boroughs in order to make room for new industrial constituencies, in other words to destroy the system by which the oligarchs had governed for more than a century. A change of such magnitude would be revolutionary, and the prospect horrified conservatives.

On this issue many Whigs were by instinct as conservative as Tories, from whom they were indistinguishable in their social connections and landed roots. But the Whigs as a party were different from the Tories in one important respect. They were out of power. They had been out since the days' of Fox, and clinging to their old ways gave them little chance of getting in again. A political party that feels itself condemned to perpetual wandering in the wilderness is a party that sooner or later will be ripe for new ideas, even unpalatable ones, if they offer some hope of tasting once more the fruits of office. So it was with the Whigs. In the late 1820s they embraced gradually, grudgingly, and apprehensively the cause of parliamentary reform, and by 1830 they were its champions.

They knew that the cause was popular, but this was not their reason for embracing it. They were willing to use the people for generating pressure, and even to exploit the theme that Whiggism had always stood for popular rights; but they had no intention whatever of obtaining a popular franchise. The unenfranchised whose support they really sought were the wealthy, not

---

[6] For the composition of the eighteenth-century House of Commons see above, pp. 29, 32–33.

the masses. The Whigs held to Edmund Burke's view that the vote, far from
being a right, was a privilege necessarily associated with property, and that
universal suffrage would be the prelude to despoilment of the rich by the
poor. They were as oligarchical as the Tories, and differed from them only in
advocating the enlargement of the oligarchy.

The Whigs' political program had two parts, the rationalization of
the franchise and the reapportionment of borough representatives. Landed
property, they argued, deserved no more influence in government than any
other form; and voting qualifications should be adjusted so that all men of
substance had an equal voice. The existing electoral system was chaotic: at
one extreme were boroughs with only a handful of voters, and at the other a
few democratic constituencies, such as Westminster, in which almost all adult
males voted. The Whigs proposed to substitute uniformity for chaos and
to make property-holding, whatever the form of property, the prerequisite for
the ballot. The same emphasis on uniformity appeared in their plan for
reapportionment: seats would be taken from the smaller boroughs and given
to the newly populous areas, particularly the industrial cities of the north; some
anomalies might be left, but the system in general would be based upon the
realities of wealth and population.

The long-term effects would be sweeping, as both conservatives and
radicals were well aware. Once admit the principle that the constitution
needed amending, then no amendment could be regarded as permanent; the
same logic that impelled the first change would lead inexorably to others, in a
never-ending process of innovation. Removing the rotten boroughs would
shake the power of the amateur country gentlemen in local government;
unseating the gentry there would be a prelude to attacking their economic
power as maintained by the Corn Laws; destroying the Corn Laws in the
interest of the people at large would lead on to enfranchising the masses, and
then how would any kind of property be safe? This line of thinking was
behind the Tory's dread of reform, and the radical's enthusiasm for it. And
both were right.

Epilogue

When the Whigs introduced their Reform Bill, in March 1831,
Britain had reached a watershed in her history. No previous ministry of the
crown had ever proposed to parliament such a deliberate and drastic
constitutional revision. The Glorious Revolution and the Hanoverian accession
had certainly brought drastic revision, but it had not been deliberate; the
intent had been to safeguard the existing constitution. In the eighteenth
century the gradual and subtle process of constitutional growth had gone
largely unperceived by the oligarchs themselves. They had not created the
cabinet, or the rotten borough, or government by "interests," but had merely
used the means that came to hand for conducting the business of the state. "In

what we improve," said Burke, "we are never wholly new; and in what we retain, we are never wholly obsolete." He was speaking for a ruling class that proved itself capable of moving with the times, slowly and hesitantly, but that had no thought of revolution even by statute.

Now, a generation after Burke's death, one segment of that class was converted to revolutionary change. Britain had been in economic revolution for the past half-century; and perceptive men could no longer blind themselves to the truth, however unwelcome, or to the need of acknowledging it in political terms. The greatest imperial and mercantile nation in the world had reached that position because it had new sources of strength. This giant was not Antaeus, who drew his power from the earth as the aristocracy did. Power now flowed as well from steam engines and factories, mines and blast furnaces. When the wielders of this industrial force, having grown rich by it, were moved to reach for political influence commensurate with their wealth, the concept of government as an aristocratic monopoly became obsolete.

Aristocracy, oligarchy, and the ruling class had hitherto been substantially synonyms for the landed interest. But oligarchy is a broader term than aristocracy and covers any form of rule by a minority. The Britain of 1830 had two wealthy minorities, agrarian and industrial. The question at issue was whether the former, the traditional aristocracy, would share power with the latter, thereby compromising the aristocratic principle in order to maintain the oligarchical — abandoning the obsolete predominance of land, in other words, to preserve a system of government by the few. The aristocrats agreed to this compromise because, at bottom, they had no choice. The extinction of oligarchy was unthinkable, and the only way to maintain it was to broaden its base.

This the Reform Bill did, and at a heavy cost to the aristocratic principle. In admitting the industrialists, the landed class that had ruled the country since the Glorious Revolution began to surrender its birthright. The newcomers brought with them concepts of administration, of poor relief, of colonial and economic policy, that rapidly altered the character of government; and soon the accelerating pace of industrialization brought an even more basic change, as the working classes came of age and demanded further adjustment of the franchise. When the settlement of 1832, which Whigs and Tories hoped would be permanent, disappeared in the second Reform Bill of 1867, the whole principle of oligarchy was eroded. The practice of a ruling class persisted until recent times, and in some degree still persists. But the principle that power should be vested in a small minority, and secured to it by constitutional means, survived the first Reform Bill by only thirty-five years.

A survey of the Age of Aristocracy may reasonably end in 1830, for the tumult that followed Wellington's resignation that autumn belongs more to the new age that was dawning than to the twilight of the old. The Britain of 1830 was a far cry from that of Lord Chesterfield. The frock coat and top hat had replaced the finery of a gentleman's brocade and sword and wig; factories, clattering in the middle of workers' slums, had appeared in parts of the countryside that had hitherto known nothing busier than grazing cows; the workshop of the world was a bustle of activity, and portents were everywhere of the greater bustle to come. The first Atlantic crossing by a steamship, British-built, had occurred in 1827; and in 1830 the opening of a rail line between Liverpool and Manchester, designed to carry passengers, inaugurated the railroad age. Steam and machinery, as they came into their own, were making the social order of the eighteenth century more and more archaic. Since the 1790s the Tories had defended and preserved that order by setting their faces flintlike against change in the structure of parliament, when change was prerequisite for adapting public policy to the needs of the new era. Now the Tory party, and the society out of which it had grown, were disintegrating together.

That eighteenth-century society need not evoke nostalgia, but it does demand respect. Aristocrats ruled it as never before or since; they loved their country, and by and large they served it well. The list of their accomplishments is long, and a few examples in conclusion may stand as a summary of their rule. They did not resolve the Irish problem, but they did consolidate the British Isles into a single kingdom, and direct the armies and navies that brought it out of insularity to world empire. They maintained a financial structure that was both stable and flexible enough to survive disruptive economic change. They governed in a manner that was sometimes lax, sometimes repressive, and always inefficient, but that permitted in the long run the growth of individual freedom. Their self-confidence matched their energy. They had a refinement and sureness of taste that made both the Jacobean and the Victorian era seem boorish by comparison, and they were experts in the fine art of living.

Most important of all, they knew by instinct when their power was ebbing, and were able to surrender it with good grace. The grace did not come easily, yet in the end they achieved it; for, hard as they battled against the inevitable, they did not battle to the death. They had a saving gift for compromise, which may be one of the humdrum but is also one of the great political virtues; and by compromising they made peaceful change possible. Their best epitaph is the observation of a shrewd foreigner, Prince Louis Napoleon, the heir and eventual successor of his uncle as Napoleon III. "In England you make reforms," said the Prince; "in France we make revolutions."

BIBLIOGRAPHY

General Works

Briggs, Asa *The Age of Improvement, 1783–1867* (1960; W. N. Medlicott, ed., *A History of England*).

Bryant, Arthur, *The England of Charles II* (1935).

———, *The Years of Endurance, 1793–1802* (1942).

———, *Years of Victory, 1802–1812* (1945).

———, *The Age of Elegance, 1812–1822* (1950).

Churchill, Winston S., *A History of the English-Speaking Peoples* (4 vols., 1956–58), Vol. III.

Clark, George N., *The Later Stuarts, 1660–1714* (1934; *Oxford History of England*).

Halévy, Elie, *A History of the English People in the Nineteenth Century* (2nd ed., 6 vols., 1949–52), Vols. I–II.*

Marriott, John A. R., *England since Waterloo* (1913; Charles W. C. Oman, ed., *A History of England*).

Marshall, Dorothy, *Eighteenth Century England* [1714–1783] (1962; W. N. Medlicott, ed., *A History of England*).

Ogg, David, *England in the Reigns of James II and William III* (1955).

Plumb, John H., *England in the Eighteenth Century* (1963).*

Robertson, Charles G., *England under the Hanoverians* (10th ed., 1930; Charles W. C. Oman, ed., *A History of England*).

Trevelyan, George M., *England under the Stuarts* (21st ed., 1949; Charles W. C. Oman, ed., *A History of England*).

* Available in paperback.

————, *England under Queen Anne* (3 vols.,
1930–34).

————, *British History in the Nineteenth Century and
After, 1782–1919* (2nd ed., 1938).

Trevelyan, George O., *The American Revolution* (4 vols.,
1905–12).

————, *George the Third and Charles Fox: the Concluding
Part of the American Revolution* (2 vols., 1915).

Watson, J. Steven, *The Reign of George III, 1760–1815*
(1960; *Oxford History of England*).

Willcox, William B., *Star of Empire: a Study of Britain
as a World Power, 1485–1945* (1950).

Williams, Basil, *The Whig Supremacy, 1714–1760* (2nd
ed., 1962; *Oxford History of England*).

Woodward, E. Llewelyn, *The Age of Reform, 1815–1870*
(1938; *Oxford History of England*).

Legal, Constitutional, and Governmental

Butterfield, Herbert, *George III and the Historians*
(1957).

Cone, Carl B., *Burke and the Nature of Politics* (2 vols.,
Lexington, Ky., 1957–64).

Feiling, Keith G., *A History of the Tory Party, 1640–1714*
(1924).

————, *The Second Tory Party, 1714–1832* (1938).

Foord, Archibald S., *His Majesty's Opposition, 1714–1830*
(1964).

Holdsworth, William S., *A History of English Law* (3rd
ed., 12 vols., 1922–38), Vols. X–XVI.

Keir, David L., *The Constitutional History of Modern
Britain, 1485–1950* (1953).

Namier, Lewis B., *England in the Age of the American
Revolution* (1933).

————, *The Structure of Politics at the Accession of George
III* (2nd ed., 2 vols., 1957).

Pares, Richard, *King George and the Politicians* (1953).

Walcott, Robert, *English Politics in the Early Eighteenth
Century* (1956).

Webb, Sidney and Beatrice, *English Local Government
from the Revolution to the Municipal Corporation
Act* (9 vols., 1906–29).

Williams, E. Neville, *The Eighteenth Century Constitution,
1688–1815: Documents and Commentary* (1960).

Economic and Social

Ashton, Thomas S., *An Economic History of England: the Eighteenth Century* (1955).
————, *The Industrial Revolution, 1760–1830* (1948).
Clapham, John H., *An Economic History of Modern Britain* (3 vols., 1930–38), Vol. I.
Deane, Phyllis, *The First Industrial Revolution* (1965).
Hammond, John L. Le B. and Barbara, *The Town Laborer, 1760–1832: the New Civilization* (1917).
————, *The Skilled Laborer, 1760–1832* (1920).
————, *The Village Laborer, 1760–1832: a Study in the Government of England before the Reform Bill* (4th ed., 1932).
Lipson, Ephraim, *The Economic History of England* (3 vols., 1937–53), Vols. II–III.
Mantoux, Paul J., *The Industrial Revolution in the Eighteenth Century in England* (1928).
Marshall, Dorothy, *Dr. Johnson's London* (1968).
————, *English People in the Eighteenth Century* (1965).
————, *The English Poor in the Eighteenth Century: a Study in Social and Administrative History* (1926).
Nef, John U., *The Rise of the British Coal Industry* (2 vols., 1932), Vol. II.
Prothero, Rowland E., *English Farming Past and Present* (1913).
Traill, Henry D., ed., *Social England: a Record of the Progress of the People . . . by Various Writers* (6 vols., 1893–97), Vols. IV–VI.
Trevelyan, George M., *English Social History* (3rd ed., 1946).
Usher, Abbot P., *An Introduction to the Industrial History of England* (1920).
Webb, Sidney and Beatrice, *English Poor Law History* (3 vols., 1927–29), Vol. I.
Williams, E. Neville, *Life in Georgian England* (1962).

Intellectual and Religious

Becker, Carl, *The Heavenly City of the Eighteenth-Century Philosophers* (1932).
Gay, Peter, "Carl Becker's Heavenly City," in *The Party of Humanity* (1964).

Gooch, George P., *English Democratic Ideas in the Seventeenth Century* (2nd ed., 1927).

Halévy, Elie, *The Growth of Philosophic Radicalism* (1928).

Laski, Harold J., *English Political Thought from Locke to Bentham* (1920).

Maccoby, Simon, *English Radicalism* (5 vols., 1935–55), Vols. I–II.

Stephen, Leslie, *History of English Thought in the Eighteenth Century* (3rd ed., 2 vols., 1902).

Sykes, Norman, *Church and State in England in the XVIIIth Century* (1934).

Willey, Basil, *The Seventeenth Century Background: Studies in the Thought of the Age in Relation to Poetry and Religion* (1934).

———, *The Eighteenth Century Background: Studies on the Idea of Nature in the Thought of the Period* (1941).

Biographical

Butler, Geoffrey G., *The Tory Tradition: Bolingbroke — Burke — Disraeli — Salisbury* (1914).

Churchill, Winston S., *Marlborough, His Life and Times* (6 vols., 1933–39).

Kenyon, John P., *The Stuarts: a Study in English Kingship* (1959).

Mahan, Alfred T., *The Life of Nelson* (1897).

Marshall, Dorothy, *John Wesley* (1965).

Ogg, David, *William III* (1956).*

Plumb, John H., *The First Four Georges* (1956).

———, *Sir Robert Walpole: the Making of a Statesman* (1956).

———, *Sir Robert Walpole: the King's Minister* (1960).

Rose, John Holland, *William Pitt* [the Younger] (2 vols., 1911).

Trevelyan, George O., *The Early History of Charles Fox* (1904).

Valentine, Alan, *Lord North* (2 vols., 1967).

Wallas, Graham, *The Life of Francis Place, 1771–1854* (4th ed., 1925).

Willcox, William B., *Portrait of a General: Sir Henry Clinton in the War of Independence* (1964).

Williams, Basil, *The Life of William Pitt, Earl of Chatham* (2 vols., 1915).

Imperial and Foreign

The Cambridge History of the British Empire (John
Holland Rose *et al.,* eds.; 2nd ed., 8 vols., 1929–36),
Vols. I–II.

The Cambridge History of British Foreign Policy, 1783–1919
(Adolphus W. Ward and George P. Gooch, eds.; 3
vols., 1922–23), Vol. I.

Gipson, Lawrence H., *The British Empire before the
American Revolution* [1748–1776] (15 vols.,
1958–70).

Sutherland, Lucy S., *The East India Company in
Eighteenth-Century Politics* (1952).

Williamson, James A., *A Short History of British Expansion*
(1922).

Military and Naval

Atkinson, Christopher T., *Marlborough and the Rise of
the British Army* (1921).

Corbett, Julian S., *England in the Seven Years' War:
a Study in Combined Strategy* (2nd ed., 2 vols.,
1918).

Fortescue, John W., *History of the British Army* (13
vols. in 20, 1899–1930), Vols. I–X.

Mackesy, Piers, *The War for America, 1775–1783* (1964).

Mahan, Alfred T., *The Influence of Sea Power upon
History, 1660–1783* (32nd ed., 1928).

———, *The Influence of Sea Power upon the French
Revolution and Empire* (10th ed., 2 vols., 1898).

Oman, Charles W. C., *The Peninsular War* (7 vols.,
1902–30).

Potter, Elmer B., and Chester W. Nimitz, eds., *Sea
Power: a Naval History* (1960).

Bibliographical

Davies, Godfrey, ed., *Bibliography of British History: the
Stuart Period, 1603–1714* (1928).

Pargellis, Stanley McC., and D. J. Medley, eds.,
*Bibliography of British History: the Eighteenth
Century, 1714–1789* (1951).

INDEX

Act of Settlement. *See* Settlement
Adam, Robert, 108
Addington, Henry, later Viscount Sidmouth, 156, 158, 160, 194, 200
Adrianople, Treaty of (1829), 203
Agriculture. *See* Revolution, agrarian
Aix-la-Chapelle, Peace of (1748), 73–75; Congress of (1818), 191
Alexander I, Czar of Russia, 151, 166–67, 169, 175, 178–80, 190–91, 202
America, North, Anglo-French rivalry in, 59, 76–77, 79
American colonies, British, 85–87. *See also* American Independence; American Revolution; Canada
American colonies, French. *See* Canada
American colonies, Spanish. *See* Spain
American Independence, War of (1775–83), 95–105, 126–27, 152
American Revolution: causes of, 85–95; effects of, 105–106, 124: *see also* American Independence
Amiens, Peace of (1802), 156–58
Anglicanism. *See* Church of England
Anne, Queen of England, as heiress presumptive, 3, 6, 16; as queen, 8, 13, 18, 19, 21–24, 28, 36, 47
Annuities, governmental, 14, 49
Arbuthnot, Admiral Marriot, 101–102, 104
Arkwright, Richard, 119
Army, British, 51, 66, 95, 142, 172
Army, French, 139–40, 159–60
Arnold, Benedict, 98, 101–102
Asiento agreement (1713), 22, 49, 61, 73
Austen, Jane, 122, 168
Austerlitz, Battle of (1805), 165
Austria, in eighteenth century, 17–19, 58, 67, 69, 73, 74, 77, 83; in Revolutionary and Napoleonic wars, 133, 138–39, 149–50, 165–66, 173–74, 179–80, 182; after Waterloo, 187–88, 190–91, 193, 202. *See also* Charles VI; Habsburg; Maria Theresa; Metternich
Austrian Netherlands. *See* Belgium
Austrian Succession, War of the (1740–48), 70–71, 73, 76, 84, 150

Balance of power, European, 8, 17, 22, 59, 66, 82, 138
Bank of England, 14–16, 48–50, 113, 194
Bavaria, 8, 19

Beggars' Opera, 41–42
Belgium, in eighteenth century, 17, 19, 20, 22–23, 35, 71, 73, 75; in Revolutionary and Napoleonic wars, 138–39, 182; after Waterloo, 187
Bengal, 77, 79, 127–28
Bill of Rights (1689), 4–6, 134
Blenheim, Battle of (1704), 19, 20
Blenheim Palace, 36, 108
Blockade, British naval, 70, 79, 96, 100; in Revolutionary and Napoleonic wars, 142–43, 150, 152, 156, 158, 160, 162, 170, 176, 185–86
Blücher, Gebhard von, Prussian marshal, 182, 184
Bolingbroke, Lord (Henry St. John), 23–24, 47, 136
Bombay, 59, 127–29
Bonaparte. *See* Napoleon
Boroughs, parliamentary, 29–32, 82, 92, 108, 113, 126, 207–209
Boston, 90, 93–95, 97
Boulton, Matthew, 120, 134
Bourbon, House of, 17, 67. *See also* Louis XIV, XV, XVI, XVIII; Philip V
Boyne, Battle of the (1690), 10, 71, 152
Braddock, General Edward, 74, 79
Brest, French naval base, 78, 150, 152, 160, 162, 165
Bunker Hill, Battle of (1775), 95, 98
Burgoyne, General John, 95, 98–99, 102, 104
Burke, Edmund, 129–30, 135–37, 200, 209–10
Bute, Lord (John Stuart), 83–84, 89, 91
Byron, Lord (George Gordon Byron), 107, 121, 199, 201

Cabinet, evolution of, 27–29, 32–33, 88, 209
Calcutta, 59, 77, 79, 128–29, 131
Canada, 67, 73, 74, 79, 83, 85, 98–99, 105, 178
Canning, George, 175, 192–93, 200, 202–205
Cape Breton Island, 73, 83
Cape of Good Hope, 176, 189
Cape St. Vincent, Battle of (1797), 143, 147, 163
Caribbean, 49, 61, 66, 99, 162–63. *See also* West Indies
Carleton, General Sir Guy, 97–98

Caroline of Anspach, George II's queen, 34, 54, 56, 58
Caroline of Brunswick, George IV's queen, 199–200
Castlereagh, Lord (Robert Stewart), 175, 190–92, 194, 200
Catholics, Roman, 1–2, 6–9, 11, 23, 26, 94, 111, 113, 152–55, 176, 205–206
Charles I, King of England, 1, 2, 4, 48, 54, 130, 152
Charles II, King of England, 3, 7, 8, 16, 28, 199
Charles II, King of Spain, 16–17, 60
Charles VI, Holy Roman Emperor: as archduke, 17, 19–20, 171; as emperor, 22, 58, 60, 66
Charles Edward, Young Pretender. See Stuart, Charles Edward
Chatham, Lord. See Pitt
Chesterfield, Lord (Philip Stanhope), 19, 25–27, 32, 34, 43–46, 52, 56, 72, 76, 89, 108
Church of England: in Stuart period, 1, 7, 11, 12, 23, 26; in Hanoverian period, 51, 114–16, 134, 154
Churchill, John. See Marlborough, Duke of
Churchill, Sarah. See Marlborough, Duchess of
Clarendon Code, 7, 26
Clinton, General Sir Henry, 95, 99–102, 104
Clive, Robert, 79, 127
Combination Act (1799), 196–97, 204; (1825), 204
Commons, House of, 3–4, 6, 45, 50–52, 55–58, 62–63, 65, 76, 82, 89, 91–93, 104, 154; composition of, 28–34, 154–55, 206; reform of. See Parliament
Concert of Europe, 190–93
Concord, Battle of (1775), 95
Congress system, 190–92
Consolidated Fund, 125
Continental System, 169–71, 173, 175, 179
Convention, French (1792–95), 138
Convention Parliament (1689–90), 2
Copenhagen, Battle of (1801), 151; (1807), 170
Corn Laws, 195–96, 204–205, 209
Cornwallis, Lord (Charles Cornwallis), 101–102, 104
Cotton manufacture, 118–19, 122
Cromwell, Oliver, 11, 136n., 152, 155
Culloden, Battle of (1746), 72
Cumberland, Duke of (son of George II), 72

Customs duties, 55, 85, 204; in America, 87–88, 90

Debt, national or public, 14–15, 49, 79, 85, 125–26, 155, 168, 195
Declaration of the Rights of Man (1789), 134–35
Denmark, in Napoleonic wars, 150–51, 170
Directory, French (1795–99), 139, 147, 149, 155–56
Dissenters, 1, 3, 7, 23, 26, 134, 205
Duncan, Admiral Adam, 144

East India Company, 50, 59–60, 78–79, 84, 93–94, 118, 126–29, 131, 173
Eden Treaty (1786), 124–25
Egypt: in Revolutionary and Napoleonic wars, 145–49, 151, 153, 156, 158–59; and Greek revolt, 202
Elba, 157, 180, 182
Eldon, Lord (John Scott), 194, 200, 205
Elizabeth, Empress of Russia, 74, 83
Enclosure movement, 40, 110–11, 117, 167–68, 195
Excise tax, 55, 85, 111, 125

Ferdinand, Duke of Brunswick, 77–78
Fifteen, the (1715–16), 48
Finance, public, 3, 9, 14–16, 79–80, 125–126, 194–95. See also Debt; Taxation
First Coalition, War of the (1792–97), 138–40, 142–43
Fleury, Cardinal André Hercule de, 57
Florida, 62, 83, 85, 105
Forty-Five, the (1745–46), 71–73
Fox, Charles James, 126, 128, 134, 137–38, 141–42, 165–66, 194, 200, 208
France: under Louis XIV, 2, 8–11, 13, 18–23; under Louis XV, 57–62, 67, 69, 71, 73, 74, 78, 79, 82–85; under Louis XVI, 88, 96, 105, 124–28; after Waterloo, 187–88, 190–93, 202–203. See also Army, French; Bourbon; French Revolution; Navy, French
Francis, Philip, 127–29
Frederick II, King of Prussia, 67, 71, 73–75, 77, 83–85
Frederick, Prince of Wales (son of George II), 34, 58, 64, 77
French Revolution: first (1789), 114, 116, 133–53, 155–86, 189; second (1830), 206–207

Gage, General Thomas, 94–95, 97
Gay, John, 41–42

Gentry, landed, 1, 9, 29, 33, 35–38, 108–11, 209; and Walpole, 52, 55

George I, King of Great Britain, 6–7, 23–24, 27, 33, 36, 47, 50, 54, 80

George II, King of Great Britain, 27–28, 33, 36, 51, 54, 56–58, 64, 71, 72, 75–80

George III, King of Great Britain: before 1783, 34, 77–78, 80, 82, 83, 86, 89–93, 96, 104–105, 107; later years, 122, 126, 128, 131, 135, 151, 154–55, 175, 188, 199

George IV, King of Great Britain: as Prince of Wales and Regent, 34, 175, 185, 190, 198–99; as king, 199–200, 203, 206

Georgia, 62–63, 100

Germain, Lord George: in Seven Years War, 77–78; in War of American Independence, 96–97, 99

Gibraltar, 20, 22, 23, 64, 146

Glencoe, Massacre of (1692), 12

Glorious Revolution (1688–89), 1–16, 26, 117, 134, 209

Godolphin, Lord (Sidney Godolphin), 18–19, 21

Gordon Riots (1780), 111, 113

Grafton, Duke of (Augustus Henry Fitzroy), 89, 90, 92, 93

Grand Alliance (1689), 8–10

Grand Tour, 38, 45, 108

Grasse, Admiral Comte de, 102–104

Graves, Admiral Thomas, 104

Greece, revolt against Turks, 200–203

Greene, General Nathanael, 102

Grenville, George, 90, 91

Habeas corpus, 140, 198

Habsburg, House of, 16–17, 20, 22–23, 59, 67, 189. See also Charles VI; Maria Theresa

Hanover: House of, 3, 6–7, 17, 21–24, 26–28, 33–34, 48, 50, 57, 72. See also George I, II, III, IV; Sophia; William IV; Electorate of, 23, 34, 35, 67, 69–71, 73–77, 80; Kingdom of, 188

Hargreaves, James, 119

Harley, Robert (later Earl of Oxford), 23–24

Hastings, Warren, 127–31

Hessians, in America, 97–98

Highlanders, Scottish, 12, 48, 71–72

Holy Alliance (1815), 190–93, 200, 203

Hood, Admiral Sir Samuel, 104

Howe, General Sir William, 95, 97–100

Howe, Lord (Richard Howe), 97–98, 100

Huskisson, William, 200, 204

Impeachment, 4; of Hastings, 129–30

India: in eighteenth century, 59–61, 67, 73, 74, 76, 78, 83, 84, 99, 126–31; in Revolutionary and Napoleonic wars, 145, 147, 158–59, 173; in Vienna settlement, 188–89. See also East India Company

India Act (1784), 129

Industrialization. See Revolution, Industrial

Intolerable Acts (1774), 95

Ireland: in late Stuart period, 2, 7, 9–11, 16; in Hanoverian period, 104, 124, 142, 151–55, 158; and Catholic emancipation, 205–206

Italy: before 1789, 10, 16, 22, 58, 71; in Revolutionary and Napoleonic wars, 138–39, 149–50, 156, 158, 165–66, 170, 176, 180; after Waterloo, 187–92. See also Savoy

Jacobins, 138–41

Jacobites, 3, 11, 15, 27, 48, 57, 71–73

James II, King of England, 1–3, 5–12, 17–18, 72, 138, 152

James "III," Old Pretender. See Stuart, James

Jenkins, Captain Robert, 62–63

Jenkins' Ear, War of (1739–48), 64–67

Jervis, Admiral John (later Lord St. Vincent), 143, 146–47, 150

Johnson, Samuel, 44, 108, 166

Judiciary, 6, 56, 140

Junius, 92–93

Kay, John, 119

Kedleston Hall, 108

King's Friends, 92

King William's War (1689–97), 8–11, 16

Laud, William, 114

League of Armed Neutrality (1780), 104; (1800), 150–51

Leipzig, Battle of. See Nations

Lexington, Battle of (1775), 88, 95

Limerick, Treaty of (1691), 11

Lisbon, 20, 170, 173–74, 179

Liverpool, Lord (Robert Jenkinson), 194, 205

Locke, John, 4, 6

Lombardy-Venetia, 187–89

Long Island, Battle of (1776), 98

Lords, House of: in seventeenth and eighteenth centuries, 4, 6, 13, 22, 32, 45, 51, 55–56, 65, 76, 89, 91, 92, 93n, 131, 154; and Catholic emancipation, 206. See also Parliament

Louis XIV, King of France, 8, 9, 17, 19, 21, 22, 28, 57

Louis XV, King of France, 57–58, 71
Louis XVI, King of France, 99, 133
Louis XVIII, King of France, 180, 182, 187
Louisbourg, 73, 75, 76, 79, 83
Louisiana, 83–84, 105, 159
Low Countries: in eighteenth century, 19, 21, 23, 71, 73; in Revolutionary and Napoleonic wars, 138, 158, 170, 176; after Waterloo, 187–88. *See also* Belgium; Netherlands, Dutch
Luddite riots, 175–76, 198

Madras, 59, 73, 127–29
Mahan, Alfred, 70*n*.
Malta, 146, 149–50, 156, 158, 176, 188
Manchester, 118, 198–99
Maria Theresa, Archduchess of Austria and Queen of Hungary, 60, 66–67, 71, 73–75
Marlborough, Duchess of (Sarah Churchill), 18, 21, 36
Marlborough, Duke of (John Churchill), 18–21, 36, 70, 71, 75, 82, 165
Mary II, Queen of England, 2–3, 5–6, 12, 134
Massachusetts, 73, 90, 93–94
Masséna, André, Napoleonic marshal, 174–75, 179
Mauritius, 176, 188–89
Mediterranean: in eighteenth century, 20, 23, 64, 78, 100; in Revolutionary and Napoleonic wars, 143, 145–49, 151, 158, 160, 176; after Waterloo, 188, 202–203
Methodism, 114–16, 141
Metternich, Prince Clemens von, 182, 189–91, 200, 202–203
Minden, Battle of (1759), 77–78, 97
Ministry of All the Talents (1806–07), 165–66
Minorca: in eighteenth century, 20, 22, 23, 64, 74, 76, 78, 83, 105; in Napoleonic wars, 149
Mohammed Ali, 202
Monroe Doctrine, 193
Moore, General John, 173
Mutinies, British naval (1797), 143–45
Mutiny Acts (1689 and after), 6

Napoleon Bonaparte: as general and First Consul, 139, 145–50, 156–59; as Emperor, 159–60, 162–63, 165–67, 169–80, 182, 184–85
National Assembly, French (1789–91), 133, 134, 137–38
Nations, Battle of the (1813), 157, 180
Navarino, Battle of (1827), 202

Navy, British: in late Stuart period, 9–10, 15–16, 20–21, 23; in Hanoverian period, 35, 64, 66, 70, 73, 75, 78, 84, 95–96, 99–104; role in American history, 105–106, 159, 193; in Revolutionary and Napoleonic wars, 142–45, 155, 160–65, 177. *See also* Blockade
Navy, French, of Louis XIV, 10, 15; of Louis XV, 78–79, 82, 84, 95–96; of Louis XVI, 99–104; in Revolutionary and Napoleonic wars, 142–45, 149–50, 158–65
Navy, Spanish: in eighteenth century, 23, 63, 82; in Revolutionary and Napoleonic wars, 143, 160, 163
Nelson, Admiral Horatio (later Lord Nelson), 143, 146–47, 151, 160, 163, 165
Netherlands, Austrian. *See* Belgium
Netherlands, Dutch: in seventeenth and eighteenth centuries, 2, 6, 8, 16, 18–20, 34, 73, 104; in Revolutionary and Napoleonic wars, 138–39, 143–44, 149, 156, 158, 160; Kingdom of (1815), 187, 189
Netherlands, Spanish. *See* Belgium
Newcastle, Duke of (Thomas Pelham-Holles), 64, 75–76, 79, 82, 83
Newcomen, Thomas, 120
New Orleans, Battle of (1814), 178
New York City, 97–99, 101, 104
Nicholas I, Czar of Russia, 202–203
Nile, Battle of the (1798), 146–47, 149, 165
North, Lord (Frederick North), 89–96, 104, 107, 122, 124, 127–28

Occasional conformity, 8, 23
O'Connell, Daniel, 205–206
Ottoman Empire: in Napoleonic wars, 147; and Greek revolt, 200–203
Oxford, Lord. *See* Harley

Paine, Tom, 137
Pardo, Convention of (1739), 63–64
Paris, Peace of (1763), 83–84, 89; (1783), 105–106
Parker, Admiral Hyde, 151
Parliament, English: in late Stuart period, 1, 3–8, 11–13, 16, 18–19, 134; in Hanoverian period, 28–35, 37, 49, 58, 63, 65, 82, 90–93, 107, 113, 122, 155; reform of, 126, 140, 198, 206–11. *See also* Commons; Lords
Parliament, Irish, 11, 124, 152–55
Parliament, Scottish, 3, 12–13
Paul I, Czar of Russia, 149–51
Peel, Robert, 200, 204–06, 208
Pelham, Henry, 75–76

Peninsular War (1808–14), 171–75, 180, 186
Pennsylvania, 98–100
Peterloo, or Manchester, Massacre (1819), 198–99, 207
Philhellenes, 200–201
Philip V, King of Spain, 17, 20, 22, 61
Pitt, William, later Lord Chatham, 58, 63, 71, 75, 77–79, 82–83, 87–89, 93, 122
Pitt, William, the Younger: peace-time ministry of, 122, 124–26, 129, 131; as war leader, 138, 140, 142, 145–46, 151, 153–57, 160, 165–66, 168, 186, 191, 198
Placemen, 32, 51, 82
Poland, 57–58, 179–80, 188
Polish Succession, War of the (1733–35), 57–58
Poor relief, 111, 113, 142, 168, 196
Pope, Alexander, 42–43, 46
Portugal, 18, 20, 170, 173–74, 191
Pragmatic Sanction, 60, 67
Press, British, 55–56, 62, 140, 197–98
Pretenders. See Stuart, Charles Edward; Henry; James
Price, Richard, 134–35
Priestley, Joseph, 134, 138
Prince Regent. See George IV
Prussia: in eighteenth century, 35, 67–70, 73–75, 77–78, 83; in Revolutionary and Napoleonic wars, 133, 138–39, 166, 179–80, 182, 184–86; after Waterloo, 187–88, 190–91, 193, 202. See also Frederick II

Quadruple Alliance (1814), 182, 190
Quebec Act (1774), 94

Railroads, 121, 211
Reform Bill, 207–10
Regulating Act (1773), 127, 128
Revolution, agrarian, in Britain, 39–41, 110–11, 117
Revolution, American. See American Revolution
Revolution, French. See French Revolution
Revolution, Glorious. See Glorious Revolution
Revolution, Industrial, in Britain, 116–22, 132, 142, 155–56, 167, 169, 207–11
Rochambeau, Comte de, 101, 102, 104
Rockingham, Lord (Charles Watson-Wentworth), 89–90
Rossbach, Battle of (1757), 77
Russell, Lord John, 200, 205
Russia: in eighteenth century, 74, 75, 77, 83; in Revolutionary and Napoleonic wars, 141, 149–51, 165–67, 169, 178–80, 182; after Waterloo, 188, 191, 202–203. See also Alexander; Elizabeth; Nicholas; Paul

Sackville, Lord George. See Germain
Sandwich, Lord (John Montagu), 96–97
Saratoga, Burgoyne's surrender at, 99, 102
Sardinia, Kingdom of, 138–39, 187–88, 191
Savery, Thomas, 120
Savoy, 8, 18, 20. See also Sardinia
Saxony, 8, 74, 188
Scotland, 2, 3, 9, 12–14, 16, 47, 58, 71–72, 141. See also Parliament, Scottish
Scurvy, 150, 189
Second Coalition, War of the (1799–1801), 149–51
Security, Act of (1704), 13
Seditious Meetings Act (1795), 140
Sepoys, 79, 128, 131
Septennial Act (1716), 32
Settlement, Act of (1701), 7, 21, 28
Seven Years War (1756–63), 74–85, 126–27
Shelley, Percy, 195, 198–99
Sidmouth, Lord. See Addington
Silesia, 67, 73–75, 77, 84
Six Acts (1819), 198–200
Slave trade, 22, 49, 116, 126, 166
Smith, Adam, 122, 124, 166
Smuggling: in Britain, 55–56, 125, 204; in America, 61, 87–89, 94
Sophia, Electress of Hanover, 6–7, 23
Soult, Nicholas, Napoleonic marshal, 180, 184
South Sea Bubble, 48–50, 52, 65
South Sea Company, 48–50, 61, 64
Spain, in seventeenth and eighteenth centuries, 8, 10, 16–23, 49, 57–58, 61–63, 70, 71, 79, 82–85, 96, 99; American colonies of, 49, 61, 172, 192–93; in Revolutionary and Napoleonic wars, 138–39, 143, 156, 159–60; after Waterloo, 191–92. See also Peninsular War
Spanish Netherlands. See Belgium
Spanish Main. See Caribbean
Spanish Succession, War of the (1701–13), 13, 16–21
Speenhamland system, 113, 168, 196
Stamp Act (1765), 90
Steam engine, 120–21, 211
St. Helena, 157, 185
St. John, Henry. See Bolingbroke
Stuart, Charles Edward, Young Pretender, 71–72

Stuart, Henry, Cardinal and Pretender, 72
Stuart, House of, 3, 6–7, 14, 21–22. *See also* Anne; James II; Mary II; Stuart, Charles Edward, Henry, and James; William III
Stuart, James, Old Pretender, 7, 17–18, 21–23, 47–48, 57, 71
St. Vincent, Lord. *See* Jervis
Sweden, in Napoleonic wars, 150, 165, 179–80
Swift, Jonathan, 41

Tariffs. *See* Corn Laws; Customs duties
Taxation, 9, 14, 33, 57, 85, 96, 168, 194. *See also* Customs duties; Excise; Poor relief
Test Act (1673), 7, 23, 26, 205
Third Coalition, War of the (1805–07), 165–67
Tilsit, Treaty of (1807), 166–67, 169–70, 175, 178–79
Toleration Act (1689), 7–8, 11, 26
Tories, in late Stuart period, 1–3, 5–9, 15, 20–24, 33, 48, 82; after 1714, 26–27, 33, 47; after 1815, 137, 142, 194, 200, 203–11
Torres Vedras, Lines of, 174–75
Toulon, French naval base, 20, 78, 100, 145–46, 149, 160, 162–63
Townshend, Charles, 90, 93
Trafalgar, Battle of (1805), 163, 165, 185
Treasonable Practices Act (1795), 140
Troppau, Congress of (1821), 191
Turks. *See* Ottoman Empire
Two Sicilies, Kingdom of the, 149, 191

Ulster, 10–11, 152
Union, Act of: with Scotland (1707), 3, 9, 13–14, 48; with Ireland (1801), 93*n.*, 152–55
United States, 99, 105–106, 135, 159, 170, 177–78, 192–93
Utrecht, Treaty of (1713), 22–23, 47, 49, 59, 71, 73

Vanbrugh, Sir John, 36–37, 108
Verona, Congress of (1822), 192
Vienna, Congress and Peace of (1814–15), 180, 182, 187–90
Villeneuve, Pierre de, Napoleonic admiral, 160, 162–63, 165

Walpole, Sir Robert, 48–65, 72, 73, 75–76, 78, 111, 125
War of 1812 (1812–14), 105, 177–78, 182
Warfare, nature of: before French Revolution, 68–70; after 1792, 139–40
Washington, General George, 74, 97–98, 100, 102, 104
Waterloo, Battle of (1815), 157, 184–86
Watt, James, 120, 134
Wellesley, Arthur. *See* Wellington
Wellesley, Lord (Richard Wellesley), 173
Wellington, Duke of (Arthur Wellesley); in Napoleonic wars, 68, 172–76, 180, 182, 184–87; after Waterloo, 202–203, 205–207, 210
Wesley, John, 114–16, 166
West Indies, 79, 83–84, 126; in War of American Independence, 102, 104–105; in Revolutionary and Napoleonic wars, 142, 163, 176, 188
Whigs, in late Stuart period, 1–3, 5–9, 15, 20–23, 33, 48; in Hanoverian period, 26–27, 29, 32, 33, 35, 47, 80–82, 86, 89, 107, 128, 135, 137; after 1815, 142, 194, 199–200, 205–206, 208–10
Whitefield, George, 115
Whitney, Eli, 119
Wilberforce, William, 126, 166
Wilkes, John, 91–93, 97, 207
William III, King of England, 2, 3, 5–10, 12–13, 15–18, 28, 34, 87, 134, 152
William IV, King of Great Britain, 206
Wolfe, General James, 79
Wool trade, 11, 118, 121–22
Wordsworth, William, 133–34, 168–69

Yorktown campaign, 102, 104